D0488138

AUG 15 2008

Developing School Leaders

Never before has the topic of educational leadership been so much in the public eye. Many countries face a crisis in recruitment to the most senior positions in schools at a time when arguments rage about the best way to develop our school leaders so that our educational institutions will be in the hands of the very best people, committed to enhancing the outcomes for our children.

Focusing on leadership development in ten diverse cultural contexts, this text brings together some of the most senior commentators in the field of educational leadership development to provide a global perspective on leadership development programmes and practices. Each writer examines the background history to leadership development in their nation and outlines the most recent developments.

As is the case with any major initiative, the rise of leadership development programmes has presented opportunities for some and challenges for others. These challenges are both practical and conceptual and relate to a series of questions that are unpacked in the text including:

- What is the appropriate balance between the academic and the practical in leadership programmes?
- Should provision be located in higher education institutions, in other government sponsored organizations or commissioned from the private sector?
- Are models of leadership studies derived from business and industry relevant to schools?
- How can research into impact inform leadership development policy and strategy?
- Should programmes be integrated into higher degree provision or should new and innovative forms of accreditation be developed?

This book will be fascinating reading for all those engaged in educational research and teaching, and working, in educational leadership.

Mark Brundrett is Professor of Educational Research at the Faculty of Education, Liverpool John Moores University. **Megan Crawford** is Senior Lecturer in Educational Leadership at the Institute of Education, University of London.

Developing School Leaders

An international perspective

Edited by Mark Brundrett
and Megan Crawford

LONDON AND NEW YORK

First published 2008
by Routledge
2 Park Square, Milton Park, Abingdon, Oxon OX14 4RN

Simultaneously published in the USA and Canada
by Taylor & Francis Inc
270 Madison Ave, New York, NY 10016

Routledge is an imprint of the Taylor & Francis Group, an informa business

Typeset in Garamond by Wearset Ltd, Boldon, Tyne and Wear
Printed and bound in Great Britain by TJI Digital, Padstow, Cornwall

British Library Cataloguing in Publication Data
A catalogue record for this book is available from the British Library

Library of Congress Cataloging-in-Publication Data
Developing school leaders : an international perspective/edited by Mark Brundrett and Megan Crawford.
p. cm.
Includes bibliographical references and index.
1. Educational leadership—Cross-cultural studies. 2. Educational leadership—Research. I. Brundrett, Mark. II. Crawford, Megan, 1957–
LB2831.6.D48 2008
371.2—dc22 2007040022

ISBN10: 0-415-43572-2 (hbk)
ISBN10: 0-203-92882-2 (ebk)

ISBN13: 978-0-415-43572-7 (hbk)
ISBN13: 978-0-203-92882-0 (ebk)

Contents

Illustrations

Figures

Tables

Contributors

Rina Barkol is director of leadership training programmes at Beit Berl College, Israel.

Mark Brundrett is Professor of Educational Research at the Faculty of Education, I. M. Marsh Campus, Liverpool John Moores University, UK.

Simon Clarke is Senior Lecturer in Educational Management and Administration and Deputy Dean at the Graduate School of Education, The University of Western Australia.

Mike Cowie, is Academic Coordinator for the SQH Programme, Centre for Education at the University of Edinburgh, UK.

Megan Crawford is Senior Lecturer in Educational Leadership at the London Centre for Leadership in Learning, Institute of Education, London, UK.

Clive Dimmock is Professor of Educational Management and Director of the Centre for Educational Leadership and Management, University of Leicester, UK.

David Eddy is Project Director of the First-time Principals Programme at the University of Auckland School Leadership Centre, Auckland, New Zealand.

Deidre Le Fevre is a Senior Lecturer in the Faculty of Education at the University of Auckland.

Chrysanthi Gkolia was formerly Research Associate at the Centre for Educational Leadership, School of Education, University of Manchester, UK and is now an academic in Greece.

Tim Goddard is Professor of Education and Vice-provost (International) University of Calgary, Alberta Canada.

S. Earl Irving is a Senior Research Fellow in the Faculty of Education at the University of Auckland.

Joseph Murphy is Professor and Associate Dean at Peabody College, Vanderbilt University, Tennessee, USA.

Viviane M. J. Robinson is Professor of Education at the School of Education, University of Auckland, New Zealand.

Allan Walker is Professor and Chair of the Department of Educational Administration and Policy, Chinese University of Hong Kong.

Acknowledgements

This text developed out of a special issue of the journal *School Leadership and Management* (Volume 26, Number 2, April 2006) which focused on school leadership development and brought together work by scholars from Europe, East Asia, Australasia and the USA. The editors would like to thank the Board of that journal for their support. Special thanks go to the Editor of *School Leadership and Management*, Professor Alma Harris, of the University of Warwick, for her ready agreement that the material from the journal could be developed, with the addition of new items, in order to create this text. Louisa Hopkins, the administrator of the journal, was, as always, unstinting in her helpfulness, and unfailingly polite when confronted with the inevitable complexity of drawing together the work of leading academics from around the world.

The journal special edition was developed whilst one of the editors was a member of staff at the Centre for Educational Leadership at the University of Manchester. Thanks are extended to all the staff of CEL for their assistance during this period. It is important to note that Chapters 2 and 5 of this text, which focus on leadership development in England and the Czech Republic respectively, are derived in part from an article in the special edition of the journal noted above that originally compared experiences in the two countries. In turn that article grew out of a conference at Charles University in Prague, organized by CEL and funded by the British Council. Special thanks are offered to Brendan Murden and Ann Dering, respectively the overall Director and Director of Research and Development at CEL, who were instrumental in organizing the conference and in supporting subsequent research activity.

More recently the editors, Mark Brundrett and Megan Crawford, have been based, respectively, at Liverpool John Moores University and The University of London Institute of Education. The Editors would like to thank colleagues at those institutions for their support. Ms Emma Fitzgerald, who undertakes the administration for the Centre for Educational Research and Evaluation at John Moores University, is to be singled out for her hard work and diligence. Mrs Rachel Anderson De-Cuevas, Research Assistant at the same institution, is thanked for all of her efforts on research projects within the Centre but specifically for her assistance with various literature searches that have assisted with the production of this work.

Chapter 1

Introduction

Educational leadership development in a global environment

Mark Brundrett and Megan Crawford

Numerous studies have affirmed the pivotal role of the school leader as a key factor in school effectiveness (see, for instance, Rutter *et al.*, 1979; Mortimore *et al.*, 1988; Teddlie and Stringfield, 1993) and as a change agent (see, for instance, Leithwood and Jantzi, 1990; Reynolds 1996). As Shields aptly describes it:

> Educational leadership is widely recognised as complex and challenging. Educational leaders are expected to develop learning communities, build the professional capacity of teachers, take advice from parents, engage in collaborative and consultative discussion making, resolve conflicts, engage in educative instructional leadership, and attend respectfully, immediately, and appropriately to the needs and requests of families with diverse cultural, ethnic, and socioeconomic backgrounds. Increasingly, educational leaders are faced with tremendous pressure to demonstrate that every child for whom they are responsible is achieving success.
>
> (Shields, 2004, p. 109)

Despite this ample evidence for the importance of good leadership practice Hallinger has argued that surprisingly little interest was shown in school leadership preparation programmes outside North America prior to the mid-1990s (Hallinger, 2003, p. iv) and that 'both pre-service and in-service training for principals and other school leaders were non-systematic, optional, and sparsely provided globally' (Hallinger, 2003, p. 4). This text developed out of a special issue of the journal *School Leadership and Management* (Volume 26, Number 2, April 2006) which focused on leadership development and brought together work by scholars from Europe, East Asia, Australasia and the USA. The central argument for devoting a text to leadership development is the same as that for the journal special edition – that leadership development has, suddenly and in some ways quite dramatically, become a major focus of educational systems around the world and yet remains under-examined and under-researched in many, probably most, nations. Indeed, one can only concur with Hallinger's analysis that, until the last decade, few countries other than the USA have paid close attention to the systematic development of school leaders and the concept of actually leading, rather than managing or administering a school, is quite new in many nations. The reasons for this are complex and culturally specific but focus around the fact that traditional conceptions have tended to view the role of head teachers and principals as leading practitioners rather than as financial or resource managers. The dramatic shift to forms of site-based management that emerged as a transnational trend during the 1980s and 1990s caused a paradigm shift in the perceived role of principals, who suddenly found it necessary to acquire skills in financial and human resource management and leading an organization in the context of a rapidly changing environment, in addition to supervision of curriculum and pedagogy that would inevitably have formed the focus for their initial professional training.

As is the case with any major initiative, the dramatic rise of leadership development programmes has presented opportunities for some and challenges for others. The opportunities have included the exciting possibilities of creating new programmes that may help to enhance leadership and transform schools. The challenges are both practical and conceptual and relate to a series of questions such as:

- What is the appropriate balance between the academic and the practical?
- Should provision be located in higher education institutions, in other government-sponsored organizations or commissioned from the private sector?
- Are models of leadership studies derived from business and industry relevant to schools?
- How can research into the impact of leadership on outcomes inform leadership development policy and strategy?
- Should programmes be integrated into higher degree provision or should new and innovative forms of accreditation be developed?

As the chapters in this text reveal, some countries, such as the USA, have chosen to locate leadership training in university departments and have built clear links with academic programmes; some have chosen to develop new forms of programmes and qualifications based in specially created institutions, such as the National College for School Leadership in the UK; others have chosen a middle route that uses established and prestigious university departments in conjunction and collaboration with private organizations, as is the case in New Zealand. Wherever programmes are located it is undoubtedly true that there has been an international trend to draw on broad frameworks that integrate leadership development models and conceptions of leadership from business and industry. For some this is a dangerous dalliance with market-driven ideologies that may diminish the social dimension of education; for others it is viewed as a sensible way of ensuring that best practice is seized upon and used in schools, wherever its origins lie.

We must remember, however, that generalizations are themselves dangerous. We may justifiably view the enormous increase of interest in educational leadership development as a global phenomenon but it would be wrong to see such developments as being unidimensional and following the same trajectory around the globe. What some in Western countries may view as a worrying tendency to train leaders in order to increase the privatization of education may well be perceived by those in Eastern Europe as a laudable attempt to provide the skills that will enable leaders to develop schools that are independent of the state and thus contribute to a budding democracy. For this reason the editors have attempted, quite deliberately, to elicit papers that provide examples of leadership development initiatives from different cultural contexts.

Structure of the book

In Chapter 2 Mark Brundrett notes that school leadership training and development in England has witnessed a rapid shift from ad hoc provision to a structured and more coherent framework for leadership learning, most notably evidenced by the creation of the National College for School Leadership. The chapter outlines the developments which led up to the creation of the National College and examines and analyses the wide-ranging activities now undertaken under the aegis of the College. The chapter subsequently progresses to unpack the emerging critique of the standards-based approach to leadership development which underpins most of the recent initiatives in leadership development in the England and the wider UK.

In Chapter 3 Mike Cowie examines the case of the Scottish Qualification for Headship. He argues that the development of leadership programmes in Scotland has tended to mirror the initiatives that have emerged in the wider UK but the creation of the Scottish Qualification for Headship has its own cultural inflections designed to meet the needs of the Scottish context as part of the burgeoning regional democracy. This chapter goes on to outline the sometimes complex educational circumstances and challenges that obtain in Scotland and delineates the approach to leadership development that has emerged during a time of significant political change in the landscape of national and local governance.

In Chapter 4 Mark Brundrett and Chrysanthi Gkolia point out that leadership training in Greece has been undeveloped due to the centralized nature of the education system since they note that the main responsibility of a school principal in a Greek school is to implement ministerial directives and to coordinate the activities of teaching staff. Notably, principals in

Greece have not traditionally received any compulsory training prior to or upon their appointment as school leaders. However, the role of principal is increasingly being reconceptualized as leader rather than administrator and as a person who is capable of setting the vision of his or her institution, changing or shaping the culture of the school, inspiring and empowering the staff and cultivating a partnership between teachers, pupils and parents. The chapter goes on to review an emerging critique of the requirements for developing a training scheme that will bring leadership training in Greece into line with modern initiatives and movements across other countries of the European Community.

In Chapter 5 Mark Brundrett examines the dramatic changes in the governance of schools in the Czech Republic prior to, and since, the democratization that followed the collapse of communist hegemony in the 1980s and 1990s. The chapter charts the dramatic shifts in school leadership preparation that mirror broader historical and cultural changes in Eastern Europe including the Austro-Hungarian Empire, the period of the independent republic after the First World War, the period of Nazi occupation, the subsequent dominance of communist ideology, and the more recent attempts to democratize the Republic.

In Chapter 6 Tim Goddard suggests that, like the Czech Republic, Kosovo has been subject to powerful cultural and ideological forces that have shaped its national history and impacted on all aspects of national life, including education. This chapter reports on an initiative designed to develop a leadership learning programme that will address the needs of educational in Kosovo leaders at a time of burgeoning democracy. The chapter outlines the policy changes in Kosovo education that have flowed from the recreation of the democratic state after the fall of the Soviet Union and the nature of the leadership development programmes that have emerged since that time.

In Chapter 7 Rina Barkol examines principals' training and development in Israel where systematic courses for principals started at the end of the 1970s in two academic institutions: Beit Berl College and the University of Haifa. She points out that in the 1980s, additional academic institutions took up the challenge of school leadership preparation and this trend continued in the 1990s, to the point where, more recently, there have been 12 academic institutions offering training programmes where the courses have been fully or mostly supervised and budgeted by the Ministry of Education. However, principals' training in Israel has been subjected to increasing scrutiny over the last decade based on the growing understanding about the centrality of the principal's role in enhancing student outcomes and, more recently, discussions have been held about establishing an institute, funded privately, that will hold the remit for principals' training and development.

In Chapter 8 Allan Walker and Clive Dimmock argue that corroborative evidence of what works in leadership training and development to influence principals' knowledge, skills, values and behaviours, is now emerging. They describe a model of best practice in Hong Kong, called 'Blue Skies', which was founded on, and derived from, a body of international research-based evidence from successful principal leadership programmes, together with evaluation evidence from another recent Hong Kong leadership programme. They outline the policy background to leadership preparation in Hong Kong since 1990 and go on to provide an explanation of the structure for school leader training and development established by the Hong Kong government since 2000. They argue that, with this structure in place, attention has been shifted to the design principles of effective leadership programmes that maximize leader learning.

In Chapter 9 Simon Clarke examines the Australian agenda for school leadership development. He points out that the National Institute for Quality Teaching and School Leadership is the culmination of a national dialogue in the advancement of excellence in school leadership and its story captures many aspects of Australian thinking and policy. The chapter examines recent Australian progress in the advancement of a national agenda for developing the quality of school leadership focused on the Institute including the logistics of promoting a national approach to quality of school leadership according to the complex sharing of responsibilities for education that exists between the federal level of government and the states and territories. The chapter also reports some promising initiatives in shaping a national agenda for enhancing school leadership.

In Chapter 10 Viviane Robinson S. Earl Irving, David Eddy and Deirdre M. Le Fevre indicate how recent governmental reforms in New Zealand have created a situation where school leaders have assumed responsibility for the financial, property, human resource and health and safety aspects of their schools in addition to the pedagogic aspects of school activity. In response to these challenges sets of standards have been developed for principals of both primary and secondary schools but the authors suggest that arguably, the most significant challenge to identifying and responding to the learning needs of the first-time principals in New Zealand is their extraordinary diversity. The chapter outlines the nature of the changes in governance in New Zealand schools that have brought about the need for enhanced leadership training; the creation of the national programme of leadership development that has emerged; and, finally, the creation of the evaluative tool which seeks to establish the needs of leadership learners working in diverse contexts.

Finally, in Chapter 11, Joseph Murphy suggests that for much of the last 15 years the academic arm of the school administration profession in the United States has been in a period of considerable turmoil. At the heart of the ferment has been some roiling debate over the effectiveness of preparation programmes. At the outset of this period of reflection, the critique was largely internal to the profession but, more recently, internal scrutiny has been supplemented by critique from outside the school administration community. Murphy reviews findings about the nature of research on leadership preparation and, based upon that data, the writers outline an agenda for strengthening research on preparation programmes.

The chapters in this text reveal that the rise of leadership development programmes is both a global phenomenon and a complex web of interconnected, but culturally specific, patterns of provision. In this sense the movements in leadership development evident in this text fit within the paradigm of 'glocalization' developed by Robertson (1992, 1995) whereby global trends are subject to the disposition brought about by local historical and cultural contexts. The editors hope that this text will go some way to assist in setting out both the commonalities and differences in provision around the world and help to set an agenda for research and international collaboration that will further enhance leadership development.

References

Hallinger, P. (ed.) (2003) *Reshaping the landscape of school leadership development: contexts of learning* (Lisse: Swets and Zeitlinger).

Leithwood, K. and Jantzi, D. (1990) Transformational leadership: how principals can help reform school cultures, *School Effectiveness and School Improvement*, 1(3), 249–281.

Mortimore, P., Sammons, P., Stoll, L., Lewis, D. and Ecob, R. (1988) *School matters: the junior years* (Somerset: Open Books Publishing Ltd).

Reynolds, D. (1996) Schools do make a difference, *New Society*, 223–225.

Robertson, R. (1992) Globalization (London, Sage).

Robertson, R. (1995) Glocalization: time-space and homogeneity-heterogeneity, in: M. Featherstone, S. Lash and R. Robertson (eds) *Global modernities* (London: Sage), 25–44.

Rutter, M., Maughan, B., Mortimore, P. and Ouston, J. (1979) *Fifteen thousand hours* (London, Open Books).

Shields, C. (2004) Dialogic Leadership for Social Justice: Overcoming Pathologies of Silence, *Educational Administration Quarterly*, 40(1), 109–132.

Teddlie, C. and Stringfield, S. (1993) *Schools do make a difference: lessons learned from a ten year study of school effects* (New York: Teachers' College Press).

Chapter 2

Educational leadership development in England

Mark Brundrett

Introduction

Although the antecedents of school leadership development can be traced back to the nineteenth century, for much of the history of state-funded education in England, school leadership training and development has lacked coherence. Despite frequent and consistent calls for more systematic training, especially in relation to the training of head teachers, for much of the twentieth century responsibility for leadership education fell under the remit of Local Education Authorities, which adopted a variety of models and approaches, many of which failed to address in full the needs of those undertaking the most senior roles in schools. During the latter part of the twentieth century the academic study of approaches to what was then termed 'school management' became established in many university departments of education and, more latterly, both masters' and doctoral programmes became comparatively common. However, the most striking feature of school leadership development in England in recent decades has been the unprecedented level of government intervention, initially operating through higher education institutions and then, over the last decade, through government or quasi-government organisations.

A number of accounts, and associated models, of the evolving development of school leadership programmes have been offered (see, for instance, Bolam, 1997, 2003, 2004; Brundrett, 2000, 2001, Brundrett *et al.*, 2006a), all of which suggest a construction that included: ad hoc provision in the 1960s and early 1970s; towards increased coherence in the 1970s and 1980s; and growing national programmes from the 1990s, including a National College from 2000–2002. This account extends the timeline of analysis back into the nineteenth century and traces the subsequent journey of school leadership development activities in England until the present day in broader periods covering the Victorian era to 1960; 1960 to 1996, when Higher Education Institutions often took the lead; and then 1996 to the present when national programmes of leadership development first appeared. The chapter then goes on to outline some of the critique that has accompanied government colonisation of leadership studies. Finally, an attempt is made to discuss some of the key challenges that may be faced in the field in the near future.

From Victorian foundations to local authority control

At the beginning of the nineteenth century, elementary schools were sponsored by private individuals or the churches and, in particular, the Church of England. Local authorities also had the power to finance schools, however, public funding for schools did not begin until 1833 when parliament voted for the provision and maintenance of church schools (Eurydice, 2005). This effectively marked the beginning of state involvement in education in the United Kingdom. With the Elementary Act of 1870 school boards in England were established. In 1880 school attendance was made compulsory. It was not until ten years later, in 1890, that attendance became largely free. By the end of the nineteenth century a national system of education had been established. This system provided free, compulsory education for all children between the ages of five and ten. The 1902 Education Act provided for the establishment of the Local Education Authorities (LEAs) and these LEAs assumed responsibility for the education provided in their areas. At the turn of the century secondary education was still the privilege of those who were able to pay for it. However, LEAs offered a number of scholarships to pupils who had successfully passed a specific examination (ibid.).

This period has been associated with the 'hero-innovator leadership model' (Thody, 2000: 162) and it has been argued that the first 'competency' lists for school managers came in 1816 with Jeremy Bentham's *Chrestomathia* which created the vision of a utopian school and contained an instruction table with the title 'Principles of School Management' (Thody, 2000: 166). There seems to have been a thriving publication industry relating to what we would now term school leadership and management, particularly in relation to the management of teaching and learning, which consisted of textbooks containing abundant detail on lesson plans and notes explaining the precise order and content of what was to be taught (Thody, 2000: 48). Indeed, reading management texts seems to have been a 'recreation' for school leaders during this period (Thody, 1994: 9). It seems that such texts were popular since they were designed to meet the requirements of what was effectively the first national curriculum in England, embodied in the Revised Codes introduced in 1862 (Thody, 2000: 48). An examination in school leadership was compulsory for all teachers in training during this period and some striking similarities have been revealed between the issues addressed in assessment during the 1880s and the National Professional Qualification for Headship in the late 1990s (Thody, 2000: 51). This period seems to have come to an end as the exigencies of the initial form of centrally directed curriculum and site-based management ceased with the arrival of LEAs at the start of the twentieth century (Thody, 2000: 47). Thus, for the first half of the century, responsibility for leadership development in English schools was held at local level. Although many local authorities attempted to provide some form of induction training activities for newly appointed head teachers, leadership training for other members of staff was notable by its absence and the system, insofar as one existed, was ad hoc, localised, and lacked any overarching set of national principles (Bolam, 2004).

1960 to 1996 – higher education involvement and the first state intervention

The emergence of school leadership and management in England as a recognisable area of activity and a discipline in its own right can be traced back to the 1960s and 1970s. Amongst the trends that stimulated this was the reorganisation of the selective system, which created many large comprehensive schools. For these head teachers it meant recognition that as well as the demands of professional leadership they now had to accommodate the demands of school management. A series of reports in this period, including the Robbins Report (1963), the Franks Report (1967), the Plowden Report (1968) and the James Report (1972), identified the emerging need for more effective in-service training throughout the education sector.

The imperative for a structured ladder of training provision in all phases and at all levels of the education system was not to be addressed for many years. However, there were a small number of initiatives that paved the way for future provision. For instance the Commonwealth Council for Educational Administration and Management (CCEAM) and the British Educational Management and Administration Society (now British Educational Leadership, Management and Administration Society) were founded in 1971 and 1972 respectively. Equally, the Master of Education degree began to proliferate in the 1960s (Shanks, 1987: 122–123) and higher degree programmes with elements of educational management began to appear in the 1970s (Bush, 1999: 239). By the 1980s taught higher degrees in educational management became an increasingly important part of the portfolio of university courses in England.

Significant weaknesses have subsequently been perceived in the fitness for purpose and professional utility of these academically oriented initiatives. Higher education institutions tended to only see merit in academically orientated courses whereas schools themselves tended to see management as a purely atheoretical activity which was divorced from theory (Gill *et al.*, 1989: 78; Brundrett, 2001: 235) but, by the early 1990s, there was a growing acceptance that skills developed in the workplace should be seen as an integrated part of academic programmes (Golby, 1994: 69) and which were flexible enough to retain academic rigour whilst addressing the professional needs of teachers (Black *et al.*, 1994: 36). In response to this call educational masters' programmes were developed that offered formalised provision which linked professional experience, individual development and academic qualifications (Davies and Ellison, 1994: 363). Moreover, the 'professional doctorate' began to emerge in British universities, aimed at 'mid-career education professionals' (Gregory 1995; Brundrett, 2001: 235). By the late 1990s higher education programmes provided a comparatively structured provision of progressive academic qualifications grounded in both theory and practice (Brundrett, 1999; 2001: 235).

It may be that this eventual interconnection between the academic and the professional and practical emerged somewhat too late to meet the developing government agenda to raise the achievement and the performance of the English school system. Department of Education and Science (DES) Circular 3/83 identified educational management training as one of four priorities for teacher training and the DES consequently introduced the most influential school leadership training project of the 1980s to be known as the 'One Term Training Opportunities' (OTTOs). These were available to head teachers and senior staff to enable them to adapt to the increasingly difficult and complicated tasks of management (Huber, 2001). At the same time the National Development Centre for School Management Training (NDC) was established at the School of Education at the University of Bristol to stimulate management training and research. Again the range, quality and pattern of provision was mixed and the substantial impact required nationally was not forthcoming. The impact of the OTTO courses was summarised by Wallace (1988) who noted that although the scheme had provided a significant response to the increased need for management training, it had not made the impact that had initially been hoped for (Brundrett, 1999, 2001). The courses did have many positive outcomes since they were perceived to be valuable by head teachers, had a significant effect on management, and provided the opportunity for reflection on changes in management practice in a way that was difficult to achieve on shorter courses (Brundrett, 2000: 28–30, 2001: 236–237). By the end of the 1980s, however, the National Development Centre had been closed down and the government had set up a School Management Task Force. The Task Force was to report on a more effective national strategy for training headteachers and school staff with management roles. Its two key recommendations were for the better integration of in-school and offsite development and for the pooling of expertise nationally.

In the 1980s a number of changes and new inputs in legislation were brought forward. The Education Act 1981 put into practice the changes proposed by the Warnock Report. These related to the provision of education for pupils with special educational needs (SEN). Five years later, in

1986, the new education act provided for increased powers for the school governing bodies. In 1988, the then Conservative government passed a new Education Reform Act which introduced a National Curriculum, national testing for students at the ages of 7, 11, 14 and 16. Crucially, for the purposes of this chapter, the Act also introduced Local Management of Schools (LMS) which meant that schools' funding was determined by pupil numbers. An associated system of inspection was created in 1993 under the aegis of the Office for Standards in Education (Ofsted). The framework for inspection includes criteria for leadership and management and judged the overall 'value for money' represented by the school in terms of performance and effectiveness. These reforms are credited with driving up standards in schools but have been subject to a sustained critique (see, for instance, Myers and Goldstein, 1998; Stoll and Myers, 1998) and revisions to the Ofsted inspection framework have placed increasing emphasis on schools' self-evaluation processes.

1996 to the present – the rise of national programmes and the arrival of the National College for School Leadership

Despite such mixed outcomes, the OTTO scheme proved to be only a foretaste of the massive state intervention that occurred from the mid-1990s when the focus shifted to the increasingly influential 'national programmes' which changed significantly the power relationship between the governmental and regulatory authorities and the providers of in-service training (Brundrett, 2001: 237). It is acknowledged that the shift to school-based systems of management, along with the increased regulatory and accountability requirement embodied in the 1988 Education Act, created the need for enhanced leadership training for schools. The remit for the development and management of these programmes originally fell to the Teacher Training Agency (TTA), was held briefly under the direct control of the Department for Education and Skills, and subsequently transferred to the National College for School Leadership (NCSL) which commenced its activities in temporary premises at the University of Nottingham in 2000 before moving to purpose-built premises on the same site in 2002. The NCSL was established to ensure that current and future school leaders develop the skills, the capability and capacity to lead and transform the school education system into the best in the world (DFEE, 2001). The NCSL has subsequently played a pivotal role in the coordination of national programmes of school leadership development and now oversees the development and delivery of courses and qualifications in England. It aims to combine the intellectual, professional and practical development of school leaders, drawing on best practice, while supporting an ongoing discourse about school leadership that will inform its work (Earley *et al.*, 2002). NCSL's corporate plan for

2002/2006 put in place the largest educational leadership development programme in the world by 2004 (NCSL, 2001b).

In 2001 the NCSL produced the *Leadership Development Framework*, which outlined five areas of leadership development linked to a series of core and extension programmes including: emergent leaders – for people who are beginning to take on formal leadership roles; established leaders – experienced deputy and assistant head teachers who have decided not to pursue headship; entry to headships – for those aspiring to or embarking on their first headship; advanced leaders – head teachers with four or more year's experience can attend the Leadership Programme for Serving Headteachers (LPSH); and consultant leaders – experienced head teachers and other leaders who wish to take on the responsibility for the future development of school leadership (NCSL, 2001c). In essence this framework encapsulated and enlarged the construction that had emerged during the previous six years of development which had come to be based around preparatory, induction and further training for head teachers.

Preparation, induction and further training of head teachers

The limitations of space preclude a detailed outline of the development of all the increasingly myriad national programmes. Nonetheless, it is useful to rehearse the fact that a triumvirate of programmes that address that key agenda of preparatory, induction and further training for head teachers have formed the backbone and key functions of national intervention in leadership training. The programme designed to address the preparatory phase of head teacher training was launched in 1997 in the form of the National Professional Qualification for Headship (NPQH). In its early form, this was a complex, centrally controlled but regionally delivered, programme of training and development with an allied, but separate, system of assessment (Brundrett, 2001). In response to robust criticisms the NPQH was completely restructured in 2000 following a major review with new contractors being appointed to offer the revised scheme which commenced in 2001 (NCSL, 2001a). A further review aimed to make the programme more specifically related to those intending to move into headship and linked more closely to the Early Headship Programme was undertaken, with the revised version trialled during 2007. The Headteachers' Leadership and Management Programme (HEADLAMP) commenced operation in 1995 with a key aim to provide funds 'to support the cost of developing the leadership and management abilities of headteachers appointed to their first permanent headship' (TTA, 1999). The decision about replacement programmes was publicly announced by the NCSL in 2003 and the Headteachers' Induction Programme (HIP), designed to replace HEADLAMP, commenced in that year. The programme was subject to further review and revision and was replaced by the Early Headship Programme (EHP) in 2006 which was designed to support new head teachers in identifying and addressing their development needs and following their desired pathway through the early years of headship (NCSL. 2007c). The Leadership Programme for Serving Headteachers (LPSH) is the most significant programme for the further training of head teachers that has been developed this far (Green, 1998). Nonetheless the programme came under review in 2006 and a new programme, entitled Head for the Future (HftF), was created which is designed to 'directly tackle emerging challenges for headship, particularly the need to collaborate with other schools and agencies' and 'asks each participant to challenge perceptions about the change and outcomes they require, keeping a clear view of what their distinctive context demands' (NCSL, 2007a).

The functions and activities of the NCSL include not only the preparation, induction and development of headship initiatives but also include a wide number of other programmes. The comparatively recent inclusion of 'Leading from the Middle' (in 2003) in the NCSL portfolio is a highly significant development since it targets middle leaders in schools and is thus emblematic of a commitment to the development of leadership capacity at all levels in the teaching profession. Other NCSL activities include: online learning and network information including Talking Heads and Virtual Heads; research and development projects; and the Networked Learning Communities scheme (Bolam, 2004: 260). The NCSL also operated 'affiliated regional centres' which no longer exist but the 'Leadership Network' which now takes responsibility for developing the College's regional links involves over 2,000 schools organised in nine regions. This rapid expansion in activity can be perceived as both an achievement and a weakness. An end to end review of the NCSL, presented in 2004, noted its 'very significant, even remarkable, achievements' but called for 'streamlining the NCSL's efforts to increasing its impact, through greater role clarity, outcome focus, goal clarity and efficiency' (DfES/NCSL, 2004: 5). This was re-echoed by the Minister of Education who called for 'greater precision, discipline, outcome-focus, and depth in the future work of the College' (Minister of State for Education, 2004: 2). Nonetheless, at the time of writing, the NCSL website listed 29 programme or major initiatives (NCSL, 2007b).

The critique of leadership development programmes

The development of a national provision of leadership training in England is to be applauded since the plethora of initiatives can be seen as the fulfilment of calls for systematic training and development for school leaders that have been made over the period of a generation. In England such calls have been voiced by successive generations of serving professionals, academics and policy makers. A cogent critique of these national initiatives has emerged which eddies around at least four interconnected sets of concerns about: increasing bureaucratisation; the underpinning conceptual framework and origins of such programmes; the relationship between such national developments and academic programmes; and, the long-term sustainability of national programmes in the face of other national imperatives. To address these anxieties in order of precedent:

- First, Glatter (1997) warned of the dangers of a bureaucratisation of leadership development at the start of such national initiatives and the subsequent national framework, centred around the National College for School Leadership, can have done little to palliate such apprehension.
- Second, the leadership development framework has been underpinned the National Standards for Headteachers (TTA, 2000) thus establishing an emphasis on standards-based approaches in training and leadership development (Brundrett *et al.*, 2006a) and concerns exist that such a structure is too detailed, prescriptive and bureaucratic (Glatter, 1997; Gronn, 2003; Thrupp, 2005) and questions remain as to the extent that programmes such as the NPQH capture the principal skills required for headship (Fidler and Atton, 2004: 139).
- Third, the decline of university sector-accredited provision (Brundrett, 1999) raises questions as to whether school leadership development may be impoverished by inadequate attention to explicit theoretical and conceptual groundings (Brundrett, 1999, 2000, 2001; Thrupp, 2005).
- Fourth, the sustainability of the leadership college model, which may be sensitive to political change, is open to question (Bolam, 2004: 260).

Such concerns about the relevance and quality of leadership standards appears to be transnational, as evidenced by Murphy's typically erudite exposition of such discussions about the system of licensure for the principalship in the USA (Murphy, 2005). The potentially problematic relationship between national programmes and academic award-bearing programmes has caused incipient disquiet in England for some time (Brundrett, 1999). Whereas the United States has pursued a course of action whereby leadership standards are embedded in university programmes, such a route has been rejected in England, leaving such programmes open to accusations of state arrogation of control (Brundrett, 2001). Undoubtedly knowledge of theory, research and practice is vital if leadership is to be exercised that draws on more than the leader's own professional and personal biography (Bush and Glover, 2005) and concerns have been expressed that national programmes in England fail to engage course participants with the research-based literature since they operate outside the remit of higher education institutions (Fidler and Atton, 2004: 140). It is for these reasons that there have been persuasive arguments positing that programmes for aspiring head teachers should be at Masters' level (Bush and Jackson, 2002: 424).

Finally, potential strategic instabilities face the organisations that develop, manage and monitor national programmes, including the danger of rapidly changing priorities of governmental and institutional incumbents and more menacingly, there are questions about the overall sustainability of programmes that are funded by governments whose priorities may change over time (Bolam, 2004: 261–263). This has led to the question of whether such programmes will be an interlude or form a permanent arrogation of leadership development (Brundrett *et al.*, 2006b).

Nonetheless, and contrary to some of the less informed analysis of leadership development in the UK and beyond, there is ample evidence that national programmes of development do have a positive impact on leadership capacity and confidence but the best evidence we have suggests that this positive impact is mixed with some serious inadequacies that have yet to be addressed. The Ofsted review of leadership and management training for head teachers, published in 2002 (Ofsted, 2002), drew on a wide range of evidence and thus provides some of the most detailed analysis of the efficacy of the key national programmes of leadership development. The main findings of the report concluded that: the quality of much of the training on the NPQH programme was of good quality but there remained concerns about the selection of appropriate candidates and the capacity of the training to respond to a wide range of needs; the quality of much of the LPSH training was good and was generally well received by head teachers but the programme did not always meet the needs of head teachers from a variety of contexts; there was no clear progression in the content of the three national training programmes for head teachers; and, the various training programmes did not meet sufficiently the particular needs of participating head teachers (Ofsted, 2002: 5–6).

In part this overarching critique of the English framework can be viewed as a reaction to the fact such national programmes of school leadership development can be seen as one element of an increasingly centralising dictum within Western liberal society that has been operant since the 1980s; a dictum which, ironically, is counterbalanced by a commitment to marketisation and local management of schooling (Daun, 2004). Commitments to leadership development in education systems in other parts of the world, such as the emerging democracies in Eastern Europe, are very different in that they flow from an attempt to democratise social processes against a background of many years of communist ideology within which the new goal of education is, above all, to create 'self-confident, participating citizens' (Havel, 1993: 118). In such nations the privatisation of education, with concomitant needs for enhanced leadership skills, is seen as a method of encouraging innovative practice that lends legitimacy to the state's aspiration for democratic change (Svecova, 1994, 2000; Cerych *et al.*, 1996). Within this programme of democratisation two principal orientations emerged: one towards restoration and one towards innovation and borrowing from the West (Daun and Sapatoru, 2002). For instance as discussed in Chapter 5 of this text, the dramatic shifts in the governance of schools and the roles and associated training of head teachers in the Czech Republic and its predecessor entities exemplifies how vocational identities have been decomposed and reconstructed in that nation in a manner which reflects trends across other central and Eastern European nations (Rafal, 1998). Concerns exist that the previous totalitarian ideology has been replaced by market-driven forces which have led to an increasing privatisation of education in the Czech Republic (Jana, 2000) but, in contrast to much of the commentary in England, such privatisation is seen by many Czech commentators as a method of ensuring the 'depoliticisation' of education and training (Svecova, 2000: 128). However, it is noteworthy that, in contrast to the situation obtaining in England, higher education institutions have retained a leading role in the development of leadership programmes, as in other areas of continuing professional development for teachers (Sayer, 1995).

Whilst England, the wider UK and most Western democracies do not have to face the immense challenges posed by the geopolitical transition being undergone in Eastern Europe, Western society does face unprecedented and, at times, apparently insurmountable challenges in terms of the need to create fairer, more democratic societies during a period which has seen the creation of evermore diverse social consortia which appear to have the potential to threaten social cohesion. This is *the* pre-eminent challenge facing school leaders and school leadership development.

Future challenges: meeting an agenda for social justice or ensuring supply

Recent government legislation has set in train fundamental adjustments to the education system, through the medium of such initiatives as the Every Child Matters (TSO, 2003) agenda, which emphasises inter-agency activity with schools as central players in delivery. Undoubtedly this policy will require a much more explicit articulation of the role of school leaders in promoting social welfare and social justice during their training. However, the challenge of finding the next generation of school leaders may itself become an increasing focus of leadership training in order to develop new skill sets in head teachers and other senior managers that will enable schools to create a 'pipeline' of leadership that will meet the challenge of recruitment.

A major review of school leadership conducted by PricewaterhouseCoopers (2007) concluded that there is a 'strong need to renew leadership capacity in the sector' in order to embrace and deliver new policy objectives such as the ECM and 14–19 agendas with one in ten heads claiming to have undertaken no professional development in the three years prior to the report (p. 148). The report noted that there is mixed evidence from school leaders and stakeholders on the appropriateness of NCSL programmes such as NPQH and LPSH/Head for the Future and that aspects of these qualifications require reform in order to ensure that they are appropriate and fit-for-purpose (p. 150). PricewaterhouseCoopers noted that this suggests the need to widen the concept of leadership qualifications, and draw on the best of what is already in the market in terms of other bespoke management and leadership qualifications, for ongoing leadership development. Overall the report called for the adoption of a new approach towards leadership qualifications in which consideration should be given to reforming key aspects of headship programmes in order to ensure that the key needs articulated by school leaders are given further prominence, in particular in areas such as financial management, extended services and the associated implications for team working and people management. Further, the report suggested that delivery needed to be overhauled and modernised to include e-learning solutions, a greater element of modularisation and tailoring to individual need, and cross-sectoral inputs within which participation in national leadership programmes is understood in relation to relevant elements of other professional qualifications. No doubt the findings of this influential report will impact significantly on future policy development in this area. For those operating in traditional higher education settings the conclusion that some school leaders indicated that other qualifications such as MBAs and masters degrees have proved, in their view, to be very useful in terms of helping them deal with leadership challenges, offers the possibility of a renewed role for the university sector (p. 151).

With this enhanced focus on the ECM agenda and the reinvigorated focus on other routes for training, including academic programmes, the possibility exists that leadership development programmes may emphasise the social justice agenda as never before. Engagement with programmes based in higher education institutions holds out the opportunity that students will be required to respond to the increasingly sophisticated literature on leadership drawn from a wide range of theoretical and empirical perspectives. The achievement of the national programmes has been significant, even startling, in a little over a decade. The possibility that leadership development activity will be broadened still further will enhance leadership capacity, student achievement and associated life chances.

There are, however, dangers that all of the agenda created by the Every Child Matters initiative will be overtaken by the apparently more mundane challenge of filling leadership vacancies. There is growing evidence of a shortage of applicants for leadership posts in English schools (Rhodes and Brundrett, 2006) and details of school leadership shortages are also emerging internationally (Gronn, 2003). The need to identify and develop a pool of talent able to meet present and future leadership requirements in schools is imperative and it is increasingly clear that one element of successful leadership may itself be a commitment to enhancing the leadership skills of others (Dimmock, 2003). Thus head teachers and other senior school leaders may play a central role in the creation of a culture which fosters leadership development by interlinking these overlapping spheres of person, school and training packages. Such a culture is mediated by the school's overall vision of its preferred future and the match between the school strategic plan and professional development is seen as crucial if programmes are to have their greatest effect (West-Burnham, 1998; Davies and Ellison, 2003). Undoubtedly, programme impact is most evident where senior school leaders take ownership or, at the very least, have strong involvement in the active commissioning of leadership activities in order to ensure that there is alignment between leadership development and school improvement planning (Brundrett *et al.*, 2006b).

Walker and Dimmock (2005: 89) indicate that the processes whereby such sponsorship leads to enhanced effectiveness are complex but it is clear that head teachers can empower staff to undertake programmes and support leadership learning through providing access to knowledge, data and power structures within the school. Stoll *et al.* (2001) note that improving learning processes and outcomes entails collaboration, and school improvement research shows that decentralised and participatory leadership rather than top-down delegation is effective. Clearly, one of the ways in which head teachers support leadership learning is through control over the distribution of responsibility (Fletcher-Campbell, 2003). Such responses reinforce the findings of Jeffrey and Woods (2003), who argue that collaboration must involve 'valuing individuals, interdependence, openness and trust' (127). Moreover, Jones (2003) links feeling valued with distributed leadership as devolving responsibility wherever possible and through working together as a team makes staff feel valued and empowered, thus leading teachers to become involved in innovation.

Developing a 'leadership pipeline' of the type recommended in the wider literature on leadership development (see, for instance, the work of Charan *et al.*, 2001) within schools may be more complex than is the case in business settings because of the permeable nature of schools which causes multiple and overlapping sets of relationships and accountability structures to be taken into consideration in any initiative, including attempts to enhance leadership learning. Nonetheless, there is ample evidence that successful head teachers have an important role in directing school improvement through making crucial decisions about staff development (Collins, 2001) and one cannot overemphasise the centrality of the role of the head teacher in providing a setting which facilitated the successful interplay of forces between programme, individual and school context. Undoubtedly such intervention can help to ensure a culture which both facilitates and encourages leadership learning.

Conclusions

Although there is evidence of a nascent national system of school leadership education during the latter part of the Victorian era, for much of the twentieth century school leadership development in England was treated as a low priority by successive national governments. Repeated calls for enhanced training, especially of head teachers, fell on deaf ears and it was only during that latter part of the century that the challenge of leadership education was taken up by higher education departments. The impetus for change was created by the dramatic changes in governance of schools, most notably through the effects of the 1988 Education Act, which transformed the role of head teachers from leading pedagogic experts to something more akin to business managers. The consequent massive state intervention in leadership training set in train a major arrogation of control over the education of leaders which transferred much of the responsibility for leadership development from local authorities and university departments of education to governmental and quasi-governmental organisations. The subsequent creation of the national school leadership development framework in England has been an unprecedented achievement that can be viewed as the fulfilment of a commitment to continual professional development by successive governments since the 1960s.

Despite these significant achievements such national developments contained a series of inherent weaknesses and challenges. National programmes have challenged the traditional role of university education departments in the continued professional development of teachers, having arisen at a time of unprecedented change in andragogy brought about by new technologies such as the internet and e-learning. The fact that their rise has been co-terminous with, and in part caused by, a period of unprecedented state intervention in schooling has given rise to the criticism that such programmes are too closely allied to the delivery of the governmental agenda. Nonetheless, unprecedented opportunities now exist for leadership development that may assist in the delivery of a laudable educational and social agenda that has as its key aim the enhancement of school outcomes and associated social opportunity.

References

Black, D.R., Ericson, J.D., Harvey, T.J., Hayden, M.C. and Thompson, J.J. (1994) The development of a flexible, modular MEd, *International Journal of Educational Management*, 8, 1: 35–39.

Bolam, R. (1997) Management development for headteachers, *Educational Management and Administration*, 25, 3: 265–283.

Bolam, R. (2003) Models of leadership development, *Leadership in Education*, London: Sage Publications.

Bolam, R. (2004) Reflections on the NCSL from a historical perspective, *Educational Management, Administration and Leadership*, 32, 3: 251–267.

Brundrett, M. (1999) The range of provision of taught higher degrees in educational management in England and Wales, *International Studies in Educational Administration*, 27, 2: 43–59.

Brundrett, M. (2000) *Beyond Competence: The Challenge for Educational Management*, King's Lynn: Peter Francis.

Brundrett, M. (2001) The development of school leadership preparation programmes in England and the USA, *Educational Management and Administration*, 29, 2: 229–245.

Brundrett, M., Fitzgerald, T. and Sommefeldt, D. (2006a) The creation of national programmes of school leadership development in England and New Zealand: a comparative study, *International Studies in Educational Administration*, 34, 1: 89–106.

Brundrett, M., Slavíková, L., Karabec, S., Murden, B., Dering, A. and Nicolaidou, M. (2006b) Educational leadership development in England and the Czech Republic: comparing perspectives, *School Leadership and Management*, 26, 2: 93–106.

Bush, T. (1998) The National Professional Qualification for Headship: the key to effective school leadership?, *School Leadership and Management*, 18, 3: 321–333.

Bush, T. (1999) Crisis or crossroads? The discipline of educational management in the 1990s, *Educational Management and Administration*, 27, 3: 239–252.

Bush, T. and Glover, D. (2005) Leadership development for early headship: the New Visions experience, *School Leadership and Management*, 25, 3: 217–239.

Bush, T. and Jackson, D. (2002) A preparation for school leadership–internal perspectives, *Educational Management and Administration*, 30, 4: 417–429.

Cerych, L., Bacik, F., Kotasek, K. and Svecova, J. (1996) Reviews of national policies for Education: Czech Republic, in OECD, *Transforming Education, Part 1*, OECD: Paris: 15–94.

Charan, R., Drotter, S. and Noel, J. (2001) *The Leadership Pipeline: How to Build the Leadership Powered Company*, London: Josey Bass Wiley.

Collins, J. (2001) *Good to Great*, New York: HarperCollins.

Daun, H. (2004) Privatisation, decentralization and governance in education in the Czech Republic, England, France, Germany and Sweden, *International Review of Education*, 50: 325–346.

Daun, H. and Sapatoru, D. (2002) Educational reforms in Eastern Europe, in D. Holger (ed.) *Educational Restructuring in the Context of Globalization and National Policy*, New York: RoutledgeFalmer: 147–179.

Davies, B. and Ellison, L. (1994) New Perspectives on developing school leaders, *British Journal of In-Service Education*, 20, 3: 361–371.

Davies, B. and Ellison, L. (2003) *Strategic Direction and Development of the School: Key Frameworks for School Improvement Planning*, London: RoutledgeFalmer.

DFEE (2001) *Schools Building on Success*, London: Stationery Office.

DFES (2002) *The Leadership Development Framework*, http://www.teachernet.gov.uk/standards_framework/frmwork-stp2.cfm?position=sl.

DFES/NCSL (2004) *School Leadership: End to End Review of School Leadership Policy and Delivery*, London: DFES/NCSL.

Dimmock, C. (1998) Leadership in learning-centred schools: cultural context, functions and qualities, in M. Brudrett and R. Smith (eds) *Leadership in Education*, London: Sage.

Downes, P. (1996) The deputy head's magic roundabout, *Managing Schools Today*, 5, 7: 27–28.

Earley, P., Evans, J., Collarbone, P., Gold, A. and Halpin, D. (2002) *Establishing the Current State of School Leadership in England*, Institute of Education, University of London Queen's Printer.

Eurydice (2005) *Information Network on Education in Europe*, http://www.eurydice.org/accueil_menu/en/frameset_menu.html (accessed January 2007).

Fidler, B. and Atton, T. (2004) *The Headship Game: the Challenge of Contemporary School Leadership*, London: RoutledgeFalmer.

Fletcher-Campbell, F. (2003) Promotion to middle management: some practitioner's perceptions, *Educational Research*, 45, 1: 1–15.
Franks, O. (1967) *Report of Commission of Inquiry*, Oxford: Oxford University Press.
Gill, J., Golding, D. and Angluin, D. (1989) Management development and doctoral research, *Management Education and Development*, 20, 1: 77–84.
Glatter, R. (1997) Context and capability in educational management, *Educational Management and Administration*, 25, 2: 181–192.
Golby, M. (1994) Doing a proper course: the present crisis in advanced courses, *Journal of Teacher Development*, 3, 2: 60–73.
Green, H. (1998) Training for today's school leaders, *Education Journal*, 21: 11.
Gregory, M. (1995) Implications of the introduction of the doctor of education degree in British Universities: can EdD reach parts the PhD cannot?, *The Vocational Aspect of Education*, 47, 2: 177–188.
Gronn, P. (2003) *The New Work of Educational Leaders*, London: Paul Chapman.
Havel, V. (1993) *Summer Meditations*, New York: Vintage Books.
Huber, S. (2001) *Preparing School Leaders for the 21st Century: An International Comparison of Development Progress in 15 Countries*, Swets & Zeitlinger Publishers, Netherlands.
James, L. (1972) *Teacher Education and Training: Report*, London: HMSO.
Jana, S. (2000) Privatization of education in the Czech Republic, *International Journal of Educational Development*, 20, 2: 122–133.
Jeffrey, B. and Woods, P. (2003) *The Creative School: a Framework for Success, Quality and Effectiveness*, London: RoutledgeFalmer.
Jones, M. (2003) What makes a good school, *New Era in Education*, 84, 1.
Minister of State for Education (2004) National College for School Leadership Priorities: 2005–06, Letter to the Chair of the National College for School Leadership, London: DFES.
Murphy, J. (2005) Unpacking the Foundations of ISLLC Standards and Addressing Concerns in the Academic Community, *Educational Administration Quarterly*, 41, 1: 154–191.
Myers, K. and Goldstein, H. (1998). Who's Failing? in L. Stoll and K. Myers (eds) *No Quick Fixes*, London: Falmer Press.
NCSL (National College for School Leadership) (2001a) *What is the NPQH?*, Nottingham: NCSL.
NCSL (2001b) *First Corporate Plan: Launch Year 2001–2002*, http://www.ncsl.gov.uk.
NCSL (2001c) *Leadership Development Framework*, Nottingham: NCSL.
NCSL (2007a) *Head for the Future*, http://www.ncsl.org.uk/programmes/headforthefuture/index.cfm (accessed March 2007).
NCSL (2007b) *A-Z List of Programmes*, http://www.ncsl.org.uk/programmes/programmes-atoz.cfm (accessed March 2007).
NCSL (2007c) *Early Headship Provision*, http://www.ncsl.org.uk/programmes/ehp/ehp-benefits.cfm (accessed March 2007).
Ofsted (2002) *Leadership and Management Training for Headteachers*, HMI Document No 457, London: HMI.
Plowden Report (1967) *Children and their Primary Schools* (2 vols.) Report of the Central Advisory Council for Education in England, London: HMSO.
PricewaterhouseCoopers (2007) *Independent Study into School Leadership*, London: DFES.

Rafal, P. (1998) The educational system in Poland and other central–eastern European countries during the transition, *International Journal of Early Years Education*, 6, 2: 165–176.

Rhodes, C. and Brundrett, M. (2006) The identification, development, succession and retention of leadership talent in contextually different primary schools: a case study located within the English West Midlands, *School Leadership and Management*, 26, 3.

Robbins (1963) *Report of the Committee on Higher Education (the Robbins Report)*, London: HMSO.

Sayer, J. (1995) The continuing professional development of teachers and the role of the University, *Oxford Studies in Comparative Education*, 5, 1: 65–70.

Sayer, J., Kazelleova, J., Martin, D., Niemczynski, A. and Vanderhoeven, J. (1995) Developing schools for democracy in Europe: an example of trans-European cooperation, *Oxford Studies in Comparative Education*, 5, 1: 1–3.

Shanks, D. (1987) The Master of Education degree in Scotland, *Scottish Educational Review*, 19, 2: 122–125.

Stoll, L. and Myers, K. (1998) *No Quick-Fixes*, London: Falmer Press.

Stoll, L., MacBeath, J. and Mortimore, P. (2001) Beyond 2000: where next for effectiveness and improvement, in J. MacBeath and P. Mortimore (eds), *Improving School Effectiveness*, Buckingham: Open University Press.

Svekova, J. (1994) Czechoslovakia, in S. Karsten and D. Majoor (eds) *Education in East Central Europe: Educational Change After the Fall of Communism*, New York: Waxmann.

Svekova, J. (2000) Privatization of education in the Czech Republic, *International Journal of Educational Development*, 20: 127–133.

Teacher Training Agency (1995a) *Headteachers' Leadership and Management Programme*, London: TTA.

Thody, A. (1994) *Lessons from the Past: Portents for the Future of Educational Leadership*, Lincoln School of Management Working Paper No 20, Lincoln: University of Lincoln and Humberside.

Thody, A. (2000) Utopia revisited – or is it better the second time around, *Journal of Educational Administration and History*, 32, 2: 46–61.

Thrupp, M. (2005) The National College for School Leadership: a critique. *Management in Education*, 19, 2: 13–19.

TSO (2003) *Every Child Matters*, London: TSO.

TTA (1998) *The National Standards ('Rainbow Pack')*, London: Teacher Training Agency.

Walker, A. and Dimmock, C. (2005) Developing leadership in context, in M. Coles and G. Southworth (eds), *Developing Leadership: Creating the Schools of Tomorrow*, Maidenhead: Open University Press.

Wallace, M. (1988) *Action Learning: Practice and Potential in School Management Development*, Bristol: NDC.

West-Burnham, J. (1998) *Leadership and Professional Development in Schools: How to Promote Techniques for Effective Learning*, London: Financial Times/Prentice Hill.

Chapter 3

The changing landscape of head teacher preparation in Scotland

Mike Cowie

Introduction

This chapter outlines how the introduction of the Scottish Qualification for Headship (SQH) should be set within an international context and viewed as part of an international policy response (Hallinger, 2003) to the increased complexity and the challenging nature of the role of head teacher (Shields, 2004). It is also a contrast to the NPQH in England (Cowie and Crawford, 2007).

This global enterprise is justified by the supposed links between attainment and economic performance in the global economy (SEED, 2006a), and the linkage of the leadership of the head teacher with improvement in a wide body of research literature (Fullan, 1992a, 1992b; Eraut, 1994; Hargreaves, 1994; Sammons, *et al.*, 1995; Hallinger and Heck, 1996; MacBeath and Mortimore, 2001 and Leithwood and Rhiel, 2003). Although the influence is contested (Bell *et al.*, 2003; Searle and Tymms, 2007), and where studies have found linkage it appears to be relatively small, indirect and not fully understood, there seems to be a broad international consensus among policy makers that the capacities of those who aspire to headship need to be developed.

Scotland became part of the global enterprise through the development of the Scottish Qualification for Headship (SQH), a 'benchmark qualification' designed to enable participants develop the competences needed to meet an identified standard. The work of Reeves *et al.* (1998) was followed by consultation process which led to the publication of the Standard for Headship (SfH) in 1998 (SOEID, 1998). The SfH provided a framework for describing the practice of headship and identified standards of performance in four key management functions. It also provided a framework for developing aspiring head teachers.

Within this framework, management activity was considered in terms of competent performance, coupled with behaviour that could be described and evidenced (Casteel *et al.*, 1997; Reeves *et al.*, 1998). Although competence-based, the SfH avoided a narrow reductionist approach by developing a holistic model underpinned by the 'Why, What and How' of professional practice. This model of professional action emphasized the primacy of professional values and required the successful deployment professional abilities as well as functional competence.

The SfH supported the development of the SQH programme, which is largely based on experiential learning and critical reflection (Reeves *et al.*, 1998). The SfH was revised in 2005 (SEED, 2005) the year in which achievement of the SfH became mandatory for new head teachers. However the reality is that mandatory status has proved to be impossible to achieve, and concerns that the number of SQH graduates is unlikely to meet the demand for new head teachers led to a government commitment to develop to provide choice and alternatives to the SQH by establishing new means of achieving the SfH (SEED, 2004).

This chapter contextualizes the development of the SQH and describes some of its distinctive features. The findings of the published research literature on the SQH is then summarized and this is followed by an outline of the revisions made to the original programme. The narrative and the research review pave the way for a brief analysis of the nature and purposes of standards in general and the revisions made to SfH in particular. Revision of the SfH, in combination with the commitment to support alternative routes towards attaining the standard, is changing the landscape of head teacher preparation in Scotland and so the chapter ends with a discussion of what the future might hold for head teacher preparation in Scotland.

Background

International discourses about modernization, performance management and improvement are reflected in educational policy in Scotland as they are elsewhere and these discourses have had an impact on professional development (Gleeson and Husbands, 2003). The introduction of a standard for new head teachers in Scotland in 1998 mirrors the politically driven 'competence movement' that emerged in teacher education in the 1990s and has had a major influence on head teacher preparation in Scotland. The SfH sits within a standards-based national framework of Continuing Professional Development (CPD) (Purdon, 2003; Christie and O'Brien, 2005). This framework has emerged in a 'piecemeal fashion' (O'Brien, 2006), but it now includes standards for initial teacher training, full registration (following an initial induction year), and chartered teachers (following successful completion of a chartered teacher programme).

The SQH was designed specifically to enable aspiring head teachers to meet the requirements of the SfH prior to their application for the post of head teacher, but its introduction was also pivotal in the subsequent emergence of a framework of professional development for school leaders (SEED, 2003). This framework encourages education authorities and providers of CPD to think in terms of a continuum of leadership and management development opportunities ranging from project leadership (for teachers early in their careers), team leadership (for those leading working groups or teams of staff), school leadership (including the SQH) and strategic leadership (for more established and experienced educational leaders and managers).

Successful participants in the SQH programme are awarded a postgraduate diploma as well as the SQH and this alignment of a professional and an academic qualification is a distinctive feature of the programme. Other distinctive features include the strong commitment to work-based learning referred to above and the collaborative management and organization of the programme in three regional consortia. Each consortium is a collaborative partnership of Education Authorities (EAs) and at least one university. The consortia provide systems of support for programme participants, with university tutors, the participants' head teachers, education authority officers and other head teachers involved in different supportive roles. The partnership model for planning and delivery ensures that prevailing orthodoxies can be challenged and that current Scottish practice is situated in a broader academic framework (Murphy *et al.*, 2000a; 2000b).

SQH participants are selected and sponsored by their education authorities (who receive funding from the Scottish Executive Education Department (SEED)). Participants must be fully registered with the General Teaching Council for Scotland and have at least five years' teaching experience. They must also demonstrate the potential for school leadership by having established a basic understanding of management principles and having successfully undertaken leadership and management tasks in school at either project leadership or team leadership level (SEED, 2002, 2003). Because much of the programme is workplace-based, participants must also have, or be able to obtain, access to an appropriate work environment to enable them to undertake whole school leadership responsibilities. The number of places available to candidates was initially based on the national requirement for new head teachers currently agreed by SEED. Education authorities were provided with 'ring fenced' funding specifically to support SQH participants, but funding for the SQH is now subsumed within general resource allocation and is now no longer protected, making it difficult for staff development officers within authorities to ensure that funding is available.

The SQH programme became fully operational in 2000, when license to deliver the programme was granted by the Scottish Executive to the three regional consortia. Operationally, the programme works within a national template, with specified units and associated learning outcomes. This national template frames local programmes, developed and delivered by the three consortia.

The original SQH programme was based on a set of design principles and a model of learning derived from research into professional learning (Eraut,

1994). At the heart of this model is the belief that learning has to influence professional practice and what goes on in schools. The 'Why, What and How' model meant that participants had not only to learn about what is involved in headship but to be able to justify decision making and also focus on the development of their intellectual and interpersonal abilities (SOEID, 1998). These three elements, Professional Values (the Why?), Management Functions (the What?) and Professional Abilities (the How?) were brought together in the programme, with learning and assessment designed to connect with each participant's school context, the wider policy context and the conceptual and research framework discussed in literature on school leadership and management and professional development.

Participants in the programme evaluate their experience against the SfH and identify their learning needs. Learning takes place through taught sessions, seminars, online activity, workshops and supported self study with reading and reflection, but the programme is predominantly workplace-based with candidates being required to manage and lead whole school projects and provide portfolios of evidence containing a claim for competence against the Standard supported by reflective commentaries. Within the final portfolio and commentary, participants are required to demonstrate that their leadership has improved an aspect of the school's ability to improve and made a difference to pupil learning through successful management practice with and through staff. The school-based element is supported by the education authority and the participants' head teachers who act as 'supporters' and are either trained for this role or given information about what is expected of them.

Quality is assured through an agreed programme descriptor, which contains performance criteria and by university quality assurance procedures. Field assessment by head teachers is an important part of the SQH programme, but assessment within the SQH also involves the rigour demanded by the requirements of the universities, with appropriate checks and balances to ensure that standards are maintained. These include moderation, double-marking and external examination.

Research findings and evaluation outcomes

Since the introduction of the SQH, several studies on the programme have been published. This work has contributed to the development of a grounded evidence base for use in decision making, both at policy and operational levels. However, at the policy level, despite general recognition of the need for decision making based on evidence and a need for effective evaluations to enable 'evidence-based' decision making (Levacic and Glatter, 2003), the outcomes of these evaluations have been ignored or poorly utilized.

The nature and purpose of these studies vary. Much of the work has been conducted by researchers in the three consortia responsible for delivering the programme. Its purpose was to improve delivery and where it has been possible to take findings into account within the operational framework the consortia have attempted to do so. However, logistical challenges beyond the scope of the consortia to resolve were identified and the Scottish Executive has been slow respond to these, or has interpreted them in particular ways, raising questions about both the commitment of the Executive towards the SQH and the extent to which evidence gained through systematic enquiry informs policy making. This failure to utilize the findings of systematic investigations and the meaning that has been attached to some findings has had implications for head teacher preparation in Scotland that will be discussed later.

The focus of published research by individuals involved in the SQH was very much on pedagogical or organizational concerns with a view to improving the quality of provision. An early study, for example, focused on issues to do with the delivery of the programme in the national pilot (Morris and Reeves, 2000). Jenny Reeves, one of the national development officers who designed the programme, and her colleagues, published a number of studies in the early years of the programme focusing on how the 'socio-dynamic nature' (Menter et al., 2003: 3) of the approach to learning within the SQH influences practice (Reeves *et al.*, 2001, 2003a, 2003b; Reeves and Forde, 2002). O'Brien and Draper (2001) looked at participant views in the first year of the programme. In government-funded evaluations, work by Simpson and her colleagues (Simpson *et al.*, 2000) focused on the role of the supporter and found that a participant's involvement in the SQH had a positive effect on the school and work by Murphy *et al.*, (2002a, 2002b) paid particular attention to the role of the EA (Education Authority) and its capacity to support and sustain delivery.

Murphy *et al.* set out a range of logistical challenges faced by those with management and coordination responsibilities. In doing so they raised a number of significant strategic issues to do with maintaining effective communication across a range of stakeholders and agencies. These included training university and education authority staff involved in delivery, support and assessment; ensuring even standards of support and delivery; integrating the SQH into a local staff development strategy at authority level; ensuring appropriate selection and candidacy; support and mentoring in-school; time and priority management for SQH candidates, who have already held demanding and responsible positions and the difficulty of maintaining national standards within a devolved delivery framework. In broad terms, however, Murphy *et al.* showed that the SQH represented a unique and valuable programme of professional learning for the Scottish teaching profession, bringing employers and universities together to provide a professionally focused but rigorous form of development, which was having a significant impact on thinking and practice within the profession.

One of the key findings, however, was the significant variety in education authority responses to and support for the programme. Murphy *et al.* found that this was having an impact on the quality of the participant experience, with some participants operating within more propitious supportive environments than others. Both in questionnaire returns and in interview, education authority coordinators were generally very positive about the SQH as a programme of continuing professional development (CPD and the partnership model of working in support of a work-based learning programme was regarded positively by coordinators, both in terms of its impact on professional learning and on schools. However, the key findings related to the complexity and significance of the coordination role within education authorities, and the critical importance of adequate resourcing for the success of the programme. Despite the concerns raised about variance in the support provided and funding, education authority coordinators across Scotland continue to have different levels seniority within their authorities and different areas of responsibility. Some coordinators, particularly those with staff development or management development responsibilities, have significant involvement in the SQH, while others, particularly in smaller education authorities, are overwhelmed with a wide range of responsibilities and coordination of the SQH is another responsibility added to a wide remit.

The most significant and wide ranging evaluation research on the SQH was a national evaluation commissioned by SEED and undertaken by Menter and his colleagues (Menter *et al.*, 2003). This study reinforced the positive findings of earlier studies and confirmed 'the significance of the SQH programme for the future of Scotland's schools' (p. 84). The aim of the evaluation was to identify the impact and outcomes of the programme where it had been completed successfully, and Menter *et al.* drew attention to its positive effect on successful participants, and indeed on their supporters (normally their head teachers) and the school as a whole, suggesting that, as had been intended, the programme is having a systemic effect. Significantly, Menter *et al.* also considered the 'high level of enthusiasm for the combination of theory and practice' to be 'extremely impressive' and recommended that the 'powerful pedagogical model' developed by the programme should be retained (Menter *et al.*, 2003: 87).

Taken together, these different studies identified significant strengths and found that the work-based learning model, with concurrent reflection on practice, and the requirement to work productively in teams to take forward whole school projects had a positive effect, not only on individual programme participants, but also on the culture of the school as a whole.

But although these studies were generally positive, concerns to do with workload pressure and variability in context and culture were also raised. As experienced teachers, most of whom hold posts of management responsibility in schools, SQH participants have demanding jobs and must balance family and work commitments. Simpson *et al.* (2000), for example, found that the programme exerts considerable workload pressures on both participants and head teacher supporters, and suggested that excessive workload demands may undermine the benefits of the programme. And although the national evaluation was not designed to identify difficulties experienced by SQH programme participants, the report noted that a small number of participants had encountered problems in the school context or had issues to do with difficulties in programme administration. Even among successful graduates, there were critical issues to do with the workload generated by the programme and the detrimental effect that this appears to have on work/life balance. This prompted Menter *et al.* to recommend devising more flexible routes to the award of the SQH as well as alternative means of demonstrating attainment of the SfH.

Although the work-based action learning model underpinning the SQH appears to be powerful and effective, it is clear that successful completion of the programme is influenced by the school context and the supportive environment provided by the EA. Murphy *et al.* (2002a, 2002b) pointed to the complexity of the role played by the coordinator within each EA and highlighted differences in how that role is interpreted. They also highlighted geographical differences, and differences in the degree and extent of support provided and contextual differences among schools. This suggests that even exceptionally able participants may find it difficult to thrive in stagnant schools with poorly developed systems and an impoverished culture, while the converse may be true in a more supportive school environment.

My own work also raised concerns about workload and equity in the Northern Consortium among participants who failed to complete the programme (Cowie, 2005). Workload and changing individual and family circumstances seem to make it difficult for some to balance family and work commitments and this work recommended that more flexibility was needed within the SQH to cater for the particular difficulties that individuals in scattered rural communities have to cope with. Perhaps contrary to what might have been expected, however (because one might expect a degree of disaffection from participants who fail to complete), most respondents valued the programme and thought that their involvement had been worthwhile.

Pressure of work and the demands of the programme mean that the nature and quality of the support provided is critical, and it is reasonable to assume that where there is a well-developed, supportive environment achievement of success is more likely. Regular EA network meetings to support participant learning, where participants meet together on a monthly or six weekly basis to discuss issues or themes from the literature or in relation to the development of their projects, were an important part of the original design of the programme, although the implications of this for rural communities was not considered. These implications were highlighted by Murphy *et al.* (2000a, 2002b) who found considerable diversity with regard to the purpose, content, structure, timing, frequency and regularity of local network meetings, with variation also in the role played by the coordinator.

There are also organizational concerns. The design of the SQH assumes that participants have some experience of school management at deputy head teacher level. However, concern over low numbers of applicants for head teacher posts, particularly in predominately rural authorities, has led some EAs to select some participants with little or no experience of senior management in schools. In some EAs participants undergo a rigorous selection procedure to gain entry to the programme, while in others, until recently, all applicants were accepted (Cowie, 2005). The absence of a well-developed framework of leadership and management opportunities at other levels has intensified concerns about readiness.

Despite these concerns, the partnership model for planning and delivery, with its combination of theory and practice, appeared to work well for most participants. However research findings challenged the consortia into thinking about how the majority could be planned for while ensuring that others are not excluded.

Programme revision

Until 2005, the three consortia operated within a template provided by SEED. Following 'deregulation' in 2005, each consortium agreed to continue to act as a partnership provider. The consortia collaborated with each other and substantially revised the original programme to take account of research and experience of delivering the programme in an attempt to accommodate different needs and contexts. Proposals were developed that were accredited by the General Teaching Council in Scotland (GTCS).

Participation in the SQH means that aspiring head teachers engage in a programme that they make their own in their particular contexts. Through 'personal formation' (Daresh, 2002) they integrate academic theory and personal and professional knowledge practice, underpinned by professional values and commitment. Research on the SQH suggests that this is a powerful model and in the redesign of the programme this emphasis on the development of theory in practice was retained.

Overall, however, the content, delivery, assessment and patterns of support were reshaped to take some account of variability in school contexts, levels of support in EAs and the workload demands on participants. In the revised programmes, participants are brought together on a more regular basis (to counter isolation in scattered rural areas) and there are more directed study activities between face-to-face teaching sessions, supported in the north of Scotland by distance learning models.

It was clear that the fairly simple 'Why, What and How' model worked particularly well and had helped emphasize the primacy of values and purpose in the functional aspects of management. However, it was felt that participants needed more time before beginning the work based project to understand and practice the skills of evidence-based evaluation, to investigate, debate and critique current practice and policy in education and the wider field of public services, and to develop a greater understanding of managing people and change.

Each consortium therefore increased the amount of time that participants engage in taught and study activities at the beginning of the programme, to try and ensure that participants are better prepared to manage and lead whole school projects. A number of shorter practical activities to develop understanding and skills in relation to managing change and evidence-informed evaluation were incorporated in the study activities to ensure that a focus on practice in the workplace is maintained throughout the programme.

The research evidence suggests that the work-based element of the programme is a considerable strength because it is embedded in school improvement processes. However, experience of delivering the programme suggested that running two projects focused on different aspects of management divided the process somewhat artificially, and that projects were too brief to ensure a clear impact on learning. There was also an element of repetition and overload in preparing two separate portfolios and commentaries for assessment.

In the revised programme participants are required to manage a single but more substantive and holistic project over 18 months, rather than two as was previously required. The intention was to limit the assessment demands on participants and allow them to address all the elements of the Standard in one portfolio and commentary, with time for evaluative activity to determine the extent to which the projects influence pupil learning.

Other revisions include a change in pedagogy, with participants in the revised programme positioned as active collaborators in fostering both their own learning and that of others. Online learning, both for the delivery of the formal programme and in order to provide means of networking and support, was developed in the Northern Consortium, where many participants are isolated geographically and local network meetings are not possible. There is now increased and more sophisticated use of e-learning, with networked peer support through action learning sets focused on structured tasks.

Supporter training was revised in each consortium and in the Western Consortium, formal sessions with a mentor are now written into participants' workbooks, with a study guide providing, through a mix of readings and practical activities, a focus for participants to work together during networking sessions.

Another change involved repositioning an investigative piece of work (the comparative study), where the participant visits an organization outside of the schools' system to investigate an aspect of leadership and management.

This part of the programme had been highly valued by participants in the original programme, but because it fell at the end of the programme, participants were unable to translate insights gained from the study into the projects. Repositioning the study means that the outcomes of the comparative study can now inform implementation of the work-based projects.

The role of field assessors in the SQH adds to the professional credibility of the programme and helps emphasize that the programme is about good practice as judged by practitioners who are themselves head teachers. In the revised programme field assessment serves a more formative function than in the original programme.

Although the programme structure and design was radically redesigned to take account of evaluation outcomes and experience of delivering the programme, the design principles and the model of learning did not change. The programme continues to be grounded in reality, with participants still required to lead and manage whole school projects, reflect upon, analyse and evaluate their experience of leading and management practice, and to apply what they have learned, drawing on the ideas and experience of others through reading and professional dialogue with peers, supporters/mentors and tutors.

Overall, the SQH represents a success story and while various studies have identified concerns to do with workload pressure and variability in context and culture, researchers and others involved in the community of practice that has developed over the years since the SQH was first introduced, have ensured that these concerns have not been lost sight of and that they are addressed. However, the landscape of head teacher preparation in Scotland is changing and an alternative route towards attaining the Standard has been proposed and is being piloted by the Scottish Executive since, it has been argued, the SQH programme does not meet the needs of all potential applicants (SEED, 2006a).

The changing landscape

Attainment of the SfH became mandatory for new head teachers in Scotland in August 2005, although authorities do not adhere to this requirement. The decision to make attainment of the SfH mandatory presented the Executive with a problem because the only way of demonstrating attainment of the Standard was by gaining the SQH and the number of people completing the programme, particularly from the primary sector, is unlikely ever to be large enough to fill the number of posts likely to become vacant over the next decade. It is this shortfall that the alternative route is supposed to address.

The alternative proposed was intended to sit alongside the SQH and interact with elements of it (SEED, 2006a). From the consultation document, it is clear that education authorities are expected to accept more responsibility for supporting individual head teachers through increased mentoring and coaching supported by attendance at personal development courses and disconnected leadership and management development courses, with candidates presenting portfolios of evidence in support of competence, gathered over time, to a panel chaired a representative of the GTCS.

Reaction to the proposal was mixed (SEED, 2006b). Although the need for more flexibility was recognized a number of issues were raised including concerns about coherence, a lack of detail in the proposals, an over-reliance on coaching, a lack of rigour in the proposed assessment arrangements and the lack of university involvement, Nevertheless, the CPD Leadership Group recommended to SEED that a pilot be established to test flexible approaches to meeting the SfH (SEED, 2006c). Pilots were subsequently set up in two education authorities. Following the combined consortia response to the consultation proposals that economies of scale and the proven value of the collaborative arrangements suggested that the universities could be instrumental in bringing authorities together to work on alternative means of achieving the standard (SEED, 2006b) a funded flexible approach was also initiated in one of the three consortia. The lack of university involvement in the consultation document, however, suggests an increased emphasis on functional competence with responsibility for preparation moving towards employers, practitioners and other providers. It also revisits issues surrounding the nature and purpose of Standards (Mahoney and Hextall, 2000), and some of these are worth discussing in this context.

Standards for head teachers define what is expected of head teachers, and they set the terms in which the performance, disposition, behaviour and attitudes of aspiring head teachers can be controlled, measured and assessed. If standards can be seen in terms of the attempts to control quality, specify outputs and reconstruct meaning and identity among head teachers, then these considerations raise interesting questions to do with how standards are derived, who is involved in this process (and who is not) and how the process of deriving any 'Standard' or set of 'Standards' is controlled. One problem with standards is that they give a spurious impression of rationality and precision in defining what competence is and who is certified as 'competent'. This is attractive to politicians, and perhaps goes some way towards explaining why in Scotland attainment of the SfH is mandatory (at least theoretically) for all new head teachers. How a standard or set of standards is interpreted, however, and how aspiring head teachers demonstrate attainment of a standard, are matters of debate and within these debates there are arguments about power and about who has responsibility for the process of accreditation.

In Scotland, the SfH was reviewed and revised (SEED, 2005) by a leadership sub-group (comprising a range of selected individuals with an interest in leadership development) of a national CPD Advisory Group. This group also developed the alternative routes proposal (SEED, 2006a). Analysis of the revised SfH reveals a tension between competing ideologies. This power dimension is highlighted in two opposing narratives and although the narratives overlap, the tension between their underpinning values and principles is evident, because one thread about development, improving practice, self reflection, learning and improving capability, while the other is more to do with managerialism, accountability and policy implementation. The powerful 'Why, What and How' model is dispensed with in the revised standard, which means that values are no longer seen as permeating actions, and there is no requirement to reflect critically on these actions. Management is eschewed in favour of leadership in the revision, but the autonomy of head teachers is weakened with a clear reminder of their accountabilities as 'officers' of education authorities in the very first line of the revised SfH. There is limited reference to collegiality and participative management and the leadership model espoused is expressed in term of motivating staff and ensuring their compliance in pursuit of priorities set externally.

Even more so than the original SfH, the revised version reflects the ambiguous mix of bureaucratic central control that standards represent (Gronn, 2003) and the rhetoric of increased professional autonomy. Menter *et al.* (2004) point out that this is characteristic of 'new public management' (Clarke and Newman, 1997) because it subordinates professional autonomy and judgement to managerial control. It also brings into question the role of the universities in head teacher preparation.

The dominant role of the universities within the consortia in designing and delivering the SQH programme has meant that although the SfH is set within prevailing orthodoxies and focused on helping participants demonstrate that they have attained 'the standard', there is considerable emphasis placed on critical thinking and professional values, with discussion and reflection on practice. SQH participants are encouraged to challenge orthodoxy, to look outward to hard social and political issues and to interrogate their own position and perspectives. As postgraduate students, they are required to adopt a critical approach but even within the SQH the need to adhere to a defined standard may inhibit aspiring heads and encourage them to configure their professional identities in ways that are consistent with the features of 'new managerialism'. A 'dialect *of managerialism*' (Reeves and Forde, 2004: 87) may enhance the credibility of the new heads and can be used to allow increased control over practice, but it may also be disabling and 'blinker them to a particular point of view and set of values' (p. 96).

This locates the SQH within the debate about the nature of contemporary professional identity and places aspiring and new headteachers in a 'complicated nexus between policy, ideology and practice' (Stronach *et al.*, 2002: 109). It may also go some way towards explaining the Executive's commitment to alternative routes towards attaining the SfH. The proposals marginalize or exclude universities, when it would have been possible to work with and within the three consortia to provide more flexibility and to explore ways of encouraging more people to aspire to headship. Despite general consensus that the role of the head teacher matters, the SQH story suggests that disagreement how head teachers should be trained and who should be responsible for and involved in that process reflects deeper and more fundamental disagreement about what kinds of head teachers are needed and what skills and attributes they need. Head teachers who are independent and critical thinkers may not be required in a system that prides itself on its arrangements for 'tough, intelligent accountability' (SEED, 2004).

An uncertain future

This chapter has outlined the development of head teacher preparation in Scotland, highlighted some of its distinctive features and described changes to the structure and the components of head teacher preparation that are being developed. I argue that these changes have been proposed without deep consideration of the evidence base that has been developed since the conception of the SQH, the outcomes of the national consultation undertaken by SEED and the changes made to provision within the three consortia. What this suggests is that alternative means of attaining the SfH may be introduced for ideological reasons rather than authentic concern for the needs of schools.

Although the SQH stood up well to intensive scrutiny in the studies noted earlier, these studies focused largely on participants' and other stakeholders' perceptions and satisfaction studies cannot give us an understanding of either the utility or the influence of the programme. This appears to be true internationally as few studies have focused on if or how preparation programmes influence change in participants' leadership practices, although attention is now being paid to this issue (Kottkamp and Orr, 2005; Bush and Glover, 2005).

However, we do not yet have a clear picture of how preparation programmes and participant practice are connected. The lack of evaluation linking the capacities developed through the SQH and the deployment of these capacities in the actual practice of participants following appointment is a concern that is being addressed in the work of Cowie and Crawford as part of an International Study of Principal Preparation. They have found some evidence to suggest that the overall influence of the SQH on individuals in the first year of headship appears not to be related to specific areas of content, but to processes that helped construct their identity as head teachers (Cowie and Crawford, 2006). Identity seems very important to the head teachers interviewed in this study and the personal narratives of the head teachers interviewed suggest clear connections between them in terms of developing an identity as a head teacher that the SQH seems to have embedded and enhanced.

Cowie and Crawford also found that collaborative activity and networking with colleagues had also helped develop their professional identities.

Participants valued the cohort approach and through engagement with others in collaborative groups a sense of trust appears to have been developed. This allowed the new heads to share their experience and knowledge with people they had come to know and trust beyond the term of the preparation programme and to develop their networks into something approaching small communities of practice (Wenger *et al.*, 2002). It would be overstating the case to say that these networks had become fully fledged communities of practice focused on individual and organizational learning, with individuals co-constructing their knowledge through interaction, but the way in which they construct and share knowledge suggests that the networks have at least the potential to become communities of practice.

The advent of alternative routes may have serious consequences for the SQH because the pool of potential applicants is relatively small and any drift away from the programme is likely to threaten its continued viability. This would be unfortunate because the acknowledged success of the SQH has been based on preparing aspiring heads for the complexities of the job through changing and developing their practice. The model of collaborative working created through the SQH and the alignment of an academic award with a professional award are remarkable achievements and this structural arrangement recognizes the higher order skills that head teachers require. Running a school involves complex, practical and interactive processes, but there is much more to it than that. If school management and leadership is as complex as the literature suggests, head teachers will need a deep understanding of school contexts and cultures and a firm grasp of relevant theory and research to enable them to develop frames of reference to guide their behaviour and decision making (Bush, 1998, 1999).

It remains to be seen if preparation for headship will encourage the next generation of head teachers to settle for the managed school 'mandated and directed' by government and focused on predefined outcomes, or will help head teachers to develop the confidence and self belief to work towards 'the renewed school', centred on educational values 'in which open, collaborative, self critical, and professional cultures produce a renewed focus on teaching and learning and on affirming professional development' (Gleeson and Husbands, 2003: 507–508). These concerns lie at the heart of the debate about where responsibility for preparation programmes should lie, the processes of preparation and the content of preparation programmes, and explain why this debate is critically important.

The future direction of head teacher preparation may be uncertain but the research outlined earlier suggests that the sophisticated relationships developed between universities, education authorities and schools have been to the benefit of individuals, schools and the system as a whole. In reconceptualizing and restructuring head teacher preparation in Scotland, it would be sensible therefore to maintain and develop the collaborative partnerships developed through the SQH consortia, to plan and deliver programmes of leadership and management development at all stages of the leadership and management continuum within these partnerships (without excluding other providers), and to work on how alternative possibilities can be integrated with the SQH in ways that allow flexibility and sensitivity to the individual contexts and needs, but also ensure that the preparation experience of all aspiring head teachers is meaningful, coherent and developmental.

References

Bell, L., Bolam, R. and Cubillo, L. (2003) *A Systematic Study of the Impact of School Leadership and Management on Student Outcomes*, London: EPPI Centre, Social Sciences Research Unit, Institute of Education.

Bush, T. (1998) The National Professional Qualification for Headship: the key to effective school leadership? *School Leadership and Management*, Vol. 18(3), pp. 321–333.

Bush, T. (1999) Crisis or crossroads?: The discipline of educational management in the late 1990s, *Educational Management, Administration and Leadership*, Vol. 27(3), pp. 239–252.

Bush, T. and Glover, D. (2005) Leadership development for early headship: the New Visions experience, *School Leadership and Management*, Vol. 25(3), pp. 217–240.

Casteel, V., Forde, C., Reeves, J. and Lynas, R. (1997) *A Framework for Leadership and Management Development in Scottish Schools*, Glasgow: QIE: University of Strathclyde.

Christie, F. and O'Brien, J. (2005) A CPD Framework for Scottish Teachers: steps or changes, continuity or connections?, in *Continuing Professional Development of Educators: Emerging European Issues*, Alexandrou, A., Field, K. and Mitchell, H. (eds), London: Symposium.

Clarke, J. and Newman, J. (1997) *The Managerial State*, London: Sage.

Cowie, M. (2005) A silver lining with a grey cloud? The perspective of unsuccessful participants in the Scottish Qualification for Headship Programme across the north of Scotland, *Journal of In-Service Education*, Vol. 31(2), pp. 393–410.

Cowie, M. and Crawford, M. (2006) *Principal Preparation Programmes in England and Scotland: Do they Make a Difference for the First Year Principal?* Paper presented at the Commonwealth Council for Educational Administration and Management, Cyprus.

Cowie, M. and Crawford, M. (2007) Principal preparation – still an act of faith? *School Leadership and Management*, Vol. 27(2), pp. 129–146.

Daresh, J. (2002) U.S. school administrator development: issues and a plan for improvement, in *Proceedings of International Conference on School Leader Preparation, Licensure/Certification, Selection, Evaluation, and Professional Development*, Wen-liuh Lin (ed.), Taipei, Taiwan: National Taipei Teachers College, 2002.

Eraut, M. (1994) *Developing Professional Knowledge and Competence*, London: Falmer Press.

Fullan, M.G. (1992a) *Successful School Improvement*, Buckingham: Open University Press.

Fullan, M.G. (1992b) *What's Worth Fighting for in Headship*, Buckingham: Open University Press.

Gleeson, D. and Husbands, C. (2003) Modernizing schooling through performance management: a critical appraisal, *Journal of Education Policy*, Vol. 18(5), pp. 499–511.

Gronn, P. (2003) *The New Work of Educational Leaders: Changing Leadership Practice in an Era of School Reform*, London: Paul Chapman Publishing.

Hallinger, P. (2003) Leading educational change: reflections on the practice of instructional and transformational leadership, *Cambridge Journal of Education*, Vol. 33(3), pp. 329–351.

Hallinger, P. and Heck, R.H. (1996) Reassessing the principal's role in school effectiveness, *Education Administration Quarterly*, Vol. 32 (1), pp. 5–44.

Hargreaves, A. (1994) *Changing Teachers, Changing Times: Teachers' Work and Culture in the Post Modern Age*, New York: Teachers College Press.

Kottkamp, R. and Orr, M.T. (2005) Taskforce on Evaluating Educational Leadership Preparation, *UCEA Executive Committee and the TEA-SIG of AERA*, http://www.aera.net/Default.aspx?id=451, accessed 2 March 2006.

Leithwood, K. and Rhiel, C. (2003) *What we know about Successful School Leadership*, Paper presented at the American Research Association Meeting, Chicago.

Levacic, R. and Glatter, R. (2003) Developing evidence informed practice in school leadership and management: a way forward, in *Developing Educational Leadership: Using Evidence for Policy and Practice*, Anderson, L. and Bennett, N. (eds), London: Sage.

MacBeath, J. and Mortimore, P. (eds) (2001) *Improving School Effectiveness*, Buckingham: Open University Press.

Mahoney, P. and Hextal, I. (2000) *Reconstructing Teaching: Standards, Performance and Accountability*, London: RoutledgeFalmer.

Menter, I., Holligan, C. and Mthenjwa, V. with Hair, M. (2003) *Heading for Success: Evaluation of the Scottish Qualification for Headship*, Paisley: School of Education, Faculty of Education and Media, University of Paisley.

Menter, I., Mahony, P. and Hextall, I. (2004) Ne'er the twain shall meet? The modernisation of the teaching workforce in Scotland and England, *Journal of Education Policy*, Vol. 19(2), pp. 195–214.

Morris, B. and Reeves, J. (2000) Implementing the National Qualification for Headship in Scotland: (a) critical reflection, *Journal of In-Service Education*, Vol. 26(3), pp. 517–531.

Murphy, D., O'Brien, J., Draper, J. and Cowie, M. (2000a) *Education Authority Co-ordination of the Scottish Qualification for Headship*, Edinburgh: Faculty of Education, the University of Edinburgh.

Murphy, D., Draper, J., O'Brien, J. and Cowie, M. (2000b) Local Management of the Scottish Qualification for Headship (SQH), *Journal of In-Service Education*, Vol. 28(2), pp. 277–295.

O'Brien, J. (2006) *The Professional Learning of Headteachers: a Forgotten Species?* Paper presented at the Commonwealth Council for Educational Administration and Management Conference, Cyprus, October.

O'Brien, J. and Draper, J. (2001) Developing effective school leaders? Initial views of the Scottish Qualification for Headship (SQH), *Journal of In-Service Education*. Vol. 27(1), pp. 109–121.

Purdon, A. (2003) A National Framework of CPD: continuing professional development or continuing professional dominance, *Journal of Educational Policy*, Vol. 28(4) pp. 423–437.

Reeves, J. and Forde, C. (2002) *The social dynamics of changing professional practice.* Paper presented at the annual conference of the British Educational Leadership, Management and Administration Society, 20–22 September, University of Birmingham.

Reeves, J. and Forde, C. (2004) The social dynamics of changing practice, *Cambridge Journal of Education*, Vol. 34(1), pp. 85–102.

Reeves, J., Forde, C., Casteel, V. and Lynas, R. (1998) Developing a model of practice: designing a framework for the professional development of school leaders and managers, *School Leadership and Management*, Vol. 18(2), pp. 185–196.

Reeves, J., Forde, C., Morris, B. and Turner, E (2003a) Social processes, work-based learning and the Scottish Qualification for Headship, in *Leading People and Teams in Education*, Kidd, L., Anderson, L. and Newton, W. (eds), London: Paul Chapman Publishing, pp. 57–69.

Reeves, J., Morris, B., Forde, C. and Turner, E. (2001) Exploring the impact of continuing professional development on practice in the context of the Scottish Qualification for Headship, *Journal of In-Service Education*, Vol. 27(2), pp. 184–202.

Reeves, J., Turner, E., Forde, C. and Morris, B. (2003b) *Changing Their Minds: The Social Dynamics of School Leaders' Learning*, Paper presented at the British Educational Research Association Conference, Edinburgh, September.

Sammons, P., Hillman, J. and Mortimore, P. (1995) *Key Characteristics of Effective Schools: A Review of School Effectiveness Research*, London: Office for Standards in Education and Institute of Education, University of London.

Searle, J. and Tymms, P. (2007) The impact of headteachers on the performance and attitude of pupils, in *The Leadership Effect: Can Headteachers make a Difference?*, O'Shaugnessy, J. (ed.), London: The Policy Exchange.

SEED (Scottish Executive Education Department) (2002) *The Scottish Qualification for Headship: Information about the Scottish Qualification for Headship*, http://www.scotland.gov.uk/Publications/2002/11/15818/1398.

SEED (2003) *Continuing Professional Development for Educational Leaders*, Edinburgh: SEED.

SEED (2004) *Ambitious Excellent Schools: Our Agenda for Action*, Edinburgh: Scottish Executive.

SEED (2005) *Ambitious, Excellent Schools, Standard for Headship*, Scottish Executive Education Department: Edinburgh.

SEED (2006a) *Achieving the Standard for Headship – Providing Choice and Alternatives*, Scottish Executive Education Department: Edinburgh.

SEED (2006b) *Achieving the Standard for Headship: Providing Choice and Alternatives – Consultation Responses*, http://www.scotland.gov.uk/Publications/2006/05/23095411/0.

SEED (2006c) *Achieving the Standard for Headship: Providing Choice and Alternatives*, http://www.scotland.gov.uk/Publications/2006/10/05134157/1

Shields, C. (2004) Dialogic leadership for social justice: overcoming pathologies of silence, *Educational Administration Quarterly*, Vol. 40(1), pp. 109–132.

Simpson, M., Gooday, M. and Payne, F. (2000) *SQH Programme Evaluation: The Role of the Supporter of Candidates on the Standard Route of the SQH: The Effects on the School of Having a Candidate on the Standard Route of the SQH*, Edinburgh: Scottish Executive.

SOEID (Scottish Office Education and Industry Department) (1998) *The Standard for Headship in Scotland*, Stirling: SQH Development Unit.

Stronach, I., Corbin, B., McNamara, O., Stark, S. and Warne, T. (2002) Towards an uncertain politics of professionalism: teacher and nurse identities in flux, *Journal of Education Policy*, Vol. 17(1), pp. 109–138.

Wenger, E., McDermott, R. and Snyder, W. (2002) *Cultivating Communities of Practice: A Guide to Managing Knowledge*, Harvard: Harvard Business School Publishing.

Chapter 4

Educational leadership development in Greece

Chrysanthi Gkolia and Mark Brundrett

Introduction

> to close the office door and stay closely with the government's minimum requirements or open the door to find opportunities for improving the school.
>
> (Greek Headteacher as cited by OECD, 2001)

Schools, globally, are facing a complex world and an endless set of pressures as they are being asked to do more than ever before. In recent years, processes characterizing education systems worldwide, such as a growing interest in quality, efficiency and effectiveness and the transfer of business management principles to schools, have created a situation where school head teachers increasingly require a blend of skills that include those of a manager, leader, economist, lawyer, team builder and evaluator. For many nations already, those who manage schools must take responsibility for a strenuous task. Nobody has discovered a perfect way of dealing with all the demands of school management, yet head teachers are increasingly expected to 'manage themselves' at a professional level.

For the past decade, the training of educators in leadership and senior management positions has been regarded as vital for improving the standards of the education system. However, there remained relatively little interest in school leadership preparation programmes outside the United States until the mid-1990s (Hallinger, 2003) but the past decade has witnessed a dramatic rise in interest in such programmes both in East Asia (ibid.) and in Europe (Huber, 2002). According to OECD (1998), teacher development has recently and in many countries become more closely related to organizational change rather than just individual objectives such as career progression.

In Greece, where the most striking features of the educational administration system are its centralization, bureaucratic complexity and traditional methods of work, the research and practitioners' community is taking the first steps in redefining the role of the school head teacher. Even now, nonetheless, the organizational structure of the school is characterized by legislative imprecision as far as its functions are concerned (Saiti, 2000). In Greek schools, educators in senior management positions are facing challenges to which they are unable to respond, emasculated as they are by the concentration of all decision making power to the central government.

In this chapter we try to explain the situation of leadership development in Greece while seeking the historical, cultural and political forces that have shaped the present form of educational administration and management of the country. We present a rationale for the design of school leadership and management programmes through the research work of Greek scholars and the observations of practitioners that can help to outline the structure of a future model of leadership development for Greek educators.

The structure of the Greek educational system

Greece has a long tradition in education, starting with the philosophical schools of the classical period (Saiti, 2000). However, the development of a structured system started when Greece gained its independence, after 1821. The act of 1834 made school education compulsory for all children. Since then a number of laws and acts have made education a basic mission of the Greek state and its provision is free at all levels, regardless of family background, origin and gender. State educational institutions are financially supported by the government as part of its aim to provide intellectual, moral and physical instruction for all living within Greece. The Greek educational system remained a centralized hierarchical system with a strong ethnocentric orientation until the 1980s. However, after 1981 when the socialist party, PASOK, formed a new government, fundamental reforms were announced that transformed not only the educational system, but also addressed wider state changes. In education, in particular, the decentralization of the education sector was attempted through the institutionalization of the administrative division. Nonetheless this took the form of a top-down model consisting of the Ministry of Education, Prefectural Education Authorities and School Units (Tsalagiorgou, 2002). The purpose of this decentralization was to bring authority to local units, give power to individual schools to manage and administer their own resources, and also to increase teacher autonomy. Despite good intentions, however, 'real' decision making power was never devolved to local educational authorities or to schools themselves. Thus, centralization remains the most problematic feature of Greek education and has been receiving constant criticism over the years from the research community and the public.

> Educational policy in Greece heavily depends on the personal whims of the Prime Minister and the Minister of Education ... The continuous and persistent participation of central government in education policy makes the system highly insensitive to local circumstances.
>
> (Saiti, 2003, p. 34)

The Greek parliament has the responsibility for passing national laws that govern the education system and overall responsibility for the system lies within the jurisdiction of the Ministry of Education and Religious Affairs. The Ministry is responsible for the coordination and evaluation of the regional services and schools, and provides financial support for relevant educational activities. However, it is also assisted at a central level by other organizations and education related bodies such as the Pedagogical Institute. This is an autonomous public body that acts under the supervision of the Ministry. Some of its main responsibilities are the formulation of guidelines, preparation of curricula, the commissioning of textbooks and research into relevant education matters.

School education consists of two main phases; compulsory from the age of three to 15 and non-compulsory from 15 to 18 years old. The latter, upper secondary education, is not compulsory and is divided into a general and a technical/vocational strand. Graduation from the general strand enables students to take part in general examinations leading to university studies. Graduates of the technical one can only enter a part of higher education, technological institutes, which generally hold lower prestige than universities (Antoninis and Tsakloglou, 2000). Figure 4.1 provides a schematic representation of the structure that eventually leads to the labour market.

Until very recently (1997) teacher recruitment in Greece depended totally on a waiting list called epetirida, from which appointments to schools were made according to the date of application for registration, which usually coincided with the year of graduation from university (Pigiaki, 1999). Until then there had been a complete lack of any criteria for entering the teaching profession apart from a university degree, the lack of a criminal record and absence of serious health problems. The epetirida list officially closed to new graduates in 1998 with the aim of complete abolition by 2003. Since then it has been replaced by a national examination system that runs examinations for teachers of all levels of education and in

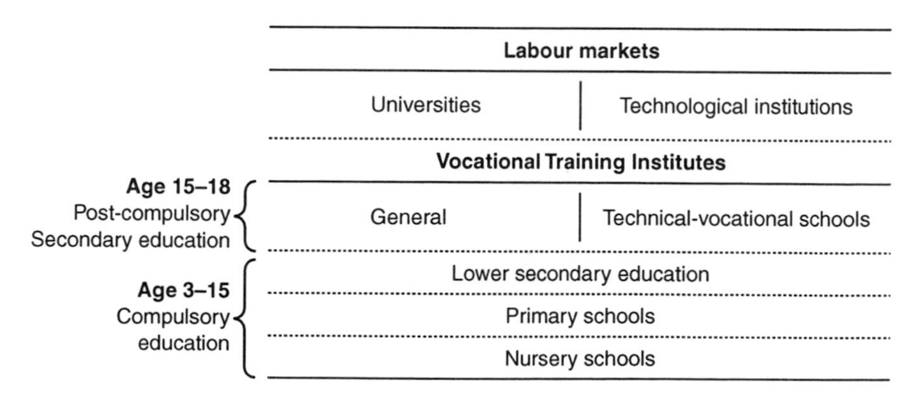

Figure 4.1 Structure of the Greek education system (source: Saiti, 2003, p. 35).

all specialist areas every two years and tests participants in subject knowledge, lesson planning and modern pedagogical theories. When the decision to replace the epetirida with national examinations was taken it was also decided that candidates sitting recruitment exams from 2003 onwards would be required to hold a 'Certificate in Pedagogy and Didactics' before they are able to sit the examination (Pigiaki, 1999). However, this part of the law remains in abeyance and candidates sitting recruitment tests are examined on pedagogical knowledge and didactics without prior training. Once successful in examination, teachers are appointed to schools all over Greece by the Ministry of Education. They gather 'points' throughout their service depending on age, marital and family status, years of service and health condition that allow them to get a permanent position in a school of their preference after a number of years. However, the freedom to choose their working environment (i.e. school) remains very limited for a substantial part of their career.

In terms of in-service teacher training, regional teacher training centres were established by law in 1985 but only began functioning in 1992. These centres offered three-month mandatory training to primary and secondary school teachers but their existence ceased four years later. Saeed (1999) reported that the majority of teachers that attended the training scheme did not find it related closely enough to the practical needs and the demands of the average school. Since 1996, the Ministry of Education has made attempts to offer longer training schemes through the education departments of universities and regional centres but these attempts were often interrupted and inconsistent in content, duration and purpose and were attended by a fraction of the teaching population.

No form or mechanism of teacher assessment has been in place for the last 20 years in Greece. The function of school inspector was notionally replaced in 1983 by advisory staff, the school counsellor, whose role is to deliver advice but not judgement to school staff. The Ministry of Education has repeatedly attempted to prepare a plan for the evaluation of teachers but it has always met the fierce opposition of the teachers' union whose position on teacher assessment has been the following:

> The union rejects any form of individual evaluation of teachers as untrustworthy and ineffective. Instead, evaluation should refer to the whole work of the school, which is done by the teaching staff itself, so that it does not differentiate among teachers, it has no effect on teachers' promotion or on their salary, it does not create competition and it respects their professional freedom and initiative.
>
> (OLME as cited in Pigiaki, 1999, p. 60)

Leadership hierarchy and the profile of the Greek head teacher

Saiti (2000) and Saitis and Menon (2004) provide a detailed description of the administration and leadership structure of the Greek education system and the duties and rights entailed within each body and position. The present administrative system consists of three main levels: the national (the Ministry of Education and Religious Affairs); the Regional (the regional education authorities) and the school level (head teacher, deputy head teacher, teachers' council). Figure 4.2 shows schematically the levels of hierarchy.

The largest amount of power rests with the Ministry, which makes every important decision about the curriculum, the allocation of time to subject areas, books that should be used in schools for each subject, books directing the teachers how to teach the 'imposed' subject bibliography, models of pupil assessment, and so forth (Pigiaki, 1999). The OECD (2004) reported that, in Greece, 88 per cent of decisions regarding education are taken at the central government level.

At the regional level, the responsibility lies with the directors of primary and secondary education who report back to the Ministry. The main responsibilities of the directors of primary and secondary education regional

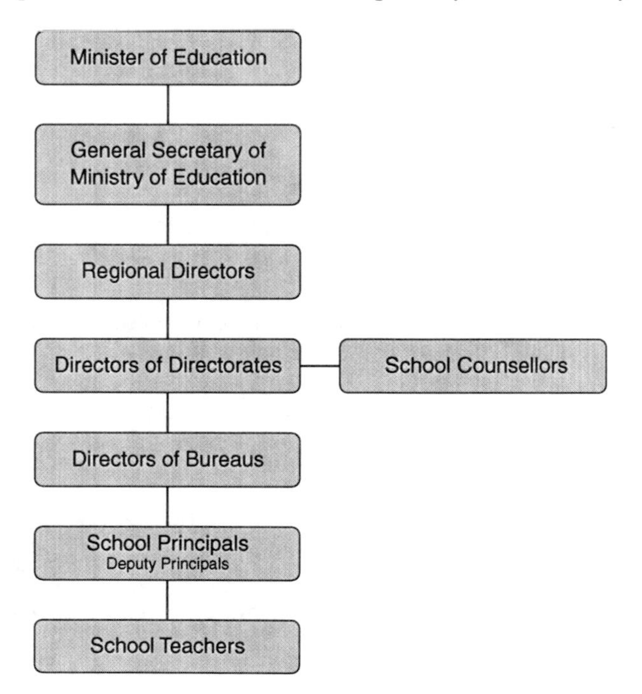

Figure 4.2 The organizational hierarchy of the Greek educational system (source: Saitis and Menon, 2004).

authorities is basically the coordination of the education offices in their region; the supervision of head teachers and the maintenance and resourcing of school buildings. In large prefectures, there are also education directorates. At the institutional level school head teachers, along with their deputies and the teachers' council, are responsible for the administration of the schools. However, schools do not have decision making autonomy. In this sense the Greek system remains an organizational hierarchy (Saitis and Menon, 2004).

The teaching staff of each school unit are the ones who are mainly responsible for the smooth day-to-day running of the school. However, the overall supervision of everyday activity lies mostly within the jurisdiction of the head teacher. Saitis (1992) outlines the main responsibilities of a school head teacher within the Greek educational system:

- the organization, supervision and general management of the school;
- being present at school during working hours in order to supervise the smooth running of the school unit;
- the keeping and regular updating of school records and files;
- facilitating school correspondence, and enforcing laws and legislation relevant to teaching and learning taking place in the school;
- to sign certificates the school awards the pupils/students;
- to supervise the teaching and non-teaching activities, and monitor teachers' work;
- to chair staff meetings;
- to review and decide on the development of the school buildings; and
- to address any behaviour and/or discipline matters arising in the school.

Thus, head teachers in Greek schools devote most of their time to procedural matters as they hold very limited powers to address the need for major school adjustments or reforms (Saitis and Menon, 2004).

The deputy head teacher is responsible for substituting the head teacher when he or she is absent and in most schools his or her role is limited to only that. According to Saiti (2000) very often heads of Greek schools do not show confidence in their deputies, entrust them with significant power or encourage them to advance their skills as deputies are often seen as 'threats' to their authority. In large urban secondary schools, there is usually more than one deputy head teacher, each one responsible for a particular section or level of the school, known as 'middle managers' in the research literature, whose responsibility is to make sure the decisions made by the head teacher are applied to their group/department and to communicate requests made by their group of teachers to the head teacher.

Leadership development programmes in Greece

The criteria for headship in Greece are de facto age-related since it is only when practitioners reach maturity in teaching experience that they are allowed promotion to a head teacher's position. There is no formal requirement to demonstrate ability to lead, manage or develop educational establishments (Kabouridis and Link, 2001).

A new law (*National Newspaper of the Greek Democracy*, 2006, Law No. 3467) that was passed in 2006 changed the selection criteria and processes for senior educational officers – such as regional directors, directors of bureaus and school counsellors – requiring that they sit a formal examination covering aspects of educational management and leadership. Furthermore their selection is now supervised by a council consisting of three members of university academic staff, one counsellor from the Pedagogical Institute, the regional director and two representatives of the central civil service. Although this was a welcome change for those who were concerned about the abilities and skills of senior education officers, it was unfortunately not extended to the head teachers of school units. The latter are still selected based on the number of in-service years (minimum 12 for heads and ten for deputies) and their selection is made by the regional director only. There is an exception, however, when it comes to small rural schools, particularly primary ones. Those usually offer less than four teaching positions, many only one, and the position of head teacher is temporary. The head has to be selected every year and whoever is appointed *acts* as the head, without being appointed officially to the position. In most cases the candidates do not fulfil the formal criteria for headship as these schools are 'undesirable' and not preferred by the more senior teaching population.

Even though, under normal circumstances, head teachers have several years of service in the educational system prior to their appointment, their experience is confined to teaching and does not extend to managerial responsibilities (Saitis and Menon, 2004). Head teachers do not receive any specific compulsory training prior or upon their appointment to becoming school leaders.

There are two non-compulsory accredited courses of further education for teachers and public managers, requiring examinations upon entry. One of them is offered by the National School of Public Administration which includes a 16-month training programme aimed at administrators and leaders in the public and civil services. Although its content covers some important general aspects of organizational development and administration, educational management and leadership are not mentioned. The other training programme is offered by *Maraslio* School and it is aimed specifically at teachers who wish to further develop aspects of the knowledge they gained through their undergraduate studies in education. The course lasts two years and one of the specialization areas offered in the second year of study is that of 'Educational Planning and International Studies in Education'. This includes modules on educational management, planning and financing. However, the course is rather theoretical in nature and does not relate directly and practically to the real school experience.

Furthermore, in response to head teachers' interest in self-evaluation (OECD, 2001) the Greek Open University offers a small number of modules on school management and leadership as part of its postgraduate degree course in education. Those distance learning modules can be studied on a voluntary basis by educators who are interested.

Historically, there has been an attempt to promote staff development associated to headship that would be available through the Greek Pedagogical Institute and local institutions of further and higher education, but 'unfortunately, these were undertaken in an ad hoc, unplanned way with no formal structures to the content of the courses' (Kabouridis and Link, 2001, p. 106).

According to Saitis (2002), almost 90 per cent of primary school head teachers have never received training on educational management. There exist, today, some seminars of shorter or longer duration that cover updates on new developments in pedagogical matters, evaluation and monitoring, new teaching methods etc. However, none of these are usually compulsory and attendance is left to the individual's discretion. The law allows head teachers and teachers to take paid and unpaid leave for postgraduate studies or further training within the country or abroad but governmental bodies do not promote those opportunities sufficiently.

However, lack of leadership development programmes is only a very small part of a greater problem regarding teachers' professional development and training in Greece. Therefore, in order to realize what is really missing and what needs to be done with educational leadership training within the cultural and historical context of the country, it is important to set it against the bigger picture.

Research that appears in international research journals in the area of educational management and leadership in Greece is very limited. This may be associated with the comparative absence of studies in the effectiveness of Greek schools which may, in turn, be associated with the fact that the Greek government has been committed to the delivery of an equality agenda for the education of all pupils. However, education stakeholders have started to reconsider this view after the first publication of the names of 'best' and 'worst' secondary schools in the country and some statistical analyses of educational data published in national newspapers with the associated emergence of parental interest in school effectiveness (Verdis *et al.*, 2003). Moreover, recent research on school effectiveness in Greece analysed the examination results of 375 *lyceia* (upper secondary education) and found that there is a difference in the performance related effectiveness between schools (Verdis *et al.*, 2003). However the effect of management and headship quality on the effectiveness of the schools was not investigated and any differences were attributed mainly to students' socio-economic background and the effect that parallel education has on student achievement (ibid.).

Pamouktsoglou (2006) too brought up the issue of school effectiveness and investigated the opinions of candidate teachers as to what constitutes effective schooling. The majority of the participants were able to name and list the factors that contribute to effective schooling, as identified from much of the international research bibliography, but also made it clear that they felt insufficiently trained to put theory to practice. This they attributed to the absence of 'transit' teacher training programmes that would support their move from their undergraduate studies to the reality of the school classroom and to the limited existence of in-service training that would help them cope with the challenges of modern schooling, such as multiculturalism and the new demands of the information-society.

Saiti and Saitis (2006) found, through a survey, that almost half of the teaching population today has never received any in-service training which, according to the authors, means that a large percentage of teachers are inadequately skilled in modern pedagogical strategies, classroom management and organization. The respondents of the survey attributed their lack of professional development to a lack of support from the Ministry of Education which has failed to develop an interesting and relevant training scheme and has not put in place a mechanism for covering their teaching duties and their expenses during training periods.

Teachers' dissatisfaction, however, has not been limited to absence of quality skills development programmes for their own classroom needs but has extended, lately, to the management and leadership skills of their head teachers. According to a study by Saitis and Menon (2004), many trainee teachers express concern about the perceived authoritarian manner of Greek school leaders, whilst experienced teachers express concerns about the ability of school leaders to manage schools effectively. Such complaints focus on the lack of transparency used for the selection of school head teachers, the lack of 'official' managerial training provision by the government and the restrictive and bureaucratic nature of the existing educational system that strips away from head teachers all ability for initiative.

A recent Greek conference, in 2006, presented by mostly senior education officers from different regions of Greece, explored, probably for the first time so extensively, a number of concepts, terms and models of school leadership. Even though many of the presentations did not include original research data but were rather theoretical and based on previous foreign literature in the area, that the conference took place was in itself an important step towards an organized initiative to change the way school leadership is viewed in Greece. Even more important is that the presenters were not academics but people with high administrative and leadership positions in the school education system. That could mean that the form of school leadership today and the ways it can be changed has started being an active concern of the practitioners' community who are engaging in reflective thinking about their role in the quality of education provided.

The set of papers presented critically examined the characteristics, role and responsibilities of today's Greek head teacher and compared them to those of their counterparts in other European countries. They looked into foreign literature for the results of research studies concerned with the qualities of the effective educational leader and tried to draw a picture of the successful Greek leader while giving consideration to the cultural context and the existing education structure of the country. One of the presenters (Marinos, 2006) also tackled the role of the middle manager, a position very much undervalued and overlooked in Greek schools.

Several of the papers included (e.g. Anthis and Kaklamanis, 2006; Tzifas, 2006) focused on the communication aspect of leadership and outlined the most important means and mediums of communication that can support a model of distributed leadership, while others debated the required changes in the decision making processes and mechanisms (Tasoula, 2006; Res, 2006) as part of an attempt to promote a more participatory model of school management (Kousoulos *et al.*, 2006).

For the first time, terms like vision, inspiration and staff empowerment are being mentioned in the educational management and leadership scene of the country at the school unit level, since the traditional way of managing education, so far, was synonymous to central and uniform rule-enforcing throughout all of the nation's schools. Vision, until now, was seen as the job of politicians while most education officers and people in leading education posts were viewed and treated as managers with minimum rights and authority. It is probably the first time that vision is referred to as something that should be expected from school head teachers. In the past, it was neither required nor hoped that head teachers would bring new ideas to their school and be proactive regarding its improvement and effectiveness (Dimitropoulos, 2007).

Reasons for developing leadership training in Greece

Publications from Greek scholars and practitioners in both international journals and national periodicals have provided a rationale for developing a model of leadership training that can be translated into structured training programmes and will be made compulsory for all educators who wish to pursue a leadership career in school education.

One of the main reasons provided by the literature (Saiti, 2005; Saiti and Prokopiadou, 2004) for doing so is the abundance of rural schools in Greece. Almost 40 per cent of pupils in primary education are being educated in the rural schools of Greece. As mentioned earlier many of those schools are run by a single teacher who is responsible for the totality of the teaching hours as well as managing the school in the position of head. Due to the way the teacher appointment system is organized, the majority of teachers in those schools are either newly appointed or in their first years of teaching experience. Hence, those practitioners have to deal with headship not only without formal leadership training but with the further shortcoming of limited school experience. This evidently puts them at a disadvantage compared to their counterparts in bigger schools in urban areas who are, at the very least, more mature in age and have, in all likelihood, many more years of service behind them.

Another compelling reason for developing a formal training scheme for educational leadership is the under-representation of women in senior school leadership (Kyriakoussis and Saiti, 2006). Female under-representation is the case for other countries too (Cubillo and Brown, 2003). The international literature (Coleman, 1996; Cubillo, 1999) has drawn attention to the fact that women, given the chance, can bring particular strengths and skills to educational management, such as their strong collaborative style, and has also pointed out that although men tend to lead in a different way to women, this does not mean that they lead in a better way too. In Greece in 1995, only 17 per cent of secondary school head teachers were women (Kantartzi and Anthopoulos, 2006). Kyriakoussis and Saiti (2006) who examined this situation in Greek schools and attempted to find the reasons behind it, came to the conclusion that the present situation is due to the following reasons:

- family responsibilities (the widely accepted perception that women are naturally suited to the primary roles of mothers and wives);
- women's view that promotions into school administration are discriminatory according to gender; and
- women's perceived failure of the Greek administration to motivate them in seeking promotions early on in their careers.

The authors found that the women that had received postgraduate pedagogical training (i.e. *Maraslio*) were actually the ones who applied for promotions into administration. This latter finding prompted the authors to propose the development of a formal and organized leadership training scheme that would attract equally women and men and will ensure that women are encouraged to advance their skills and develop the motivation to seek more senior positions.

The changing face of the Greek society and particularly the challenges that urban schools are facing due to the multicultural student intake of the last decade have put new stress on the practitioners' community. Greece has not historically been a nation of immigrants and the contextual culture was not diverse between its members (Saiti, 2007). The nature of these changes and the challenges that ensue are entirely alien to Greek teachers who are so far coping with them based on their personal instincts, feelings and attitudes to classrooms of mixed ethnicities. The international literature about multicultural education and the challenges it poses for the management and leadership of a school is extensive particularly in the USA and the UK. Scholars have warned that the challenges posed by the education of students of diverse ethnic backgrounds are frightening as 'they confront prejudice, injustice and historical misconceptions that are so profoundly entrenched in the fabric of our systems that they often appear insurmountable' (Walker, 2004, p. 3). They have also found that effective multicultural schools are usually led by proactive head teachers who recognize the many dimensions of students' identity (Henze *et al.*, 2000); anticipate the future problems, needs and changes (Walker, 2004); and endorse inclusive cultures by positioning schools within community, organizational, and service-related networks (Riehl, 2000).

Finally, teachers themselves have expressed dissatisfaction with the current promotional opportunities available in Greece. Koustelios (2001) in his investigation of teachers' job satisfaction found that even though most teachers are happy with the work itself, they wish they had better prospects and more options regarding career advancement.

Proposals for leadership training

Although the present state of leadership training in Greece is rather disappointing, this does not mean that worthy propositions have not already been brought forward to the Ministry of Education about a possible reform of teacher training that encompasses the development of leadership training programmes.

Barkatsas (1999), however, has argued that what is needed first and foremost is the development and firm establishment of a general teacher professional development plan (pre- and in-service) that will be mandatory for all teachers.

> There is an urgent need to encourage staff to view P.D. as a platform for developing co-operative, shared and innovative practices; to extend and broaden the knowledge of experienced teachers; to enable staff in managerial roles – including principal class personnel – to realise that their training should be part of an overall strategy of change and development related to school development; and to encourage the incorporation of exemplary practice.
>
> (Ibid., p. 78)

Tzifas (2006) discussed a model of management for the Greek education system and outlined the knowledge requirements for the modern head teacher. Those he claims span from the scientific to the legal, financial and managerial fields:

- educational management;
- school unit organization;
- education financing;
- organizational psychology;
- legal education framework;
- classroom management;
- professional coaching;
- models of leadership;
- professional assessment;
- communication.

He cautioned, however, against an uncritical and 'blind' adoption of foreign models of educational leadership as the history, societal and political conditions of Greece are as unique as any other nation's. More particularly he suggests that a new approach to management and leadership, within the Greek context, should be less centralized than it is now, but not as decentralized as the one seen in other countries such as the UK. More specifically, he recommends that the Ministry keeps the role of general coordinator and chief inspector but the regional authorities and school units gain the power to make decisions regarding the needs of their district.

Mantas *et al.* (2006) attempted to lay out in a more structured way the requirements and content of a possible leadership development programme in Greece. He debated the 'teachability' of leadership skills and whether a leader is 'made or born', deciding finally on a combination of both, accepting the existence of inherent traits but also supporting the theory that leadership skills can be developed and improved. The authors went a step further from a theoretical model of leadership and suggested a concrete structure and content for a possible leadership course. Such a programme would consist of three distinct levels:

- Basic transferable skills (encompassing finance, ICT, mathematics and writing skills).
- Advanced personal skills (on school management, organizational development, leadership models, ethics, change and crisis management and communication).
- Skills application (hands-on experience of management and leadership in schools or regional authorities with the possible cooperation of universities and existing training centres).

At the time of writing it was notable that, in December 2007 a large national conference on 'Assessment and Educational Management' was due to take place in Greece. The scheduled presenters come from both the practitioners' community and the Greek academia and the proposed presentations promise an in-depth analysis of all of the issues discussed in this chapter. Also, suggestions and propositions regarding the creation and establishment of a development training scheme for educational leaders will be brought forward.

These are changing and interesting times in Greek education and the administration needs to be transformed in order to contribute to the country's economic and social development. Conversely, frequent changes, *sans* powerful vision and well-planned strategies to realize it, can prevent the modernization of the system. However, the emerging picture is not yet clear. 'It rather represents the tensions between tradition and modernity in the Greek social, political and cultural context' (Zambeta, 2002, p. 637). Although the state has made some steps forward, in recognizing a number of powerful determinants for school effectiveness, such as organizational support, devolution of power, school leadership and teacher training, it has not translated, thus far, good intentions into good practice.

Conclusion

The head teacher's role in Greek schools is significantly underdeveloped. So far, his or her main responsibility is to implement ministerial directives and to coordinate the activities of teaching staff. Participation at head teacher training seminars still remains at the discretion of the head teacher and appointments and promotions are still based mainly on seniority levels.

A significant number of academics in Greece (Papanaum, 1995; Persianis, 1998; Pigiaki, 1999; Saitis 2002) have repeatedly pointed out the need for decentralization and the shift of considerable power and responsibility from the Ministry of Education to the individual head teachers as a measure that will not only revive the educational system but will also bring it into line with modern initiatives and movements across other countries of the European Community. In-service training and further training and development are also recognized as important steps that need to be taken in order to facilitate leadership development in the Greek system.

> The highly centralised function of Greek education, the total absence over decades of any pedagogical criteria for teacher recruitment, the lack of teacher evaluation for more than the past 20 years, the failure to correlate teacher training to the needs of practice and the demands of curriculum development, the absence of teachers' self-reflection and self-development, the intense demands made on pupils of 'parallel education', all these generate an almost pathological condition.
>
> (Pigiaki, 1999, p. 62)

A situation as critical as the one described above urgently demands realization from the government that a substantial number of factors related to school effectiveness has to do with the abilities and skills of individuals much closer to schools, in terms of hierarchy.

> OECD countries are today confronted with new challenges arising from the determination of politicians to reform educational systems. It is no longer enough for principals 'just' to be good managers: they must now don the cloak of leader, for their efficiency is perceived as being of prime importance for setting up educational reform and improving learning conditions.
>
> (Gaussel, 2007, p. 1)

Consequently, the role of the head teacher needed to be further developed and built on in order to correspond more with similar initiatives in other countries. As educational leadership becomes more devolved across Europe the Greek system is coming under increased scrutiny by those interested in education.

References

Anthis, K.C. and Kaklamanis, T.T. (2006) Social and communication skills of educational leaders (in Greek), in proceedings of the 1st Educational Conference organized by the Epirus Regional Centre for Primary and Secondary Education, titled 'The Greek School and the Challenges of the Modern Society', Ioannina, 12–14 May.

Antoninis, M. and Tsakloglou, P. (2000) Who benefits from public education in Greece: evidence and policy implications, *Education Economics*, 9 (2), 197–222.

Barkatsas, A. (1999) The development of effective professional development programs for teachers, *Mentor*, 1, 76–92.

Coleman, M. (1996) Barriers to career progress for women in education: the perceptions of female headteachers, *Educational Research*, 38 (3), 317–332.

Cubillo, L. (1999) Gender and leadership in the NPQH: an opportunity lost? *Journal of In-service Education*, 25 (3), 545–555.

Cubillo, L. and Brown, M. (2003) Women into educational leadership and management: international differences? *Journal of Educational Administration*, 41 (3), 278–291.

Dimitropoulos, G. (2007) School change through everyday development (in Greek), http://www.de.sch.gr/kvoutsin/Dimitropoulos.doc (accessed 08/06/2007).

Gaussell, M. (2007) Leadership and educational change. La lettre d'information (Veille Scientifique et Technologique), no 24.

Hallinger, P. (2003) *Reshaping the landscape of school leadership development: a global perspective*, Lisse: Zeitlinger.

Henze, R., Katz, A. and Norte, E. (2000) Rethinking the concept of racial and ethnic conflict in schools: a leadership perspective, *Race Ethnicity and Education*, 3 (2), 195–206.

Huber, N.S. (2002) Approaching leadership education in the new millennium, *Journal of Leadership Education*, 1 (1), 25–34.

Kabouridis, G. and Link, D. (2001) Quality assessment of continuing education short courses, *Quality Assurance in Education*, 9 (2), 103–109.

Kantartzi, E. and Anthopoulos, K. (2006) The participation of the two genders in educational administration positions (in Greek), *Epitheorisi Ekpedeftikon Thematon*, 11, 5–19.

Kousoulos, A., Bounias, K. and Kabouridis, G. (2006) Participatory management and decision making processes in primary (in Greek), in proceedings of the 1st Educational Conference organized by the Epirus Regional Centre for Primary and Secondary Education, titled 'The Greek School and the Challenges of the Modern Society', Ioannina, 12–14 May.

Koustelios, A.D. (2001) Personal characteristics and job satisfaction of Greek teachers, *The International Journal of Educational Management*, 15 (7), 354–358.

Kyriakoussis, A. and Saiti, A. (2006) Underrepresentation of women in public primary school administration: the experience of Greece, *International Electronic Journal for Leadership in Learning*, 10 (5).

Mantas, P., Pamouktsoglou, A. and Reppa, A. (2006) Training of educational administration officers: the role of lifelong learning in the development of managerial skills (in Greek), in proceedings of the 1st Educational Conference organized by the Epirus Regional Centre for Primary and Secondary Education, titled 'The Greek School and the Challenges of the Modern Society', Ioannina, 12–14 May.

Marinos, E. (2006) Middle managers in schools: the forgotten link of hierarchy (in Greek), in proceedings of the 1st Educational Conference organized by the Epirus Regional Centre for Primary and Secondary Education, titled 'The Greek School and the Challenges of the Modern Society', Ioannina, 12–14 May.

National Newspaper of the Greek Democracy (2006) Law No. 3467, Issue I, p. 128.

OECD (1998) *Staying ahead, in-service training and teacher professional development*, Paris: OECD.

OECD (2001) *What works in innovation in education: new school management approaches*, Paris: OECD.

OECD (2004) *Education at a glance: OECD Indicators – 2004 Edition* (in Greek), Paris: OECD.

Pamouktsoglou, A. (2006) Effective school: characteristics and observations in an evaluation attempt (in Greek), in proceedings of the 1st Educational Conference organized by the Epirus Regional Centre for Primary and Secondary Education, titled 'The Greek School and the Challenges of the Modern Society', Ioannina, 12–14 May.

Papanaum, Z. (1995) *The management of the school* (in Greek), Thessaloniki: Kyriakides.

Persiannis, P. (1998) 'Compensatory Legitimation' in Greek educational policy: an explanation for the abortive educational reforms in Greece in comparison with those in France, *Comparative Education*, 34 (1), 71–84.

Pigiaki, P. (1999) The crippled 'pedagogue': discourses in education and the Greek case, *Educational Review*, 51 (1), 55–65.

Res, I. (2006) Decision making processes in schools: review and redefinition (in Greek), in proceedings of the 1st Educational Conference organized by the Epirus Regional Centre for Primary and Secondary Education, titled 'The Greek School and the Challenges of the Modern Society', Ioannina, 12–14 May.

Riehl, C.J. (2000) The principal's role in creating inclusive schools for diverse students: a review of normative, empirical, and critical literature on the practice of educational administration, *Review of Educational Research*, 70 (1), 55–81.

Saeed, M. (1999) The in-service training of primary school teachers in Greece: views of directors and vice-directors of PEK, *International Journal of Educational Management*, 13 (4), 180–186.

Saiti, A. (2000) Organisational deficiencies in school management: the case of Greek primary schools, *Mediterranean Journal of Educational Studies*, 5 (2), 39–55.

Saiti, A. (2003) Evidence from Greek Secondary Education, *Management in Education*, 17 (2), 34–38.

Saiti, A. (2005) The staffing of small rural primary schools in Greece, *Management in Education*, 19 (4), 32–36.

Saiti, A. (2007) School leadership and educational equality: analysis of Greek secondary school data, *School Leadership and Management*, 27 (1), 65–78.

Saiti, A. and Prokopiadou, G. (2004) Teacher education as a crucial determinant of the effectiveness of small rural schools in Greece, in proceedings of Teacher Education 7th Spring University Conference, 6–8 May, 2004, University of Tartu, Estonia.

Saiti, A. and Saitis, C. (2006) In-service training for teachers who work in full-day schools: evidence from Greece, *European Journal of Teacher Education*, 29 (4), 455–470.

Saitis, C. (1992) *The management and organisation of education: theory and action*, Athens: University of Athens.

Saitis, C. (2002) *The principal of the contemporary school: from theory to practice* (in Greek), Athens: Self-publication.

Saitis, C. and Menon, M.E. (2004) Views of future and current teachers on the effectiveness of primary school leadership: evidence from Greece, *Leadership and Policy in Schools*, 3 (2), 135–157.

Tasoula, V. (2006) Decision making processes in schools – challenges and contradictions of the modern Greek reality (in Greek), in proceedings of the 1st Educational Conference organized by the Epirus Regional Centre for Primary and Secondary Education, titled 'The Greek School and the Challenges of the Modern Society', Ioannina, 12–14 May.

Tsalagiorgou, E. (2002) Understanding the implementation of curriculum change: a study of practice in Greece, Unpublished PhD thesis, University of Manchester, UK.

Tzifas, A. (2006) The headteacher of the modern school (in Greek), in proceedings of the 1st Educational Conference organized by the Epirus Regional Centre for Primary and Secondary Education, titled 'The Greek School and the Challenges of the Modern Society', Ioannina, 12–14 May.

Verdis, A., Kriemadis, T. and Pashiardis, P. (2003) Historical, comparative and statistical perspectives, of school effectiveness research: rethinking educational evaluation in Greece, *The International Journal of Educational Management*, 17 (4), 155–169.

Walker, A. (2004) *Priorities, strategies and challenges: proactive leadership in multi-ethnic schools*, Nottingham: National College for School Leadership (NCSL).

Zambeta, E. (2002) Modernisation of educational governance in Greece: from state control to state steering, *European Educational Research Journal*, 1 (4), 637–655.

Chapter 5

Educational leadership development in the Czech Republic

Mark Brundrett

Introduction

As noted in the introduction to this text, this chapter developed out of a previous article that compared leadership preparation in England and the Czech Republic (Brundrett *et al.*, 2006), this in turn drew on a publication sponsored by the British Council (Slavíková *et al.*, 2003). Both the British Council and all those involved in those previous publications are thanked for their assistance. Both those previous publications point out that over the last decade, in many European countries, external as well as internal social, economic and political changes have created a dramatic shift in the way in which educational institutions are managed and have led to a marked need for enhanced professional training of managerial staff, especially principals (Huber, 2003: 315). The impetus for such training springs out of a growing realization that the role of schooling is undergoing transformation based on an acceptance that the individual's educational achievement determines his or her subsequent economic category and that school socializes and integrates young people into the community (Slavíková *et al.*, 2003: 6).

As in many other European countries, the education system in the Czech Republic developed during the nineteenth and twentieth centuries as a centralized system, with the government in the decision-making role. During much of this period the Czech Republic and its precursor entities was subject to external hegemonic forces from imperial Austria, Fascist Germany, and communist domination. The role and function of senior and managerial staff were subject to changes during the development of the national educational system which, to some extent, mirrored the changing political and intellectual milieu. This chapter draws on the work of Slavíková *et al.* (2003) to examine three key periods in the development of the Czech education system; it goes on to chart the emergence of leadership programmes in the Czech Republic and, further, attempts to examine the origins of leadership development in the Czech Republic and outline and analyse themes in the patterns of training and development.

The structure of the chapter is based around a brief historical evocation of the nature of the education system and the associated methods of educational leadership training and development, followed by an analysis of the key overall emergent themes that can be distilled from the national experience.

1867 to 1945 – the period of the Austrian–Hungarian monarchy and the independent Czech state after 1918

The first attempts at building a modern education system, responding to contemporary needs in what was to become the Czech Republic, can be found in the Imperial Educational Act no. 62/1869 of 14 May 1869. This replaced the decree of 1805 applicable to elementary and lower secondary education. The basic philosophy, undoubtedly already obsolete at the time, was expressed in the statement: 'Austria does not need educated people. What Austria needs is loyal subjects'. The Act introduced compulsory eight-year education; established free four-year teacher training at educational facilities; limited the teaching load; reduced the authority of the church in the domain of school management and supervision; stipulated the responsibilities of municipalities with respect to schools; and put schools into public or private categories. Elementary and lower secondary school head teachers' powers were divided into two basic domains: school management and teaching. The head teacher was obliged to teach to the same extent as teachers, i.e. 30 hours per week. However, many municipalities considered this burden too high and attempted to intervene. For example, in 1888 the municipal council in Prague set teaching duty to ten hours weekly for head teachers at combined elementary-lower secondary schools and 14 hours weekly for headteachers at lower secondary schools. In large schools, with many classrooms, the head teacher's teaching duty was reduced to three lessons per week.

1948 to 1990 – the period of communist domination

After the communists seized power in 1948, fundamental changes took place in the whole community, the education sector being no exception. Overall the educational system during this period was characterized by a highly centralized administration based on the totalitarian principles of communist ideology (Svecova, 2000: 127). The majority of legislative acts valid until then, which had proved useful for decades, were degraded by the Education Act no. 95/1948, whereby any legal document which failed to comply with that act was quashed. The situation subsequently became very unclear with laws being superseded by circulars issued by government agencies. From 1950, schools reported to the regional level of state administration, known as Regional National Committees; specifically to their Education and Sports Departments (Zøízeny naøízením vlády è. 14/1949 Sb). Regional councils controlled schools both from the educational and from the staffing and administrative aspects. Head teachers were no longer appointed through a selection process; instead, they were appointed by the relevant Regional National Committee, the candidate's membership of the Communist Party playing a major role in their likelihood of success. Head teachers' responsibilities and some school management issues were partly defined by a series of education acts including: Act no. 95/1948, which set out that 'gymnasia' (grammar schools) were replaced by 11-year secondary schools; Act no. 31/1953 which established 'general education secondary schools'; and by Act no. 186/1960. Individually and cumulatively the above acts removed head teachers' powers in the domains of school management and administration, education of students, or staffing since these were proclaimed tasks of the government, ministry, councils and national committees.

In 1976, the Central Committee of the Czechoslovak Communist Party approved a comprehensive conceptual document entitled 'Further Development of the Czechoslovak Educational System'. Within this project, the task was set to implement the restructuring programme for the elementary school; to continue in developing the scope of the middle school; and the programme of restructuring the scope and organization of vocational training facilities was to be continued in secondary schools. The Czechoslovak secondary education system comprised three basic streams: grammar schools, secondary vocational schools and secondary vocational training facilities, and it was decided that all of these should provide mutually equivalent full secondary education. Act no. 77/1976, the first law to address the issue of governmental administration in the education sector, only came into effect in 1978. Article 4 defined head teachers' responsibilities. Under this legislation the head teacher was made responsible for the ideological, educational and professional standards of the educational process and for the school's performance. He/she was placed in charge of creating a favourable environment for all staff, whose performance the head teacher had to control and supervise. The duty to promote in-service political, educational and professional training of the school staff was stressed. The head teacher was granted decision-making powers in many matters of administrative nature, such as: admission of students to secondary schools, granting or withdrawing scholarship, students' temporary suspension from study etc.

During this period teachers' in-service education and training was directed by the Czech Ministry of the Interior (Sayer *et al.*, 1995). Crucially in terms of the remit of this article, requirements in relation to the qualifications for headship were identified by Education Ministry Regulation no. 59/1985. The head teacher was to be appropriately educated for the given type of school, which usually meant: university-level education or equivalent as listed in the appendix to the regulation; a minimum of seven years' experience as a teacher; and, successful completion of professional training as defined by Education Ministry Regulation no. 61/1985.

Compulsory in-service training for the position of head teacher lasted for two years and led to a final examination before an examining board. The head teacher was to enrol on this study within two years of the date he or she assumed the head teacher's position, because this training was a prerequisite for this managerial position. *Further Development of the Czechoslovak Educational System* was the fundamental document setting the basic educational policy principles. In order to fully implement those principles Education Act no. 29/1984 on the system of primary and secondary schools was passed by the parliament and this Act remains valid under the current legal framework. Schooling became compulsory from the ages of six to 16 and a unified system of schools became the basis of the educational system. Schools of the same level and type all over Czechoslovakia were to teach based on unified educational plans, unified curricula and using the same textbooks, while respecting national specifics of the Czech and Slovak nations.

1990 to 2003 – the period of transformation after the fall of the communist regime

The contemporary educational system in the Czech Republic strives to follow up the nation's democratic traditions, forcibly interrupted for nearly half a century by Nazi occupation in 1939 and subsequently by the communist totalitarian regime (Svecova, 2000: 129). Its current transformation and development are based, among other things, on experience gathered by developed European countries (Slavíková and Karabac, 2003: 45). The Czech educational system was subject to three transformation stages during the 1990–2003 period.

The first stage of this period (1990–1994) was characterized by extensive and rapid changes in legislation, in the funding patterns and, in particular, in the content and forms of the educational system, with impact on all school types (Beran, 1995). The start of changes in legislation entered into force on 1 June 1990, when Act no. 171/1990 replaced Education Act no. 29/1984 on the system of primary and secondary schools. The most important law governing the administration and management of the regional education system, Act no. 54/1990, on governmental administration and self-government in the educational sector, was passed in December that year. Through that act the existing rigid central administrative grip on school management was loosened, schools gained a substantial amount of autonomy, and head teachers were granted basic decision-making powers. Education Authorities were established in 1991 as an intermediate link in the implementation of state administration in the education sector. Hence, from then on there were three new management sectors: the Ministry of

Education (central level), the Education Authority (district level), and the school (local level). As a concomitant of the 1990 Act large numbers of managerial staff at all levels were replaced. Head teachers were to perform a new, rather difficult task: to execute state administration at their schools. Head teacher responsibilities were defined by the relevant provision of the act as follows.

The head teacher:

- is the manager of the school, pre-school facility or school-type facility;
- appoints and dismisses the deputy head teacher;
- acts as the head of the organization, including responsibilities vested on this position by the Labour Code;
- He/she makes a number of administrative decisions, such as: exemption from compulsory education; transfer of students to different schools; study suspension; inclusion of children into a pre-school facility; running the school canteen and after-school care centre.

The head teacher is responsible for:

- compliance with the teaching plan and curriculum;
- the school's professional and educational standards;
- effective use of school facilities;
- creating favourable conditions for school inspections;
- inspecting performance of teachers and other school personnel;
- students' learning achievements.

During the second stage (1995–1999), head teachers' powers were quite extensive. For instance, head teachers took decisions in matters such as: the use of the budget; selection of teaching plans for their school, or teaching patterns. Primary and state-owned secondary school head teachers were selected by the Educational Authority, the municipality for primary schools and the Ministry of Education, Youth and Sports for state-owned secondary schools. The demands put on the head teacher increased as all secondary, private and church-owned schools became responsible for their own legal affairs. A certain tendency to autocratic decision-making, exhibited by some head teachers, has not been eliminated to a sufficient extent through their managerial skills training so far.

During the third stage (2000–2003), the educational sector ceased to be managed by the Ministry of Education, Youth and Sports. The Educational Authorities were dismissed, and the respective administrative powers were gradually transferred from the Ministry to the Regional Authorities (for secondary schools). The District Authorities, which were not legal entities until then, were given the status of the employer for schools. The National Programme for Development in Education, 'The White Book', was adopted by the Czech Government on 7 February 2001, which promotes training for managerial staff. Managerial staff at schools must have a clear idea of what they want to achieve, and how they're going to do it, given the particular circumstances of the particular school. Within this document head teachers are encouraged to be aware of the fact that no fundamental change in school culture can be effected unless they invite committed teachers into the decision-making process. Head teachers must be prepared for situations where their colleagues will not understand their intentions, or will even oppose them, and they must know how to proceed in such circumstances. Training of managerial staff in the educational sector thus became a priority within the system of teacher training organized by the Ministry of Education, Youth and Sports. During this stage, Act no. 564/1990 on governmental administration and self-government in the education sector was amended, whereby powers in the appointment and dismissal of head teachers were changed. Now the Regional Authority grants its approval to the appointment and dismissal of head teachers at schools which fall under the authority of the municipality.

Head teachers at schools which were legal entities had a substantial responsibility even before the public administration system reform took place, and now their responsibilities are increasingly being extended in the area of curricular policy. Moreover, the head teachers will have to fulfil coordination tasks related to the accession of the Czech Republic to the European Union. In this manner the profile of the managerial staff powers, so far mainly oriented to economic and legislative issues, will change so as to encompass planning, leadership, motivation, and teamwork as well. It is the head teacher who should, together with his or her collaborators, set up the school's educational programme. Although the basic directions are included in the Educational Framework Programmes, the practical aspects such as course contents and teaching methodology will be developed by the head teachers and their teams.

Recent developments in the training and development of school leaders in the Czech Republic

The fall of the communist regime led to the demise of teacher education centres and the school inspectorate previously controlled by the Ministry of the interior and the academic community made calls for new conception of in-service teacher education and training (Beran and Kohnova, 1995). The adoption of a fundamental document, the 'Concept of In-Service Training of Managerial Staff at Schools and School-Type Facilities', was a key event in the development of school leaders. This document identifies three types of education specific management development training: Positional Training I, Positional Training II, and Other Managerial Staff Training.

Positional Training I ('PT I')

This compulsory management development training is for managerial staff at schools and school-type facilities and is designed for head teachers who have been appointed to their position quite recently or are assuming this position now, for deputy head teachers, or candidates who want to submit their bids to a selection procedure for a managerial position at a school or school-type facility. The course encompasses 60 hours of instruction, 60 hours of participants' self-study, and a four-day study visit to another school. The training course ends with a practically oriented first examination before an examining board appointed by the Ministry of Education, Youth and Sports. After passing this exam, the successful course participants will be granted a certificate. The scope of PT I is based on the key professional competences of managerial staff at schools and school-type facilities and on the description of responsibilities following from Act no. 564/92 on governmental administration and self-government in the educational sector. The programme is structured into four modules including: the basics of law; labour law; school funding; and organization of the school and the educational process.

Positional Training II ('PT II')

This training for managerial staff at schools and school-type facilities is designed for managerial staff who have held such a position for five years or more, for head teachers who want to reinforce their professional competence, and other staff wishing to gain a better insight into school management issues. This training course should provide the participants with a deeper theoretical background and related practical skills necessary for efficient management and development of schools in line with the needs of the community and the region. After passing this training course, the school manager should be able to create a school strategy; guarantee the high educational standards expected and contribute to the continual improvement of the educational process; secure equal opportunities for all staff; and be responsible for an effective and efficient use of all resources so that the school meets its targets. High levels of competence are expected in day-to-day school management; organization and administration; and favourable public relations aimed at the parents, municipality, region, social partners. PT II prepares the trainees for managerial performance at schools and school-type facilities and instructs them in state and public administration at a level considerably higher than PT I. The training is intended to give the participants not only a deep understanding of school management issues, but also good leadership, managerial, and personal skills and competencies, covering all areas of their professional responsibilities. A number of different practical training methods are used and the programme reinforces the Leadership and

Education Process Management modules so as to create stimuli for self-assessment, development of emotional intelligence areas and social skills. The training course is scheduled for two years, encompassing a total of 364 hours of combined training. This form of training respects a number of specifics, mainly determined by the trainees' position and employment relationships. The training patterns not only allow their professional and personal experiences to be used, but also creates preconditions for a complex interlinking of theory and practice, to a higher extent than is possible in a course based on instruction in the classroom. The training course is completed by the second management development examination before an examining board. Once again, after passing the training course the successful participant will obtain a certificate. The training programme is structured into six basic modules including: school management – theory and practice; law; economic and financial management; educational process control and management; leadership; and managerial practice

'Other' managerial staff training

This encompasses any managerial staff training except for positional training and advanced study. It serves to extend and/or deepen the manager's knowledge and skills in various areas, usually respecting his or her current needs. Such training provides the trainees with knowledge and skills they need within the context of the school and its plans, which they did not gain within the positional training or advanced study. The training course content is not directly controlled by the Ministry of Education and can encompass a variety of problems. Other advanced training of managerial staff in the education sector, which is highly diversified, is provided by various institutions: advanced study facilities, universities, secondary schools of education, foundations and companies.

Positional Training I is organized by educational centres, which are controlled centrally by the Ministry of Education. Specialists at the Ministry have trained the trainers for the individual modules. Evaluation tools have been developed for the assessment of both the trainers and the study scope contents through a pilot project.

Positional Training II was tested by the School Management Centre, at the Charles University in Prague through a pilot project, encompassing both combined learning and distance learning, and has been implemented at university level. Initial experiences with the proposed Positional Training I and II, suggest that this is the most comprehensive form of school management training in the Czech Republic (Slavíková *et al.*, 2003: 14). The students gain access to up-to-date information thanks to their top-level trainers and make contact with local leading lecturers in their regions. From the organizational point of view, the training course is easily accessible because the majority of the courses (90 per cent) take place regionally.

The training system encompasses a broad spectrum of professional competencies that managerial staff should possess, be it managers just starting or experienced managers or only candidates wishing to take such positions in the future. In compliance with the long-term vision of the government's National Programme of Development in Education and the requirements specified in the Life-Long Learning Memorandum and OECD documents, stress is laid upon the linking of theory and practice. The training course system for managerial staff in the education sector was developed for practical use, so as to meet the requirements of new legislation in education effective from 2004. This legislation will put more demanding requirements on the head teacher, whereby systemized training of school managers is gaining in importance. In this way improving aptitudes and skills for school management has ceased to be a voluntary decision and has become a professional requirement within which training goes hand in hand with the career path for employees in education.

Future challenges

The development of a national provision of leadership training in the Czech Republic is to be applauded since the relative initiatives can be seen as the fulfilment of calls for systematic training and development for school leaders in a nation where such pleas are part of the emergent discourse relating to the dramatic changes in national governance that occurred in the latter part of the twentieth century. The major shifts in the governance of schools and the roles and associated training of head teachers in the Czech Republic and its predecessor entities exemplifies how vocational identities have been decomposed and reconstructed in that nation in a manner that reflects trends across other Central and Eastern European nations (Rafal, 1998). Concerns exist that the previous totalitarian ideology has been replaced by market-driven forces that have led to an increasing privatization of education in the Czech Republic (Jana, 2000) but, in contrast to much of the commentary in nations such as England, such privatization is seen by many Czech commentators as a method of ensuring the 'depoliticization' of education and training (Svecova, 2000: 128). However, it is noteworthy that in contrast to the situation obtaining in England, higher education institutions have retained a leading role in the development of leadership programmes, as in other areas of continuing professional development for teachers (Sayer, 1995).

In some Western nations a critique of leadership development has emerged that can be viewed as a reaction to the fact that such national programmes of school leadership training are one element of an increasingly centralizing dictum within Western liberal society that has been operant since the 1980s; a dictum which, ironically, is counterbalanced by a commitment to marketization and local management of schooling (Daun,

2004). In this sense the historical derivations of the overall transformation of the Czech education system are very different from other societies that have not experienced the huge social and geopolitical shifts evident in that nation since leadership development initiatives in the Republic flow from an attempt to democratize social within which the new goal of education is, above all, to create 'self-confident, participating citizens' (Havel, 1993: 118). Thus the privatization of education, with concomitant needs for enhanced leadership skills, is seen as a method of encouraging innovative practice that lends legitimacy to the state's aspiration for democratic change (Svecova, 1994, 2000; Cerych *et al.*, 1996). Within this programme of democratization two principal orientations emerged: one towards restoration and one towards innovation and borrowing from the West (Daun and Sapatoru, 2002). On balance it would appear to be the latter orientation that has predominated in the case of the leadership development initiatives discussed in this chapter.

As yet, any critique of the Czech programmes is emergent and it is clear that the various incumbents and individuals who have developed and led the Republic's national programmes have striven hard to ameliorate some of the most seminal of the problematic issues noted in other nations. From the outset, the educational leadership programmes outlined earlier in the chapter were integrated into an academic award-bearing structure. The fact that the leadership programmes in the Czech Republic are integrated with the nation's higher education system augurs well for close correlation between such professional programmes and academic discourse.

Conclusions

Education leadership programmes tend to reflect the central intellectual and social concerns of the wider society in the host nation (Brundrett, 2001). As such concerns change and mutate and programmes of educational leadership development are reconceptualized and refocused. The nascent framework for leadership development in the Czech Republic has developed rapidly from a construction that was fragmented and unsystematic but with strong emergent and intellectually challenging practice based in individual institutions (Slavíková and Karabac, 2003: 50) towards one that encompasses mandatory and systematic training.

The history of such development is finely attuned to changes in broader policy, intellectual change and geopolitical shifts in doctrine and national educational governance. In some ways there is a striking correspondence between developments in the Czech Republic and Western nations such as England which mirror contemporary engagement with standards-based, competency-led systems of training that stand to one side, but interrelate with, older traditions embodied in academic programmes. Nations such as the Czech Republic are responding to hegemonic global forces in ways which demonstrate the various cultural inflections of each state. However, what is most crucial is that the Czech people have chosen to invest in the development of educational leaders as a means of driving up achievement in schools.

References

Beran, J. (1995) Transformation of the Czech education system: the common school project, *Oxford Studies in Comparative Education*, 5(1), 74–89.

Beran, J. and Kohnova, J. (1995) Proposal for the conception of in-service teacher education and training, *Oxford Studies in Comparative Education*, 5(1), 90–101.

Brundrett, M. (2001) The development of school leadership preparation programmes in England and the USA, *Educational Management and Administration*, 29(2), 229–245.

Brundrett, M., Slavíková, L., Karabec, S., Murden, B., Dering, A. and Nicolaidou, M. (2006) Educational leadership development in England and the Czech Republic: comparing perspectives, *School Leadership and Management*, 26(2), 93–106.

Cerych, L., Bacik, F., Kotasek, K. and Svecova, J. (1996) Reviews of national policies for education: Czech Republic, in: *Transforming education, Part 1*, Paris: OECD, 15–94.

Daun, H. (2004) Privatisation, decentralization and governance in education in the Czech Republic, England, France, Germany and Sweden, *International Review of Education*, 50, 325–346.

Daun, H. and Sapatoru, D. (2002) Educational reforms in Eastern Europe, in: D. Holger (ed.) *Educational restructuring in the context of globalization and national policy*, New York: RoutledgeFalmer, 147–179.

Havel, V. (1993) *Summer meditations*, New York: Vintage Books.

Huber, S. G. (2003) Methodology and methods, in: S. G. Huber (ed.) *Preparing school leaders for the 21st century: an international comparison of development programmes in 15 countries*, Lisse: Taylor and Francis, 328–340.

Jana, S. (2000) Privatization of education in the Czech Republic, *International Journal of Educational Development*, 20(2), 122–133.

Sayer, J. (1995) The continuing professional development of teachers and the role of the University, *Oxford Studies in Comparative Education*, 5(1), 65–70.

Sayer, J., Kazelleova, J., Martin, D., Niemczynski, A. and Vanderhoeven, J. (1995) Developing schools for democracy in Europe: an example of trans-European cooperation, *Oxford Studies in Comparative Education*, 5(1), 1–3.

Slavíková, L. and Karabec, S. (2003) School management preparation in the Czech Republic, in: L. E. Watson (ed.) *Selecting and developing heads of schools: twenty-three perspectives*, Sheffield: European Forum on Educational Administration.

Slavíková, L., Karabec, S., Murden, B., Nicolaidou, M. and Dering, A. (2003) *Head teacher-leader and manager: a comparative study of professional leadership qualifications in the European education sector*, Prague: British Council.

Svekova, J. (1994) Czechoslovakia, in: S. Karsten and D. Majoor (eds) *Education in East Central Europe: educational change after the fall of Communism*, New York: Waxmann.

Svekova, J. (2000) Privatization of education in the Czech Republic, *International Journal of Educational Development*, 20, 127–133.

Chapter 6

Educational leadership development in Kosovo

Tim Goddard

Introduction

The development of educational leaders is a culturally grounded process. In this chapter I offer an outsider's perspective on the professional development of educational leaders in Kosovo. First, I situate Kosovo within the social, economic, cultural and political context of the Balkan region during the early years of the twenty-first century. Second, I provide a brief overview of the processes by which school administrators were prepared in the period prior to the educational reforms initiated in 2000. Third, I describe the processes by which educational reforms were designed and developed in Kosovo during the immediate post-conflict period and then, fourth, I examine the leadership development practices currently in place. And finally, I suggest some of the complexities of change which may be considered by policy makers in Kosovo.

Context

Kosovo is located in the Balkans region of south-east Europe and is part of the former Socialist Federal Republic of Yugoslavia. Kosovo has a long history. It is known from Roman times as Dardania and, according to Kosovars themselves, was originally Illyria. Following the collapse of the Roman Empire the region came under the control of the Serbian states of Zeta and Raska and then, after the battle of Kosovo Polje in 1389, it was part of the Ottoman Empire. The Turkish regime was over thrown in the late 1800s and, in 1913, the Treaty of London returned administrative responsibilities to Serbia. The Treaty of Versailles in 1918 ceded the territory to the 'Kingdom of the Serbs, Croats and Slovenes' (Bartlett *et al.*, 2004, p. 486), which became Yugoslavia in 1929 and then the Socialist Republic of Yugoslavia in 1943. This political entity collapsed in the 1990s, and as a result of what have become known as the Balkan wars a number of independent states emerged.

Unlike Slovenia, Croatia, Macedonia and Bosnia-Hercegovina, Kosovo stayed as a territory within Serbia and, more recently, Serbia and Montenegro. This situation was resisted by ethnic Albanians within Kosovo and led to increasing repression by Serbian authorities. This, in turn, led to armed conflict within Kosovo, to the exodus of refugees, and to the NATO intervention of 1999.

Authors such as Clark (2000), Cviic (1997) and Ramet (1996) provide more detailed histories of the period following the 1980 death of President Tito. What is clear, however, is that 'the important role that formal education plays in social cohesion had begun its dreadful disintegration decades before the hostilities between Serbs and Albanians [in Kosovo] broke out ... in 1998' (Bartlett *et al.*, 2004, p. 486). As each succeeding political group took leadership and power, so textbooks and curricula were adjusted to reflect the views and ideologies of the prevailing dominant elite.

Currently, Kosovo has a population of approximately two million people, 88 per cent of whom are ethnically Albanian. The minority groups in Kosovo include those of Serbian, Gorani, Egyptian, Ashkali, Roma and Turkish background. The population of Kosovo is demographically the youngest in Europe, with some 50 per cent of the residents under the age of 20 (International Centre for Community and Enterprise Development [ICCED], 2006). As a result of population shifts which occurred due to the destruction of homes in rural areas, there was a large influx of people to the urban centres (Earnest, 2004). In Prishtina, for example, a pre-1999 population of approximately 250,000 had burgeoned to over 600,000 by 2004. Many of these new urban inhabitants were young – Stone *et al.* (2004) report that 60 per cent of the population of Prishtina are under 24 years of age. The high rate of unemployment is exacerbated among youth, with over half unemployed (Wright, 2006).

Politically, Kosovo is currently under temporary administration by UNMIK, the United Nations Interim Administration in Kosovo (ICCED, 2006). Installed in 1999 under the authority of United Nations Security Council Resolution 1244, the mandate of UNMIK is to establish a coherent structure of governance. The mandate is currently being reviewed with the possibility of a monitored form of independence being granted by the world community. This possibility, however, is being resisted by Serbia, which still claims Kosovo as a province.

The establishment of separate jurisdictions from the former Yugoslavia was often accompanied by inter-state or civil war. The specific Kosovo context has been described elsewhere (Goddard, 2007). The deployment of the Serbian army to Kosovo in 1990 predicated a series of measures which effectively suppressed the Albanian population (Clark, 2000; Ramet, 1996). The return of civil government under the auspices of UNMIK only happened following the NATO intervention of 1999 (Goddard, 2003, 2007).

Kosovo was always an economically deprived region within the former Yugoslavia. Indeed Elsie (1997) described it as 'the poorhouse of the European continent' (p. 152). It is estimated that 47 per cent of the population lives in poverty and that unemployment is currently between 44 per cent (ICCED, 2006), and 50 per cent (Wright, 2006). One of the outcomes of both civil and inter-state war is the difficulty in finding precise and accurate statistics. It is apparent, however, that Kosovo has a large proportion of young people and that the majority of them are unemployed. Further, many of these young men and women have witnessed, or engaged in, acts of extreme violence.

Exacerbating this already difficult situation is the fact that many youth are socially displaced. In addition to suffering from the psychological harm of post-traumatic stress (Davies, 2005), many also have to cope with other pressures. The educational needs of orphans (International Rescue Committee [IRC], 2006b), refugees (Ahlen, 2006; Commonwealth Secretariat, 2004) and internally displaced persons (Quick, 2006) are different from those of children from stable family backgrounds, as are the needs of nomadic youth (Commonwealth Secretariat, 2006) such as the Roma and Ashkali peoples.

The work of school administrators in Kosovo, therefore, is a difficult task. Although all the jurisdictions which emerged from the former Republic of Yugoslavia have 'followed a process of intensive educational reforms, directed towards universal developments and democracy' (Clarkson, 2005, p. 321) in Kosovo this process has been hindered by the social and physical ravages of war.

The physical and environmental infrastructures within which schools operate were devastated during the years leading up to the conflict in Kosovo, and during the conflict itself. Davies (2005) observed that many schools were physically ruined. Daxner (cited in Bartlett *et al.*, 2004, pp. 487–488) reported that 37 per cent of the schools were either completely destroyed or in extremely bad physical condition, and that following the NATO intervention some two-thirds of the educational faculties were found to have suffered damage and were in need of repair.

Further, educational records had been lost or destroyed (Davies, 2005), landmines and unexploded ordinance littered the grounds of many schools (Bartlett *et al.*, 2004) and the poor physical condition of schools included insufficient sanitary facilities, a lack of drinking water, old or broken furniture, and little in the way of sports facilities, musical instruments, and so forth (Gefferth and Zylfiu-Haziri, 2004).

To further complicate matters, many Albanian Kosovar children had no real experience of school. In 1992 the Serbian authorities had dismissed 26,000 Albanian teachers on the same day (Gefferth and Zylfiu-Haziri, 2004; Sommers and Buckland, 2004) and, as a result, a parallel system of education was established. Generally ignored by the authorities, these schools functioned from 1992 until 1999. However the parallel system was 'undisclosed, understaffed, and under resourced' (Bartlett *et al.*, 2004,

p. 489) and many children received a somewhat less than optimum educational experience. Exposed only to a traditional didactic model of learning and isolated from the digital revolution taking place elsewhere in Europe (Stone *et al.*, 2004), and forced to see their schools used for purposes which had complete disregard for their original function (Davies, 2005), the children entered the twenty-first century with multiple pedagogical handicaps.

The ramifications of these handicaps were intensified by a lack of trained teachers. Many had fled the region during the 1990s and those who took on the teaching role were enthusiastic amateurs rather than professionally trained teachers. With the influx of foreign troops under NATO, those returning teachers who had in exile learned language skills were quickly recruited as interpreters by the British, German, American, and other armed forces. The low salaries offered to teachers further exacerbated the flight from the profession (OECD, 2004) and those who remained in the classrooms were often forced to take second or even third jobs. Many were 'attracted to new opportunities in the new bureaucracy, and in the international agencies and non-governmental organizations' (Buckland, 2005, p. xviii).

Finally, it must be noted that there was a severe 'lack of trained school administrators' (OECD, 2004, p. 323). In many communities this position was simply awarded to the most senior teacher, while in other cases political sponsorship was a necessary precursor for appointment.

The professional development of school administrators must therefore be considered as an activity taking place in a post-conflict, resource-free environment fraught with uncertainty and ambiguity. Further, it involves individuals who have very limited personal exposure to professional development. During the 1980s, Kosovars of Albanian ethnicity were systematically excluded from what little professional development activities were available to Kosovars of Serbian descent.

Approximately two-thirds of the population lives in a rural village or hamlet (ICCED, 2006). To the post-conflict and resource-free environment experienced by poorly trained school administrators must therefore be added the policy arena of rural education. As Wallin and Hiebert (2007) and others have shown, rural settings often experience problems which deter educational excellence.

Indeed, research in a rural Canadian province identified educational themes which resonate in the Kosovo experience. Schools are isolated from centrally located specialized services; it is difficult to recruit teachers; accessibility to professional development activities is limited; and, students are often not motivated to excel (Wallin and Hiebert, 2007, p. 3). It is within this context that the professional development of school leaders must occur.

A traditional milieu

As noted, professional development opportunities for school administrators in the 1980s and 1990s were very limited. As a result, those who hold formal leadership positions in Kosovar schools in the early twenty-first century have had limited exposure to either the literature or practice of educational reform (Goddard, 2004, 2006).

In many countries, the last quarter of the twentieth century was marked by significant reforms in the field of education. School effectiveness researchers identified alternative ways of understanding the conceptual and methodological structures of schools. The interactions between people and policy, and between resources and outcomes, were more closely examined. The important roles of gender, culture and ethics within school administration were explored and explained (see Heck and Hallinger, 1999, for a summary of these events). Organizations were recast as a variety of metaphors (Morgan, 1986), leadership was understood to be distributive rather than hierarchical (Gronn, 2002), and the impacts of culture and diversity in schools became an important part of the educational discourse (Billot *et al.*, 2007; Goddard, 2003). In most Western jurisdictions, questions of standardization and assessment began to drive educational policy, and funding was redirected to priorities related to information technologies such as computers and the Internet.

Curricula were standardized within many countries, and accountability measures designed to document success were developed and implemented. International comparative assessments were conducted, and leadership was reconstructed as a shared or distributed function of many within a school, rather than the domain of one individual. However, the school directors, as head teachers or principals are known in Kosovo, have experienced none of this and in many cases have no idea that such changes even occurred.

Acknowledging that initial and in-service training of teachers was a widely adopted phenomenon, Bush and Jackson (2002) noted that 'recognition of the need for specific preparation for aspiring and practicing school leaders, to generate the positive effects identified in the school effectiveness research, has been slower to emerge' (p. 418). This was certainly the case in Kosovo, where the school effectiveness and improvement literature was generally unknown (Goddard and Fagnou, 2002) at the turn of the century.

Traditionally, as Tahiraj (2007) noted, school directors in Kosovo 'believe they are in the position of deciding everything' (p. 7). They have not experienced or been encouraged to learn 'inclusive democratic processes with distributed leadership of the type found in western democracies' (Anderson *et al.*, 2007, p. 80). Rather, their understanding of effective leadership is predicated on the traditional bureaucratic model. As such, their practice 'emphasized [the] rigid use of rules, close surveillance of teachers, tight hierarchical control, and clear delineation of objectives and procedures that teachers are expected to follow' (Terrence and Dolores, 2000, cited in Tahiraj, 2007, p. 8). This command and control model of leadership was mirrored throughout the hierarchy. In the same way that school directors closely monitored and directed the work of their teachers, so their work in turn was monitored and directed by school inspectors employed by the Ministry of Education (Goddard and VanBalkom, 2007).

A time of reformation

Following the NATO intervention of 1999, a Department of Education and Science (DES) was established by UNMIK. The immediate issues of concern were to repair or reconstruct schools damaged during the conflict and to provide essential supplies (Anderson and Humick, 2007) necessary for schools to function. Concurrently the two co-heads of DES, one a Kosovar and the other an international, laid the policy groundwork for the establishment of a Ministry of Education, Science and Technology (MEST).

MEST was operationalized in 2002 and immediately began to address the 'qualitative issues of educational reform such as teacher training, curriculum reform and the creation of a pluralistic and multi-ethnic education system for Kosovo' (Anderson and Humick, 2007, p. 7). A focused programme of leadership development was part of that reform agenda. The educational reforms which were implemented in Kosovo during this period were identified by MEST and then addressed by various organizations contracted for the purpose.

Essentially, UNMIK and DES identified major areas of reform and tasked different national governments, through their various development arms, to design and implement a programme of reform in each area. Thus Finland was awarded the area of special education, Germany was awarded vocational education, and so forth. Canada was awarded a leadership role in teacher training.

Subsequently the Canadian International Development Agency (CIDA) called for competitive proposals to execute reforms in teacher education. A consortium of the University of Calgary and Universalia Management Group submitted the successful bid and the Kosovo Educator Development Project (KEDP) was launched in May 2001. Working closely with officials from DES and, later, MEST, the KEDP staff designed and implemented a programme of teacher training and leadership development.

Initially planned as a three-year project, KEDP was subsequently extended to six years and also expanded to include Serbia and Montenegro. In this chapter, however, the focus is limited to the Kosovo experience.

Considering change

As the educational reconstruction process proceeded in Kosovo, so a number of challenges became apparent. First, a 'lead agency' approach was implemented. Through this different aspects of educational reform were made the responsibility of different national agencies. Thus, for example, special needs education became the domain of a Finnish development organization, GTZ of Germany took responsibility for vocational education, and CIDA was the lead agency for teacher education. This approach led to some confusion and overlap in service delivery as there was political resistance to any one agency having power or control over the others. As Olson (2007) has argued in the Afghanistan context, donor coordination is an important organizational strategy. In Kosovo this responsibility was jealously guarded by MEST. The ministry, however, had little implementation capacity in the initial post-conflict era. Officials were largely untrained and there was no infrastructure capacity to coordinate the activities of multiple international actors.

A second challenge was the financial focus on physical reconstruction efforts (IRC, 2006a). Although many of the school buildings were in disarray, such 'prioritization of infrastructure can lead to neglect of teacher training, capacity building, curriculum issues and sustainable financing' (Nicolai, 2006, p. 23). Although teacher training was considered a policy priority, it was not supported with large-scale budget allocations.

There are those, such as Greeley and Rose (2006), who argue that it is essential to focus on teacher training 'as teaching can play a key role in supporting post-conflict transition' (p. 14). A counter-argument is that such programmes, where the focus is 'on pedagogical aspects of teaching and short-term teacher training' (Spink, 2006, p. 16), ignore the deeper malaise in post-conflict situations, namely the lack of subject knowledge among the surviving teachers. Drawing on the context of Afghanistan, Spink (2006) suggests that modernizing pedagogical practices without also providing teachers with contemporary subject knowledge is a foolhardy practice.

A third challenge was the changing political and economic environments in the donor countries. In 2000 it was generally accepted that education could not be a 'a post-conflict add-on; it must be the cornerstone of state building and reconstruction' (Spink, 2006, p. 16). There was an agreement within the international community that 'conflict presents not only challenges for reconstruction but also significant opportunities for reform of educational systems' (Buckland, 2005, p. xv). As noted earlier, all of the former Yugoslav republics took advantage of their individual post-conflict periods to launch extensive educational reform agendas.

In Kosovo, this process was constrained by external global events. As Jackson (2003) reported:

> increased accountability requirements, tight budgets, and the unpredictable demands of a volatile, post-cold war (and now post-September 11) world, among other factors, have prompted most bilateral and multilateral development agencies to redefine the way they spend their money.
> (p. 42)

One consequence of this, in Kosovo, was the slashing in 2002 of the budget of one agency from $25 million USD to $5 million USD, with the balance of the funds transferred to agency operations in Afghanistan.

A fourth challenge was a limited awareness of the high democratic return on investment (DROI) offered by educational reform. In a carefully constructed programme of reform it is not only the physical infrastructure which is improved. There is also a high DROI with respect to human capacity development. As Jackson (2006, pp. 49–50) points out, benefits include: students learning about their civic rights; girls and women are empowered to participate in all aspects of the community; mutual understanding and engagement is developed among diverse (and sometimes antagonistic) groups; parents and the society at large are included in educational reform; and, labour force skills are developed.

In order for the DROI to be realized, however, educational change must take place within a conducive environment. The school must provide a safe haven for change to occur and for individual human capacity to increase. It is the responsibility of the school administrator to provide and nurture such an environment. To do this they need to have an awareness of the nuances of educational leadership, an awareness that can only be developed through an extensive and intensive leadership development programme.

Implementing change

Educational interventions in post-conflict Kosovo took place at the macro (policy), meso (institutional) and micro (individual) levels. The activities of KEDP impacted all three levels. A Teacher Training Review Board (TTRB) was established to review and create policy related to the training, credentialing, and professional accountability of educators. A Faculty of Education was established at the University of Prishtina and senior administrator development programmes were initiated at the Ministry of Education, Science and Technology. Finally, a learner-centred instruction programme for teachers and a leadership development programme for school administrators were conceived, designed and implemented.

The intent of the latter two programmes was two-fold. First, to develop individual skills and capacities. Second, to provide these individuals with the knowledge and ability to influence change in the meso and macro environments. Although it has been suggested elsewhere (CDA, 2006) that 'programme assumptions that individual change will lead to socio-political change have not been borne out in Kosovo' (p. 6), this was not the experience in the educational domain. Rather, of the 43 individuals who completed the first KEDP leadership programme in 2001–2002, over half – 26 – were employed in senior administrative positions by 2006. In these roles they acted as change agents to reform the educational system.

In their history of KEDP, Anderson and Humick (2007, p. 14) summarize the development of the educational leadership programme:

> Educational leadership development also advanced through a concentrated and coordinated process of building networks and support systems for educational administrators and school directors. A total of 43 Albanian and Bosniak trainers each received about 100 hours of training, and were subsequently able to deliver 23 educational leadership courses reaching approximately 600 school directors and educational administrators. Leadership trainers then went on to facilitate follow-up Poster Conferences in at least seven regions with some project support and mentoring. It is estimated that nearly 100% coverage of school directors had been achieved by the end of the 2002 Summer Institute – however, it was estimated that 20% of these directors had been replaced in the hiring process for school directors, which took place in later 2002/early 2003. As of 2005, they too had been successfully trained, and MEST made it compulsory for future principals to have completed such training.
>
> Strategies to transfer in-service educator development to full ownership and leadership of indigenous organizations were started, but experienced some difficulties as a result of previously unforeseen political factors as well as variable organizational capacity. However, KEDP, MEST and the Kosovo Education Centre (KEC) agreed to propose a compulsory training schedule for all school directors consisting of the basic course (KEDP program) followed by the modules developed by KEC and then by a jointly-developed advanced leadership course.

These leadership courses provide a 'laddering' of professional development opportunities for school directors. In 2001 a total of 184 in-post school administrators completed the initial leadership training programme (Goddard, 2002). Of these, 43 subsequently completed a programme which focused on the pedagogy of delivering the leadership programme and which drilled deeper in to the content. A total of 38 participants successfully completed that training programme and were then able, over the next four years, to deliver the leadership programme to all their in-post peers and to all new school directors who were hired. In 2006 the MEST made successful completion of the KEDP programme a requirement for all persons appointed to school leadership roles.

Also during this period a major reorganization of the education system took place. A programme for the newly appointed regional education officers was designed and delivered (Anderson *et al.*, 2005) to respond to these changing needs. A further reorganization led to the appointment of seven senior regional education officers, one for each region within Kosovo. As all of these individuals had completed the KEDP leadership programme, and five were trainers of the programme, it was decided to further their personal leadership skills through an advanced leadership programme (Anderson and Goddard, 2006). Concurrently, largely unsuccessful attempts to engage the minority Kosovar Serbian community in the educational reform process were attempted (Goddard *et al.*, 2006). Threaded throughout all these initiatives was an understanding of education as a tool for democracy and reconstruction, and as a means of achieving societal change.

In the 2006–2007 academic year the MEST issued legislation requiring all aspiring school administrators to follow a prescribed training programme. First, in order to be considered for a post all aspirants will be required to complete an introduction to school management course created by CIMIC, a civil–military cooperation initiative undertaken by the German elements of the NATO Kosovo Force. Second, either prior to or within two years of appointment, school directors are to complete the KEDP leadership programme, which is now 'owned' by MEST and delivered by KEDP-trained instructors. Failure to complete this programme will result in contracts not being renewed after the two-year probationary period. Third, school directors are required to complete a series of in-depth modules developed by the Kosovo Education Centre, each of which focuses on one element of administrator functions identified by the school effectiveness literature. These modules must be completed within five years of appointment and are a necessary prerequisite for employment as a regional education officer.

Those school directors who choose to continue their professional development then have the option of participating in the advanced leadership course, also now delivered by MEST. Regional education officers are required to complete this programme within five years of their appointment. It is hoped, by MEST officials, that the advanced leadership course will eventually become a bridge to, or a component of, a masters level degree programme at the University of Prishtina. Such plans, however, are still in a nascent stage as the Faculty of Education does not currently have the capacity to deliver such a programme.

This pyramid of training and continuing professional development opportunities for school administrators has been warmly received in the field. Educational administrators at all levels of the Kosovo system appear to appreciate the opportunity to advance their own knowledge, skills and competencies and to act as catalysts for reform. Teachers, especially those who have completed the learner-centred instruction and similar programmes, appreciate the support they receive from educational leaders who are no longer mired in the controlling, hierarchical and risk-averse practices of the past.

That said, the sustainability of the model will require a continued focus and allocation of resources by MEST. Currently there are no financial rewards, in the form of salary increments, for those who complete the different tiers of the training pyramid. Compliance is assured due to the job requirements attached to each programme, but resistance to this process is already being observed. Although MEST claims financial exigency as a reason for the lack of financial incentives, many school administrators are questioning why they need to commit time and effort to training programmes which carry no monetary reward. In an environment where school teachers and directors are still woefully underpaid, even by the norms of other professions within Kosovo, such reluctance is perhaps easy to understand.

Complexities of change

It is a taken-for-granted assumption of most post-conflict development initiatives that education will 'heal the psychosocial wounds of war, solve youth unemployment, deliver decentralization and democracy, build peace and promote economic and social development' (Buckland, 2006, p. 7). This assumption must be challenged. There often appears to be a disconnect between the espoused and enacted values of development. The involvement of armed-forces-led initiatives such as the CIMIC leadership programme can lead to the 'militarization' of aid (Olson, 2007). Cultural resistance (Tahirij, 2007) to imported policy strategies becomes manifested in schools, where lip-service adherence to new programmes is abandoned in the crucible of the classroom.

While many profess a sustainable assets-based approach to educational development (Kretzmann and McKnight, 1993), attempts to build educational capacity by 'harnessing the myriad of collective assets and strengths within the greater community' (Koch, 2007, n.p.) are often more successful in the conceptual rather than the applied domain. There are many reasons for this displacement between theory and practice. A major one, as Escobar (1997) relates, is that many development efforts have tended to encompass 'a top-down, ethnocentric and technocratic approach, which treated people and cultures as abstract concepts, statistical figures to be moved up and down in the charts of "progress" ' (p. 91).

A second reason, perhaps, is the narrow focus on human capital development as a means of building individual capacity, or resources. Wigley and Akkoyunlu-Wigley (2006) argue the focus ought to be improving human capabilities, that is, the ability to act. They suggest that simply increasing the 'creation of productive agents' (p. 293) available to an individual, a resource library as it were, is not useful if the individual does not also have the capability to act on those resources. Human capital resources are 'necessary (but not sufficient) pre-conditions for human agency' (p. 292). Any programme of educational leadership development must provide not only the knowledge base required for one to be an effective administrator but also the techniques and strategies required to implement that knowledge.

These processes of human agency must be considered within the socio-political context of the educational environment. It must be understood that there are inherent dangers in any programme which attempts to simply transfer knowledge from Western educational systems in to a different environment. Such transfers may bring an impression of surface legitimacy, as policy makers will present these initiatives as being representative of a 'better' system. However, 'importing policy reforms formulated elsewhere under different economic, political and cultural conditions presents challenges for the new host culture' (Dimmock and Walker, 2000, p. 307). There are many examples of situations where international education agencies, albeit unwittingly in many cases, are 'used to (1) replace diverse local sentiments with shared nationalist ones and (2) replace parochial thought patterns with rational-modern ones represented as universal' (Waks, 2006, p. 405). Always a political act, education thus becomes complicit in external attempts to establish socio-political structures which are ideologically replicative of the donor state.

The implementation of educational reforms can also be derailed due to a false understanding of the local terrain. Models of organizational decentralization often require the existence of strong district and local level structures through which the reforms will be implemented (Mundy *et al.*, 2006, p. 30). In Kosovo, however, few such structures existed and more pressing priorities of social reconstruction meant that there was neither the money nor the political will to establish or support such structures. There was a recognition that decentralizing the system would be more expensive than a centralized model and, also, a fear that central power would be diminished and transferred to local power groups.

Such indices of resistance to change are apparent across Kosovo. In a wide-ranging review of the post-conflict educational experience, Sommers and Buckland (2004) found 'consistent expressions of distance, and feeling under-appreciated and overlooked, reported by nearly every educational professional interviewed at the municipal and school levels' (p. 137). As their study was conducted at a time when all school directors had completed the KEDP leadership development programme, but the implementation of a similar programme for ministry officials was in its early stages (Anderson and Humick, 2007, p. 26), such findings are not unexpected. Indeed, they make be taken as testament to the success of the leadership programme in facilitating change at the individual level.

This increase in self-awareness and a new willingness to critique the central authority, something which would have been unthinkable under the communist structures of earlier times (Karstanje, 2001), signifies a paradigmatic shift in administrator thinking. School directors in Kosovo are no longer willing to act simply as managers, responsible for the supervision, control and coordination of staff and the maintenance of centrally dictated indicators of performance (Dimmock and Walker, 2000, p. 304). Rather, they now see themselves as educational leaders, with the responsibility to set the goals of the school and motivate staff, students and community to achieve these goals.

They are still constrained by local context. The traditional dominance of the voices of senior male teachers is culturally ingrained and difficult to overcome. Educational innovations can sometimes be perceived, and (mis)represented, as running counter to state-controlled ideology. As such, reform efforts may be understood not only as a pedagogical challenge to the status quo but also as a political one.

School administrators are also required to cope with the aftermath of conflict. The students are unused to regular hours of school, teachers are either unqualified or else lacking in contemporary subject knowledge, and the remnants of ethnic antagonism loom large over the community.

It is important, therefore, that leadership development programmes in post-conflict zones go beyond the theoretical domain and embrace practice embedded in context. In Kosovo, this required school administrators to understand the principles of staff performance appraisals and also to develop locally-appropriate mechanisms to implement these processes. Course components related to the management and effective utilization of resources (human, financial, technical, material, spatial and time-related) had to be tempered by the reality that very few resources were available to be managed and utilized.

Similarly, it was necessary to embed western notions of inclusion within the post-conflict context. Within the old system of socialist Yugoslavia, children with special needs were confined to special schools and were not integrated into the mainstream system. As a result, most teachers had little or no experience dealing with children who had severe physical or intellectual disabilities, who were blind or deaf, or who were otherwise 'different' from perceived 'normal' children. The integration of special needs children into the school system therefore required a major change in individual teacher perceptions of the role of education, and a concomitant change in school director perceptions of their role in implementing integration.

Concurrently, attempts to include children from minority and marginalized populations were being initiated. There was a call, albeit led by Western advisors to UNMIK, that all children should not only be included in their local school but should be active participants in the life of that school. In many communities this required children from families who had suffered terribly during the war to attend school with children from those families responsible for that suffering. As a result, as Sommers and Buckland (2004) noted, 'education remains one of the chief settings where tensions and conflicts among and between Albanians and Serbs [in Kosovo] play themselves out' (p. 20). The development of culturally-appropriate curricula, including that which is relevant to and resonates with minority group students, thus becomes another area of responsibility for the school director.

The restructuring of curriculum is fraught with difficulty. It is through the curriculum that children construct their identities and the norms of civil society are inculcated. It is through the governance of schools that 'relationships between government and civil society' help students develop an understanding of 'the effective, democratic and equitable management of human societies' (Mundy *et al.*, 2006, p. 4). In a post-conflict environment where both parties to the conflict are now attempting to coexist, however, the curriculum becomes a new battleground.

Davies (2005) has commented that the ways in which schools construct 'us' and 'others' are reflected in the curriculum. She observes that in Bosnia-Hercegovina, for example, the results have included separate systems of schooling, a differentiated curriculum, and different versions of history (p. 361). In Kosovo, Serbian students still tend to attend schools located in the 'enclaves' where most Kosovars of Serbian heritage now reside. Here the schools still follow the curricula established by Belgrade. Attempts to integrate all students under one system, directed by MEST from Prishtina, have to date not been successful. Once a final determination of Kosovo within the international community has been established, it is anticipated that educational integration will be mandated.

Within the Albanian Kosovar educational system there are also urgent needs for curricula reform. The curriculum needs to evolve from its current tendency to prioritize 'great works' and accumulated knowledge in a transmission model. To many older educators, education is a means of relaying known facts to the student body. School directors are faced with challenging and changing this world view.

The post-conflict reforms have provided an opportunity to infiltrate the curricula space. Information on HIV/AIDS and landmine awareness, for example, is now included in the curriculum. Psychosocial support for children suffering from post-traumatic stress and other pressures is becoming accepted as a necessary function of schools. History textbooks are being rewritten to better reflect the identity and community understandings held by the Kosovar population. However any substantial cultural change is gradual, and so multiple generations of students will have to experience the new curriculum before it becomes an accepted part of the socio-cultural fabric of Kosovo.

We know that education affects social cohesion through a number of different factors (Colenso, 2005). The distribution of educational resources, opportunities and outcomes can be targeted to address existing differentiation among various ethnic groups. Through the exercise of transparency and participation in educational policy formulation, planning and management, so it is possible for community members to become more engaged in the school. And, through the development of social and behavioural competencies in students, so a new willingness to coexist with others might be initiated and nurtured. It has been shown in the school effectiveness literature that adequately prepared school-based educational administrators play a crucial role not only in the academic success of the students but also within the wider community served by the school (Heck and Hallinger, 1999; Ryan, 2003; Silins and Mulford, 2002). In a post-conflict environment such as Kosovo, the presence of such local leadership contributes not only to the successful implementation of educational reforms but also to the wider revitalization of the community. As McMurtry (2001) has argued, sustainable development requires the building of a civil commons, where institutions of public education, healthcare and broadcasting are not driven by ideology, profit or advertising but by a deeper belief in the humanity of community. School administrators are key members of the civil commons, and their programmes of preparation must reflect their necessary ability to adapt to the complexities of change.

Conclusion

In his review of the Kosovo Education Development Project, Jackson (2006) noted five 'lessons learned' from the initiative. He concluded that in any post-conflict programme, success would only be possible if:

1 the security situation was stable and durable;
2 the dominant ethnic groups wanted peace and valued education;
3 sector interventions promoted change at multiple levels at the same time;
4 donor investment in the intervention was focused, and substantial, over a five to ten year period;
5 the project and programme strategies were sequenced or blended in order to optimize results (pp. 46–48).

These circumstances existed in Kosovo during the immediate post-conflict period (2000–2007) and contributed to the success of the leadership development programme.

That said, it is also important to recognize that many of the problems – and solutions – inherent to the educational reform process lie beyond the agency of educators. Often, necessary political and economic decisions affecting education are taken in different fora, and by different people, than are the technical planning decisions made by educators (Colenso, 2005). Young (1990) cautions those engaged in development projects to avoid cultural imperialism, the tendency to establish as a norm the experiences and culture of the dominant group. International educators who focus on ensuring that they do not import policy and practices from their own society must also be cautious not to simply endorse those of the dominant group within the recipient country.

Initiators of educational reform within post-conflict communities will also face political resistance to what appear common-sense ideas. They may find that ministry officials are willing to discuss neutral 'technical' issues but 'may not be willing, or able, to discuss sensitive political issues related to social cohesion' (Colenso, 2005, p. 424). The attempts by KEDP to include members of the Kosovo Serbian community are examples of the failure, due to ideology, of attempts to influence societal change through educational reform.

Ideologies, in essence, 'are systems of belief about what works and what does not work as individuals attempt to attain valued outcomes' (Petrick and Scherer, 2000, p. 98). When different groups value and seek different outcomes so ideology can contradict strategy.

Research into cultural difference (e.g. Hofstede, 1980; Dimmock and Walker, 2000) has posited a variety of dimensions or frameworks of difference. Hofstede (1980) initially described these as being: power distance; individualism; uncertainty avoidance; and, masculinity. Although originally based on research conducted within a large multinational business, Hofstede (1986) later applied his framework to an educational setting. Dimmock and Walker (2000) further refined the framework and developed six pairs of cultural indicators, with each pair being conceptualized as being at the opposite ends of a continuum. The six pairs were: power-distributed/power-concentrated; group-oriented/self-oriented; consideration/aggression; proactivism/fatalism; generative/replicative; and, limited relationship/holistic relations (pp. 308–410). A brief examination of these cultural dimensions shows that there appears to exist a wide degree of variance between the cultural norms and values of Kosovo and those of the western societies responsible for implementing educational reform. Although more substantive research is required to validate these observations, the following discussion is pertinent.

In Western liberal democracies such as Canada and the United Kingdom, high levels of inequality within the society are generally not tolerated, at least in rhetoric and policy. In Kosovo, by contrast, there appears to be a greater acceptance of unequal distributions of power. In school, students are generally obedient and conforming to the rules of the school. The teacher is understood to have knowledge which s/he will impart to the pupil, and respect is afforded to teachers relative to their age.

The individualistic orientation of Western societies is antithetical to the collective values of Kosovo, where the communal is prioritized over the personal. Family and group loyalties are high and ties between students are based on age, sex, kinship and language. Similarly, there is a high degree of uncertainty avoidance. Students feel comfortable in highly structured learning situations and teachers consider themselves to be experts who must not be challenged, and who cannot learn from lay people.

Perhaps as a result of its history, Kosovo has an education system which tends to be replicative rather than generative. Innovations, ideas and inventions are adopted from elsewhere and are implemented without significant critique. There is a high level of fatalism, a sense of 'what will be, will be', and gender-specific life roles are commonly accepted. Holistic relationships influence professional interactions, with kinship, patronage and friendship often trumping rules and established hiring policies when applicants are considered for employment. A gendered perspective that men take on leadership roles outside the home while women look after the family also influences hiring decisions. These cultural differences must be contemplated and acted upon when designing and implementing programmes of educational reform.

The educational development of leaders in post-conflict jurisdictions such as Kosovo requires interventions across many levels. It is not sufficient to introduce a programme of professional development which is focused on the content of educational management and leadership. School directors work with teachers, students and communities, and strategies which permit them to understand the needs and aspirations of these social actors must be incorporated in any leadership training programme. Similarly, schools function as sub-sets within a wider policy environment, and any attempts to promote organizational change must target all elements of the system.

Professional development programmes for educational leaders seek to initiate chain reactions, where input leads to activity, to output, to outcomes and to impact. For a leadership training programme to be considered successful, the impact of the training must be visible and measurable. Through this process:

> individuals are encouraged to participate in their own re-education through the active intervention of change agents with groups as a medium of re-education ... The goal is to build commitment through cognitive change not just compliance.
>
> (Petrick and Scherer, 2000, p. 104)

Sommers and Buckland (2004) argued that the three priorities of post-conflict educational reconstruction are the rebuilding of school facilities, the production and distribution of textbooks, and the raising to prominence of special needs and minority education. All are worthy goals. In this chapter, however, I have argued that the provision of a locally contextualized programme of educational leadership development, grounded in theory but nuanced by both the existing and the desired social, political, economic, cultural and policy environments, is a prerequisite of sustainable educational change. It is through the development of a critical mass of informed change agents located and acting within schools, that education will achieve its rightful place as a tool of democracy and reconstruction in post-conflict societies.

References

Ahlen, E. (2006). UNHCR's education challenges. In M. Couldrey and T. Morris (eds), *Forced Migration Review. Supplement. Education and conflict: research, policy and practice* (pp. 10–11). Oxford: University of Oxford, Refugee Studies Centre.

Anderson, G. and Humick, B. (2007). The educator development project in the Balkans, 2001–2007. In G. Anderson and A. Wenderoth (eds), *Facilitating change: reflections on six years of education development programming in challenging environments* (pp. 1–29). Montreal: Universalia Management Group.

Anderson, G., Humick, B. and Lynn, D. (2007). Governing and learning to govern democratically. In G. Anderson and A. Wenderoth (eds), *Facilitating change: reflections on six years of education development programming in challenging environments* (pp. 75–100). Montreal: Universalia Management Group.

Anderson, K. and Goddard, J. T. (2006). *Charting change: organizational and policy development for senior educational leaders.* Prishtina, Kosovo: Educator Development Program.

Anderson, K., Goddard, J. T., Hutton, S., Buleshkaj, O. and Zeqiri, S. (2005). *Regional Education Officers Training Program: curriculum materials.* Prishtina, Kosovo: Educator Development Project.

Bartlett, B., Power, D. and Blatch, P. (2004). Education in a recovering nation: Renewing special education in Kosovo. *Exceptional Children*, 70(4), 485–495.

Billot, J., Goddard, J. T. and Cranston, N. (2007). How principals manage ethnocultural diversity: learnings from three countries. *International Studies in Educational Administration*, 35(2), 3–19.

Buckland, P. (2005). *Reshaping the future: education and post-conflict reconstruction.* Washington, DC: World Bank. Online. Available http://www1.worldbank.org/education/pdf/Reshaping_the_Future.pdf. Accessed 6 December 2006.

Buckland, P. (2006). Post-conflict education: time for a reality check? In M. Couldrey and T. Morris (eds), *Forced Migration Review. Supplement. Education and conflict: research, policy and practice* (pp. 7–8). Oxford: University of Oxford, Refugee Studies Centre.

Bush, T. and Jackson, D. (2002). A preparation for school leadership: international perspectives. *Educational Management and Administration*, 30(4), 417–429.

CDA (2006). *What difference has peacebuilding made? A study of the effectiveness of peacebuilding in preventing violence: Lessons learned from the March 24th riots in Kosovo.* Cambridge: CDA – Collaborative Learning Projects. Online. Available: http://cdainc.com/publications/rpp/articles/KosovoWhatDifferencePeacebuilding.pdf. Accessed 21 December 2006.

Clark, H. (2000). *Civil resistance in Kosovo.* London: Pluto Press.

Clarkson, J. (2005). Reformation of the Macedonian teacher education programme, 1999–2001. *Educational Research*, 47(3), 319–331.

Colenso, P. (2005). Education and social cohesion: developing a framework for education sector reform in Sri Lanka. *Compare*, 35(4), 411–428.

Commonwealth Secretariat (2004). *Promoting education in crisis and post-conflict reconstruction in Africa.* London: Author. Online. Available: http://www.thecommonwealth.org/Internal/36895/38230/promoting_education_in_crisis_and_post_conflict_re/. Accessed 29 November 2006.

Commonwealth Secretariat (2006). *Promoting flexible education for nomadic populations in Africa*. London: Author. Online. Available: http://www.thecommonwealth.org/news/151685/promoting_flexible_education_for_nomadic_populatio.html. Accessed 29 November 2006.

Cviic, C. (1997). After Tito. In R. Petrie (ed.), *The fall of communism and the rise of nationalism* (pp. 66–72). London: Cassell.

Davies, L. (2005). Schools and war: Urgent agendas for comparative and international education. *Compare*, 35(4), 357–371.

Dimmock, C. and Walker, A. (2000). Globalisation and societal culture: redefining schooling and school leadership in the twenty-first century. *Compare*, 30(3), 303–312.

Earnest, J. (2004). *Education reform in post-conflict transitional societies: case studies from Rwanda, Kosovo and Timor Leste*. Paper presented to the 3rd Asia-Pacific Conference on Diversity and Equity in Continuing Education and Lifelong Learning, Perth, Western Australia. October.

Elsie, R. (1997). The last Albanian waiter. In R. Petrie (ed.), *The fall of communism and the rise of nationalism* (pp. 150–153). London: Cassell.

Escobar, A. (1997). The making and unmaking of the third world development. In M. Rahena (ed.), *The post-development reader* (pp. 85–93). London: Zed Books.

Gefferth, E. and Zylfiu-Haziri, H. (2004). *Study on the primary and secondary education in Kosovo*. Prishtina, Kosovo: Euronet & Partners.

Goddard, J. T. (2002). *School reform in Kosovë: an introduction to educational leadership*. Prishtina, Kosovo: Kosovo Educator Development Project.

Goddard, J. T. (2003). Towards glocality: facilitating leadership in an age of diversity. *Journal of School Leadership*, 15, 159–177.

Goddard, J. T. (2004). The role of school leaders in establishing democratic principles in a post-conflict society. *Journal of Educational Administration*, 42(6), 685–696.

Goddard, J. T. (2006). The role of educational leaders in professional development. In W. D. VanBalkom and S. Mijatovic (eds), *Professional development: experiences from educators for educators* (pp. 143–156). Prishtina, Kosovo: Educator Development Program.

Goddard, J. T. (2007). The professional development needs of educational leaders in post-conflict Kosovo. *Educational Forum*, 71(3), 200–210.

Goddard, J. T. and Fagnou, R. (2002). *Contemporary educational issues in Kosova: voices from the field.* Prishtina, Kosovo: Kosovo Educator Development Project.

Goddard, J. T. and VanBalkom, D. (2007). Leadership for the future. In G. Anderson and A. Wenderoth (eds), *Facilitating change: reflections on six years of education development programming in challenging environments* (pp. 127–147). Montreal: Universalia Management Group.

Goddard, J. T., Anderson, K. and Zeqiri, S. (2006). *Leadership for learning: an introduction to educational leadership for Serbian School Directors in Kosovo* (p. 79). Prishtina, Kosovo: Educator Development Project.

Greeley, M. and Rose, P. (2006). Learning to deliver education in fragile states. In M. Couldrey and T. Morris (eds), *Forced Migration Review. Supplement. Education and conflict: research, policy and practice* (pp. 14–15). Oxford: University of Oxford, Refugee Studies Centre.

Gronn, P. (2002). Distributed leadership. In K. Leithwood and P. Hallinger (eds), *Second International Handbook of Educational Leadership and Administration* (653–696). Dordrecht: Kluwer Academic Publishers.

Heck, R. H. and Hallinger, P. (1999). Next generation methods for the study of leadership and school improvement. In J. Murphy and K. Seashore Louis (eds), *Handbook of research on educational administration (2nd ed.)* (pp. 141–162). San Francisco: Jossey-Bass.

Hofstede, G. (1980). *Culture's consequences: international differences in work related values.* London: Sage Publications.

Hofstede, G. (1986). Cultural differences in learning and teaching. *International Journal of Intercultural Relations*, 10, 301–320.

International Centre for Community and Enterprise Development (2006). *About Kosovo.* Online. Available: http://icced.info/kosovo.php. Accessed 23 July 2007.

International Rescue Committee (IRC) (2006a). *The post-conflict development initiative.* Online. Available: http://www.theirc.org/what/the_postconflict_development_initiative.html. Accessed 28 November 2006.

International Rescue Committee. (2006b). *IRC programs for children in armed conflict.* Online. Available: http://www.theirc.org/what/irc_programs_for_children_in_armed_conflict.html. Accessed 21 December 2006.

Jackson, E. T. (2003). How university projects produce development results: lessons from 20 years of Canada-China cooperation in higher education. *Canadian Journal of Development Studies*, 23(1), 41–49.

Jackson, E. T. (2006). *Ten thousand agents of change: education for nation-building in Kosovo, Serbia and Montenegro.* Unpublished performance review of the Educator Development Program prepared for the Canadian International Development Agency. Ottawa: E. T. Jackson & Associates Ltd.

Karstanje, P. (2001). Centralization and deregulation in Europe: towards a conceptual framework. In T. Bush, L. A. Bell, R. Bolam, R. Glatter and P. M. Ribbins (eds), *Educational management: redefining theory, policy and practice* (pp. 29–42). London: Paul Chapman.

Koch, J. (2007). *Assets for Education (AFE) Institute: community building for educational capacity.* Unpublished concept paper.

Kretzmann, J. and McKnight, J. (1993). *Building communities from the inside out: A path toward finding and mobilizing a community's assets.* Chicago: ACTA Publications.

McMurtry, J. (2001). The life-ground, civil commons and the corporate male gang. *Canadian Journal of Development Studies*, XXII, Special Issue, 819–854.

Morgan, G. (1986). *Images of organization.* Newbury Park: Sage Publications.

Mundy, K., Maclure, R., Cherry, S., Haggerty, M., Manion, C., Meyong, C., Poulson, N. and Sivasubramaniam, M. (2006). *Civil society participation and the governance of educational systems in the context of system-wide approaches to basic education: draft report on the desk study completed January 2006.* Toronto: Ontario Institute for Studies in Education of the University of Toronto.

Nicolai, S. (2006). Rebuilding Timor-Este's education system. In M. Couldrey and T. Morris (eds), *Forced Migration Review. Supplement. Education and conflict: research, policy and practice* (pp. 22–23). Oxford: University of Oxford, Refugee Studies Centre.

OECD (2004). *Reviews of national policies for education: South Eastern Europe. Volume 1: Albania, Bosnia-Herzegovina, Bulgaria, Croatia, Kosovo.* Paris: OECD.

Olson, L. (2007). Fighting for humanitarian space: NGOs in Afghanistan. In J. Ferris and J. Keeley (eds), *Canada in Kandahar* (pp. 45–64). Calgary papers in

Military and Strategic Studies, Vol. 1. Calgary: Centre for Military and Strategic Studies.

Petrick, J. and Scherer, R. F. (2000). Global leadership, capacity for judgment integrity, and acculturized organizational knowledge. *Performance Improvement Quarterly*, 13(1), 97–116.

Quick, D. (2006). Rebuilding education from scratch in Liberia. In M. Couldrey and T. Morris (eds), *Forced Migration Review. Supplement. Education and conflict: research, policy and practice* (pp. 18–19). Oxford: University of Oxford, Refugee Studies Centre.

Ramet, S. R. (1996). *Balkan babel: the disintegration of Yugoslavia from the death of Tito to ethnic war.* Boulder: Westview Press.

Ryan, J. (2003). *Leading diverse schools.* Dordrecht: Kluwer Academic Publishers.

Silins, H. and Mulford, B. (2002). Leadership and school results. In K. Leithwood and P. Hallinger (eds), *Second International Handbook of Educational Leadership and Administration* (pp. 561–612). Dordrecht: Kluwer Academic Publishers.

Sommers, M. and Buckland, P. (2004). *Parallel worlds: rebuilding the education system in Kosovo.* Paris: International Institute for Educational Planning.

Spink, J. (2006). Education, reconstruction and state building in Afghanistan. In M. Couldrey and T. Morris (eds), *Forced Migration Review. Supplement. Education and conflict: research, policy and practice* (pp. 15–16). Oxford: University of Oxford, Refugee Studies Centre.

Stone, A., Briggs, J, Smith, T. and Olsson, C. (2004). Cultural issues in developing a leadership education program in Kosovo. In *Proceedings of the IEEE International Conference on Advanced Learning Technologies* (pp. 968–974). Finland: University of Joensuu.

Tahiraj, I. (2007). *Introducing school based management to a post-socialist and post-conflict society.* Unpublished final paper, MEd program. University of Calgary, Canada.

Waks, L. J. (2006). Globalization: state transformation, and educational restructuring: why postmodern diversity will prevail over standardization. *Studies in Philosophy and Education*, 25, 403–424.

Wallin, D. and Hiebert, J. (2007). *Building bridges between rural communities and provincial agendas.* Paper presented at the Annual Conference of the Canadian Association for the Study of Educational Administration, Saskatoon, Saskatchewan. June.

Wigley, S. and Akkonoyunlu-Wigley, A. (2006). Human capabilities versus human capital: Gauging the value of education in developing countries. *Social Indicators Research*, 78, 287–304.

Wright, J. (2006). Lost in transition: Canada and the search for a 3D solution in Kosovo. *IRPP Policy Matter*, 7(1).

Young, I. M. (1990). *Justice and the politics of difference.* Princeton: Princeton University Press.

Chapter 7

The training and development of principals in Israel

Rina Barkol

Introduction

This chapter describes the development of programmes for preparing school principals in Israel from their inception in the 1970s to the present time. The chapter is divided into two principal sections: the first section presents a comprehensive review of the field from a national perspective; the second section gives a detailed outline of its development in one academic institution in particular – Beit Berl College, where the author headed the Principals Training and Development Department during the period 1992–2006.

This chapter is based, in addition to the author's personal familiarity with the subject, on position papers, documents of the Ministry of Education, articles written by researchers in the field, as well as interviews with key figures in the Ministry of Education and the academic world who are actively involved in the field. References are included to a number of central issues that have engaged the attention of leading figures in the field of education in Israel and elsewhere: can it be said that 'management is management is management' or is educational management unique, calling for separate training? Should the inventory of principals be made up of teachers only? In which framework should principals be trained and qualified – the Ministry of Education? Academic institutions? Perhaps private agencies? What is the best way to prepare a person for this complex profession, and how is it possible to effectively tie in theory with practice? Where should the emphasis lie during the course of training – in theoretical studies or in imparting skills? What frameworks can be created for serving principals that will help them to remain abreast of developments and perform according to high standards and in a manner compatible with their surroundings?

Preparation of principals in Israel – a review

Despite the temptation to write about the subject in chronological order, the author has opted to begin with what stands out in her mind as a turning point in which all the above issues were subjected to close scrutiny. The year was 1999 (although training for the principalship first appeared on the scene in the 1970s – but this will be elaborated on later).

In January 1999, a document entitled 'Training for School Principalship – Proposal for a New Procedure' by Prof. I. Friedman, Head of the Henrietta Szold Institute for Research in Behavioural Sciences, Jerusalem, was circulated among activists in the field in universities and colleges. This document, which was published and distributed on behalf of the Office of the Deputy General Manager of the Ministry of Education and Culture, suggested a change in the methods for training principals, the implications being the transfer of greater power to representatives of the Ministry and the playing of a more limited role by academic institutions in training and qualifying personnel for the position. Accreditation would be granted to those individuals who could prove to Ministry representatives that they possessed the skills and qualifications required for principalship by virtue of their personality, experience and academic background. Accreditation, becoming divorced from the academic studies, would be based on training, whose guiding principle is 'separation between the giving and receiving of a general administrative education and the acquisition of skills and other application aspects in the job of the principal' (p. 7). In other words, a person who has, for example, completed his studies towards a master's degree in educational administration and who seeks accreditation by the Ministry of Education, would undergo a process of classification and, if found suitable, would be matched to a programme that would be in line with his background. This is in contrast to a person who has completed his master's degree in a different field, for whom, following classification, a different training programme would be determined. Such training is rooted in the concept that management is an activity that is not necessarily associated with a single field but is universal:

> Management is an activity that is not necessarily associated with one field (a school, an industrial plant, etc.): it is a science that includes subjects of study that are universally valid; differences exist between knowledge-based courses and courses oriented to the imparting of skills. The differences between the two types necessitate a reasonable separation in the process of professional training.
>
> (p. 15)

Two key researchers of the subject during the period in question, Gibton and Chen (2003), published a document that was intended to respond to and critique this proposal. The document was written against the backdrop of the strong opposition to Friedman's proposal on the part of a forum of individuals in universities and colleges who were engaged in principal training, being expressed vehemently at two meetings that were held by the Ministry of Education in that year to familiarize people with the programme. Opposition focused mainly on the attempt to strip the academic world of responsibility for training and accreditation and to entrust the government and its institutions with these tasks. There was also resistance to the claim that a person can be trained for the principalship 'as in the universal field of management'. The reactions are expressed in detail in the document, published in the form of an article, of Gibton and Chen (2003), who add that, notwithstanding the above, they do distinguish between training and accreditation, which belong to the academic world, and licensing, which should be the responsibility of the Ministry of Education. In the tendency the authorities have to claim for themselves training and accreditation as well, the above researchers see a regression to the past, when the job of school principals was more limited and less complicated.

The proposal made by Friedman (1999) intends in fact to draw a line separating administrative knowledge, whose rightful place is in academic institutions, and managerial skills and experience, which should be taught in branches of the Ministry of Education or by business entities. According to Gibton and Chen (2003), such a separation has been annulled in every established professional occupation.

Friedman claims that a change in training is called for because of the need of the school to function in a changing environment, while also referring to the complexity of the job and its conflicting demands. Gibton and Chen (2003) agree with his analysis but do not accept his conclusions: the moral neutrality arising from his document does not appeal to them. They base their claim on Sergiovanni (1995), who states that the principal must do 'not what works, but what is right'. They also express the opinion of the forum members in claiming that training is required to produce a professional principal specializing in the management of an educational institution (as opposed to general management) and having a well-formed social-political and moral stand, and that the proper place for this process is the university, an academic bastion of freedom.

They reaffirm their vehement opposition to the introduction of models from the world of business management as recommended by the proposed programme, these being based on the concept that the theory of management is a universal theory. In their opinion, successful business administration harbours values that are in contradiction to those that should be upheld by school principals. Decisions that are charged politically or ideologically are 'smothered' by bureaucratic administrative systems, and problems of a more substantial nature become merely technical. The claim regarding bureaucratic strangulation also appears in the OECD document dated 2002, which points to the bureaucratic scene as being destructive in terms of the educational system.

They express the opinion of the members of the forum in stating that the proposal totally ignores the extensive new literature on education leadership in Israel and elsewhere, which has concluded that training and accreditation must be performed by academic institutions, as these serve as a repository for up-to-date research knowledge on successful headship of schools. The practical, experiential components must be based on broad professional knowledge from the humanities and the social sciences. Decision-making on issues of a moral nature (Sergiovanni, 1995) must be based on principled considerations supported by extensive knowledge rather than on narrow technical skills. Taking this a step further, it may be added that administrative–technical knowledge is not a basis for training of the transformational leaders who are needed today (Hallinger, 2003; Leithwood and Jantzi, 1996; Leithwood *et al.*, 1996) – leaders having a symbolic, cultural, educational and moral leadership (Sergiovanni, 1995, 1996; Fullan, 1999, 2002; Barth, 2002) who can transform the school into a community of learners that is a community of leaders. In order to develop these capabilities, there is a need to undergo specialization in close association with a serving principal, acquiring knowledge together with the development of reflective processes: the learner analyses his work and the work of his peers in the wider context of social and political processes, using theories and concepts that he has acquired in the course of his studies and constructing a worldview that he will take to his job as principal.

In their article, Gibton and Chen (2003) emphasize the fact that care must be taken to ensure that all individuals joining the ranks of the school principalship are experienced in teaching and undergo training and accreditation if deprofessionalization is to be prevented. They do not negate the entry of people from other fields, but emphasize that this must be preceded by an extended process of professional retraining, citing as an example a retraining programme for reserve officers from the Israel Defence Forces (IDF) that was held for many years at Beit Berl College (details of which are presented below).

The article of Gibton and Chen (2003) as a whole, which is in line with the opinions of others in the academic field, including those of the author, states that a separation between knowledge and experience must not be allowed and that the two must be integrated judiciously in order to develop prospective principals with reflective and critical abilities, so necessary for the job in view of the changing realities.

Even though the events described above led nowhere – among other reasons due to the change of personnel that occurred around that time in the Ministry of Education, which led to the proposal's demise – they are perceived by the author as representing a milestone. The proposal can be regarded as having triggered shockwaves with respect to all aspects of principal training, forcing all concerned individuals to devote some thought to central issues such as educational versus universal management; academic institutions versus other entities; knowledge versus skills; and theory as related to practice. Reverberations were also felt in the National Mission Force for Advancement of Education in Israel (popularly known as the Dovrat Committee, see Dovrat 2005), which was established in 2003 by the then Minister of Education and whose work dealt extensively with the subject of school headship, as explained later.

During the 30 years that preceded the turning point referred to earlier, attention was being given to the training of principals, mostly courses in the framework of academic institutions. Training of principals in Israel began with the establishment of the Centre for Educational Administration at Haifa University in 1971 and commencement of its orderly operation a year later, even though proper training of principals had not yet been crystallized. The official change towards the principalship started in 1977, with the publication of E. Israeli's *Plan for Developing Preparation Programmes for Senior Educational Administrators* (Israeli, 1977). The plan's most important recommendation was the requirement that all new principals possess an academic degree or at least a diploma attesting to participation in a two-year course of study in educational administration. It also recommended that new courses of studies in educational administration be established at universities and teachers' colleges. The regulation requiring new principals to have an academic degree or diploma in educational administration was first enforced in 1984 (Chen, 1996).

The first two-year training programme for principals was formulated as a result of E. Israeli's publication, and in 1979 the Principals Training Centre was established at Beit Berl College for the purpose of implementing this programme. Subsequently, full-fledged programmes were opened at other universities and colleges as well, and in 1983 a regulation published in a General Manager's circular defined the requirements of principals, namely:

1 pedagogic training;
2 at least five years' teaching experience;
3 an academic degree or diploma from the two-year academic programme for principal training.

Individuals who had been appointed without the required training were called upon to undergo supplementary training within three years of their appointment (it should be noted that till recently strict attention was not paid to this last condition).

Academic institutions had to agree to a number of conditions in order to be allowed to hold training courses (Chen, 1996), namely:

1 only candidates recommended by the Ministry of Education would be accepted;
2 the Ministry of Education would administer the process of classification and selection;
3 the structure of the studies would be different from that existing in the educational administration tracks leading up to a master's degree, and would include, in addition to academic studies, also management skills and practical work.

Despite these special requirements, the schools of education in the universities and colleges agreed to open a two-year track for diploma studies that was funded by the Ministry of Education. Chen (1996) claims that the collaboration was based on 'a shaky compromise' and that it left 'partial control' in the hands of the Ministry of Education. He explains the consent of the institutions by the financial support and the access to schools that they gained. The course in the institutions was generally given in the framework of continuing education programmes; it was uniform in all the institutions in terms of scope but not necessarily content, with variations existing between the institutions despite the identical components, and was intended for the cohort selected by the Ministry of Education.

Following this development two tracks for preparing school principals were run in Israel's academic institutions. One was an academic track that led to a bachelor's or master's degree in educational administration, which was entirely theoretical in nature and independent from the academic point of view, with the students paying for their studies. The second track for diploma studies was offered in collaboration with the Ministry of Education, which was also the financing agency; these diploma studies lasted, as stated, two years, were composed of components including theory, practice and the imparting of skills, and took place in the framework of continuing education programmes. Whereas the academic degree reflected a theoretical, broad-based approach, an outlook that was intellectual and had no particular reference to the job itself, the diploma track was more specific, practical and to the point (Chen, 1996). The academic orientation that the colleges of education developed in the 1980s caused the programmes that operated in their framework to gradually assume a more academic nature (Gotterman, 2005).

In the 1990s some 15–18 colleges existed that held diploma programmes in the frameworks mentioned above. This was the case up to 1998–1999, a year in which no course was opened due to budgetary cutbacks. The programme was renewed a year later but in a more meagre format: one year instead of two, and the number of hours reduced from 720 to 420. These reductions occurred in parallel with personnel changes in the Ministry of Education in 1999–2000, prompting rethinking of the issue and formulation of the following principles:

1 school principalship is a special profession based on values that are unique to education;
2 essential core topics exist that must be included in the training programme.

The institutions were nevertheless autonomous as to the manner in which they chose to implement the principles (Gotterman, 2005).

After the reduced programme had been underway for a year, the programme reverted to its two-year format with a total of 600 hours. Israel's annual turnover of about 270 school principals called for about 400 graduates from the training programme every year. During those years, as a result of the accelerated academic orientation referred to above, fully one-third of the candidates had master's degrees in addition to the fact that most of them had already served in managerial positions before joining the programme.

The turnover of personnel also led to a change in the method for classification of candidates. In the initial years of the programme preference was given to candidates who had been recommended by their superiors – principals or inspectors – and these candidates appeared before a committee of the Ministry of Education that included inspectors and representatives of the training institution. In the early 1990s, in addition to the above stages, there was also another stage – candidates appeared before an assessment centre and their achievements were presented to the committee of the Ministry of Education.

In practice, most of the candidates who had come with the recommendation of a principal or inspector were admitted, so that the significance of the assessment centre is somewhat doubtful. Criticism of the assessment centres can be found in Friedman (1999) and more scathingly in Gibton and Chen (2003), who perceived their central problem as stemming from the fact that they were planned and led by people who had no connection with or understanding of education.

From 1999–2000 the method underwent a change, as follows: registration for the principals' programme was announced in a General Manager's circular and subsequently in the website of the Ministry, in notices posted in schools, and in independent notices published by training institutions. The latter could for the first time influence the scope of the training programme offered by them; this was because the new forms filled in by the candidates included a reference to the training institution of one's choice whereas previously this was fully decided by the Ministry of Education (Gotterman, 2005). Like the previous forms, the new forms included sections for filling in by the principal and inspector, and for submission directly to the relevant unit in the Ministry of Education. Changes also took place in the threshold requirements and for the first time a bachelor's degree was defined as obligatory without exception, vis-à-vis the past, when elementary schooling was sufficient for a senior teacher. Apart from academic training the candidate had to have a teacher's certificate, a tenured teaching position, and teaching experience of four years (as compared to five years in the past). Individuals who did not meet these threshold requirements were not invited for the next stage of classification. Following examination of the candidates' details, they were invited to an admissions committee in the training institutions, composed of representatives of the Ministry of Education unit, representatives of the inspectorate in the district to which they belonged by virtue of their teaching position (at times these could also be senior principals), and representatives of the academic training institution. The interviewers gained an impression of the candidate on the basis of a number of fixed parameters, including: educational conception, holistic perspective, leadership, motivation for the position, and ability to form good interpersonal relations. Following their evaluation and based on the opinion of the principal and inspector, a grade was assigned to the candidate, ranging from highly suitable to highly unsuitable. The final decision regarding acceptance of the candidate was made in the Ministry of Education unit, which also forwarded the final list of names to the institutions. This unit was also the address for appeals.

In recent years the acceptance rate of candidates dropped from 80 per cent to 50 per cent while the percentage of individuals holding a master's degree rose to 35 per cent (Gotterman, 2005). The training institutions were colleges of education and universities – centres for educational studies. There was the principle of 'renewed candidacy' by the institutions to host the principals training programme and according to the new rules, one of the conditions for opening a new course was the existence of at least 35 candidates, of whom at least 20–24 were found suitable. In addition the curriculum of the course had to receive the approval of the principals' training unit, which was nevertheless careful not to force its opinions onto the institutions but rather to be in a state of dialogue with them (Gotterman, 2005). The institutions were required to confine themselves to the selected cohorts and any exception, in the way of incorporation of students from other programmes, was allowed only with the consent of the principals training unit in the Ministry of Education.

During that period programmes were held in about 15 institutions, while principal development programmes (in addition to the training programmes) that were run in some of the institutions were expanded. In addition the activity of the forum of principal trainers, established in the 1980s, was renewed, its having slumped during years in which the programme was cut back. In its new format the forum included, in addition to the heads of the programmes in the academic institutions, also the head of the Ministry of Education unit, and his deputies and advisers, who also led the activities of the forum.

The forum became a centre for interpreting the Ministry's training policy, for exchanging ideas and for clarifying issues relating to training. It was the forum that decided on the distribution of the 600 programme hours – one-quarter devoted to internship, and an additional 150 hours to subjects including: the principal as organizational head, development of a managerial-educational perspective, and a knowledge of system fundamentals (mainly education laws). With respect to the rest – 50 per cent of the programme – each institution was free to choose the content according to its own conception. Up to the 2004–2005 academic year the Ministry of Education bore all the costs of the course, while from that year on the participants had to pay one-third of the costs.

During that period an improvement in the level of the programmes and an increase in the number of candidates and their level could be discerned (Gotterman, 2005). In 2005 the General Manager of the Ministry of Education determined that a diploma testifying to participation in a principals training programme or, alternatively, a master's degree in educational administration, would be a threshold requirement in tenders for school headship.

Against the backdrop of the dissatisfaction felt over what was happening in the educational system and the disappointment over educational achievements, the Government of Israel (at the initiative of the Minister of Education) appointed a committee on 21 September 2003 – the National Mission Force for Advancement of Education in Israel, chaired by S. Dovrat – with the aim of carrying out an in-depth examination of the educational system in Israel, recommending a comprehensive programme for change, and outlining a method to implement the programme. The committee, which included 18 plenum members and more than 100 members in 12 professional committees, dedicated itself to the task for a period of 15 months. The programme that was eventually formulated included tens of pedagogic, organizational, structural and budgetary recommendations that were intended to 'bring about the recovery and advancement of the educational system in order for it to be on a par with and even surpass educational systems throughout the world' (National Mission Force for the Advancement of Education in Israel, 2005, p. 5). The programme was to have been comprehensive and all-encompassing, relating to all aspects of education. The head of the committee was the director of a well-known high-tech firm in Israel (Shlomo Dovrat, after whom the committee came to be known) and many of the more prominent members of the committee were businessmen from the high-tech world.

One of the serious criticisms levelled against the committee during the course of its work and subsequent to it was the fact that it was not led by educationists and that it did not seek the involvement of people from the world of education, including, among others, representatives of the powerful teachers' unions. Being headed by businessmen, the committee naturally attached great importance to the subject of professionalism and status of school principals. In a report by the committee, special reference is made to the job of the school principal:

> the focus of authority and responsibility for educational activity in the school places a huge responsibility on the principal. The professionalism and status of the principals must be strengthened by training them to bear their extended responsibility and their new jobs, and by raising their salaries to reflect this responsibility. It will thus also be possible to draw on high quality manpower to head the schools.
>
> (Ibid., p. 151)

The main recommendations with respect to the requirements of the position and preparation by the candidate for the position of school principal were as follows: possession of a master's degree, graduation from a principals training course, and teaching experience of at least five years. Candidates from outside the educational system would be required to meet the same threshold requirements. Candidates with managerial experience from other systems would require, as an exceptional condition, teaching experience of three years only.

A starting principal would be accompanied by a senior principal for a period of at least one year, with a possible extension for an additional year. At the end of the two-year period, which could be extended by yet another year, a process would get under way for granting a licence for heading a school. High-standard university programmes in educational administration would be developed for individuals without a degree in educational administration as well as a shortened track for those with a master's degree and managerial experience in other fields. High-level programmes would be formulated for continued development of serving principals.

An extensive and comprehensive system for training serving principals in light of the proposed changes would be speedily established and run.

Apart from the above there were also recommendations that related to the salaries of principals, to their path of mobility and to the creation of a standard that would define their functions.

As regards training, although the report included concepts that were based on activities that were being pursued in the framework of existing training programmes (such as the inclusion of a mentor or admission of candidates from outside the educational system – steps that were taken in the Principals Training Department at Beit Berl College, described below) the committee's message was that thought should be given to new, improved frameworks for principals. At the same time, initiatives were shown by certain foundations to take over the programmes for training principals.

The Dovrat programme, which aroused great opposition, particularly by the teachers' unions, perished as the country was overtaken by political changes a short while after publication of the report in 2005. Even so, the programme served as an additional catalyst for setting up committees in the Ministry of Education to rethink the issue of principal training. It was decided meanwhile to continue the training programmes according to the format that had been in existence before the work of the committee, but to halt the development programmes that were being held in some of the institutions until a general programme on the subject was crystallized. This is the situation today. The trend for the future appears to be the development of master's degree programmes specially oriented to the field of school principals that will integrate theory, skills and practical work at the academic institutions (-service), together with the approval of a public foundation to take over the subject of principal development (in-service). There still appears to be no official decision relating specifically to the processes of classification and licensing, although the role of the academic world in training has received further strengthening, as has the recognition of school headship as a profession that warrants training on a master's degree level.

Principals training and development department, Beit Berl College

Beit Berl College was the first of the institutions of higher education to offer teachers a systematic and orderly programme for training of principals in a two-year format. The framework, which was put in place in 1979, is still operative. In 1987 an additional programme was incorporated that ran until 2006, offering retraining of reserve officers from the IDF for the school headship after undergoing a teacher training course, also in the college. Supporting a career turnaround in midlife (Barkol, 1996, 2005b), the programme is unique to the college and is unmatched by any other academic institution in the country.

Although studies in both the above programmes are on a diploma level, strict attention has been paid throughout to their academic level in terms of the standard of the lecturers and the structure of the syllabus. The two frameworks have been examined, evaluated and updated yearly on the basis of internal feedback, adapting themselves to changes taking place in the educational environment and to new knowledge gained from activities in the field in Israel and elsewhere.

The programmes in Beit Berl College are highly esteemed and are therefore in great demand, with the number of people seeking admission being disproportionately higher than the number admitted. The rich experience gained in the college over time constitutes a firm basis for a high-level master's programme that could meet future requirements for academic institutions as a condition for receiving approval for training school principals.

Towards the mid-1990s, in answer to needs on the ground, a focused framework for development of principals was formed, comprising two main projects:

1 mentoring of new principals during their first year of work;
2 creation of a 'principals' club' as a framework for support, enrichment and revitalization of serving principals.

Appearing before the Dovrat Committee, the author presented the retraining programme for reserve IDF officers and the mentoring project. These were instrumental in steering the recommendations of the committee such as to allow individuals who were not from the field of education to head schools if they had undergone appropriate training, and to have novice principals mentored in their first year by senior principals.

Both the principal development projects – the mentoring programme and the principals' club – together with training, form a four-stage study programme for the principal throughout his professional life, as follows:

- First stage: pre-service training.
- Second stage: first year of work, developing and acquiring confidence with the help of a veteran principal serving as mentor.
- Third stage: 'midway principal', when the college offers him a principals' club as a professional framework for growth and support.
- Fourth stage: veteran principal with many years of headship and proven success to his credit, when he is offered participation in a mentors' course with a view to becoming a mentor himself, who can contribute his experience to suitable novice principals (see Figure 7.1).

Rationale and conceptual perspective

In order to understand the significance of the programme as a whole, the author deems it relevant to cite a number of basic assumptions and raise a number of questions regarding the school headship that are posed frequently in the relevant literature.

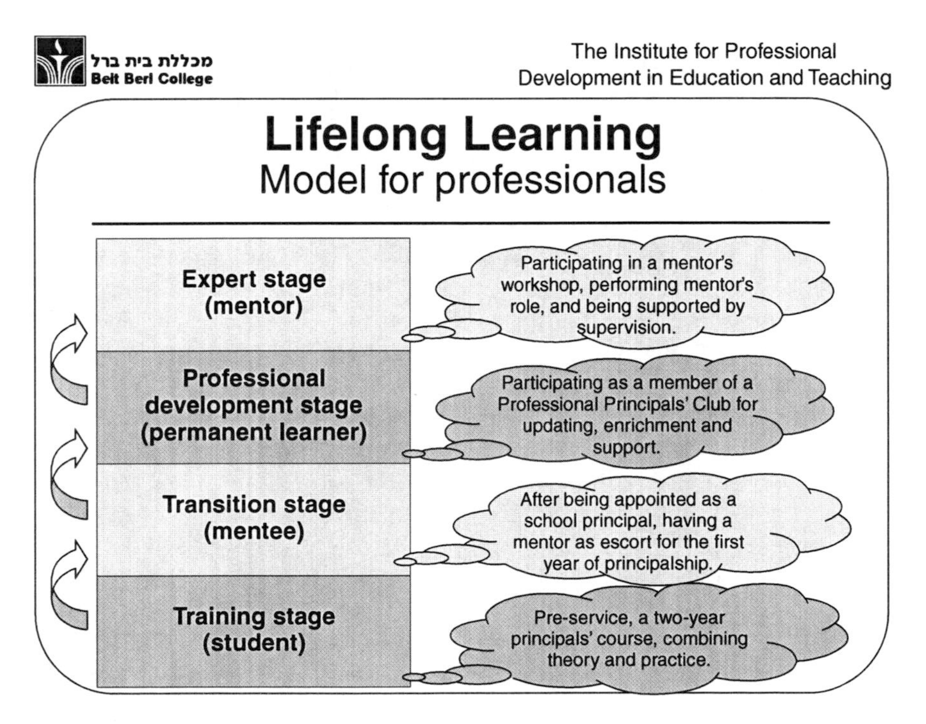

Figure 7.1 Rationale and conceptual perspective.

The first assumption relates to the principal as the figure who determines the nature and character of the school, a statement that has been a recurrent theme in the professional literature during the past three decades. Sarason (1982) refers to the principal as one who 'plays a fateful role' (p. 139). De Roche (1985) claims that the principal is the major influence in the quality of education in a school' (p. 10). Anderson (1989), Murphy and Beck (1994), Clark and Clark (1996), Fullan (2002), Caldwell (2003) and many others are only some examples of those who repeatedly emphasize that the school leadership is central to the determination of the quality of the school. Based on this assumption it may be concluded that what is required is not only strict processes of candidate selection but also suitable preparation to train the prospective principal for this responsible role.

The second assumption relates to the complexity of the job, which makes it difficult to perform. Murphy and Beck (1994) describe the multiple facets of the principal's job by calling him a 'servant leader', a definition borrowed from Greenleaf (1977). They also refer to him as a 'person within a community', a 'moral agent', but also an 'organizational architect'. He is in addition a 'social advocate and activist', while being regarded as an 'educator' and not merely an administrator. The descriptions by Murphy and Beck greatly emphasize the moral aspect and tell us about the complexity that leads to tensions between the leadership, social and educational aspects on the one hand, and the managerial and administrative aspects on the other. Bush (1995) too asks if the principal is a 'leading professional or chief executive' (p. 11) and adds that the reforms of the 1980s and 1990s 'have made it more difficult for heads and principals to sustain this dual role' (ibid.).

The complexity of the principal's role is given clear expression in the *Cambridge Journal of Education* dated November 2003, an issue that was devoted entirely to the subject of leadership in education. In the editorial, MacBeath (2003) sums up statements made elsewhere in the issue and emphasizes the fact that the uncertain environment dictates the qualities required of the leaders, so that forbearance in the face of ambiguity and a life buffeted by constant change becomes a vital attribute. Empathy, cooperation, a proclivity for dialogue and moral goals make their way in as common expressions in the new lexicon of leadership. 'Trust' too assumes a more central role, this clearly being difficult to gain in an atmosphere marked by competition and personal achievement. In the same issue of *the Cambridge Journal of Education*, Seashore-Louis (2003) emphasizes that it is no longer possible to manage the headship alone and that successful headship is contingent on collaboration with the teachers.

The 'dual role' that Bush (1995) refers to is covered in the issue in an even more radical way. In their article, Moos and Moller (2003) state that the principals must do their utmost to cultivate a culture of trust and commitment in the school, but at the same time they must also function outside the school in a competitive environment that is driven by a market culture in which 'rating' rules supreme. Such functioning necessitates the adoption of managerial behaviour patterns drawn from the business world. Thus the principal is torn between the need to convey trust and reciprocity inside and act competitively and demandingly outside – a duality that can drain him physically and mentally. The Israeli professional literature also refers to the complexity of the role and the heavy load that comes with it. Friedman (2000) emphasizes the fact that the principal must be a person with knowledge and understanding in the field of education as well as organizational and administrative systems. The specific knowledge required of him is in a constant state of flux and is being examined all the time. The multiplicity and variability of the role and tasks can be to the principal's detriment and reference is made to the high burnout rate in the profession. Lev-Chaim and Gaziel (2005) also talks about the ambiguity and conflict inherent in the job and emphasizes the need to tread a fine line between different, and at times contradictory, roles: development versus assessment, pedagogic oversight versus financial management, management of internal relations versus external relations. In a case study that analyses the success of an outstanding principal, Barkol (2006) too emphasizes the importance of an ability to manoeuvre between opposing demands: trust, caring and compassion within, together with political and manipulative skills without.

The numerous facets of the job as well as the tolerance for ambiguity and for functioning in a state of unceasing contradiction must undoubtedly find expression in the training process.

The third assumption on which the programme is based is consideration of the principal as the person who is building the school culture to be one that is characterized by collaboration, support, mutual esteem and caring (Barth, 2002; Deal and Peterson, 1999; Fullan, 2002; Friedman, 2000). In order to develop this culture the principal must behave like a transformational leader (Hallinger, 2003; Leithwood *et al.*, 1996; Leithwood and Jantzi, 1996), leadership being perceived as a mutual influence process, rather than as a one-way process in which leaders influence others (Barth, 2002).

The fourth assumption relates to the isolation of the principal – despite the statements made above – for although the principal cannot operate alone and must act in collaboration with others, when all is said and done he frequently finds himself fighting a lone battle. Daresh and Playko (1992) claim that isolation from colleagues is one of the most serious problems in educational management. Isolation is burdensome and aggravates anxieties; relieving these anxieties can spur professional growth. The prospective principal must be prepared for such isolation, and must also be taught to work in collaboration and create for him a framework for belonging, enrichment and support.

Following are the central questions that the programme attempts to answer:

1 Is school management a universal domain or a unique one? (Friedman, 1999, 2000; Gibton and Chen, 2003; Barkol, 2005a). According to this programme, the school principal is obliged to possess the knowledge and skills that serve as the basis of management, but apart from this he has a unique profession at the core of which is the concept of school leadership as moral leadership (Sergiovanni, 1995, 1996; Fullan, 1999).
2 Is proper training of school principals something that deals with the building of a management and leadership worldview or something that is primarily the imparting of different kinds of managerial skills? (Barkol, 2005a; Gibton and Chen, 2003; Friedman, 1999, 2000). According to the programme a person who learns only skills will find it difficult to perform in new situations requiring different thinking from that which he has been used to. On the other hand a person who analyses reality from a broader and more developed perspective will succeed to a greater extent in being flexible and adapting to the changes he encounters.
3 As a direct extension of the previous question: what is then the best way to relate theory and practice? The problem arises in any debate on professional training and is also the subject of discussion with those dealing with teacher training. Clark and Clark (1996) emphasize that programmes must be created in which there is close collaboration between the academic agency responsible for training and the field, and they believe that the key to effectively coping with this issue lies in such collaboration.

   In this programme too (Barkol, 2005a) there is an attempt to connect in a significant way between the theoretical and practical components, both in the training (pre-service) stage and the initial in-service stage (the first year of principalship).
4 How is it possible to create a career path for school principals? Principalship, like teaching, is a profession that does not go hand-in-hand with a career. Advancement from the headship can be to the job of inspector, which is in fact a position of a different type and not a direct continuation of the headship, or, as recently, to the position of the head of the education department in the local authority, which is also essentially different from the principalship. The lack of a sense of advancement could have an adverse effect on the principal's motivation. The question is, how is it possible to create a career path within the framework of the headship? The Dovrat Committee attempted to address this matter in their report but so far nothing has been done about it. The programme tries to create such a path, as detailed below.
5 How is it possible to create lifelong learning for school principals? The complexity of the job, performance under conditions of uncertainty and constant change oblige the principal to commit himself to a programme of study throughout his lifetime (Barkol, 2005a). Learning frameworks

with colleagues experiencing a similar reality can help to release the principal from the professional isolation he experiences at times and to relieve his anxieties.

In offering lifelong learning the Beit Berl College programme can provide some solution to the issue in question.

The programme is, indeed, built on a consideration of the basic assumptions and attempts to answer the questions raised. Based on the above, the aims of the programme were defined as follows:

1. To provide the school principal with a lifelong study framework, from training in the pre-service stage to support, updating and renewal in the in-service stage.
2. To maintain an academic level of studies equivalent to a master's degree and to advance the programme with this level in mind.
3. To provide the educational system with a reserve of principals that combines transformational leadership ability with the required managerial knowledge.
4. To build the training process in a manner that represents an optimal combination of theory and practice.
5. To make the college the principals' home, where they will find answers to the needs arising in the field.

The four stages of the programme, involving realization of the above aims, were mentioned briefly at an earlier stage of the discussion. They are now presented in greater depth. As may be seen from Figure 7.1, Stage 1 is a pre-service stage while all the others are in-service stages.

Stage I: training (pre-service stage)

This is a two-year programme that is conducted collaboratively and in coordination with the Ministry of Education, which serves as a key partner, making decisions regarding classification procedures, approving the programmes and being a joint signatory on the diploma. In addition the Ministry of Education bears two-thirds of the cost of the programme (having borne the entire cost up to three years ago). The scope of the programme (which is dictated) is 600 hours – 20 weekly hours over a period of two years. An effort was made to concentrate the lessons in one day of study lasting 8–10 hours (in addition to observations in schools) in order to allow the teachers participating in the programme an absence of only one day a week from their schools.

The programme includes all the following fields: leadership in general, and educational leadership in particular; and organization and management, including legal, budgetary, economic, policy and decision-making aspects.

The principal is treated as the head of a curricular system, in the context of which the students in the programme attend lessons in curriculum/syllabus planning and evaluation. The principal is also considered to be the head of a pastoral system, so that the students are exposed to the field of learning disabilities and inclusion. Throughout the learning processes emphasis is placed on the development of a holistic outlook, analytical–critical thinking, and the ability to cope with complex and unforeseen situations. Constant reference is made to these fields throughout the student's learning process: in theoretical lessons, which are mainly frontal in makeup, and in semi-theoretical-workshop sessions, in which skills and practical school experience are imparted.

The four semesters of the programme (two years of study) are arranged as follows:

- In the first semester the emphasis is on theory and lessons are mainly frontal; a few of the lessons stress skills and there are some visits to schools as observers.
- In the second semester there is a greater emphasis on skills, imparted through workshops in which the student takes a more active part; he also carries out observations in schools and keeps an observation log.
- The third semester (i.e. the first semester of the second academic year) takes place outside the college, in training schools; each training school accepts three to five students who stay there throughout the weekly study day (see details below).
- In the fourth and last semester the venue of the lessons is once again the college. These advanced lessons attempt to tie in the theories learned with the practical experience acquired by the students in the field. Thus theory connects with practice and practice with theory as part of a circular process.

The venue for the internship in the third semester is, as stated, the training schools; these are successful schools that were singled out by the programme leaders, in which the principals were willing to serve as mentors. The principals concerned participate in a preparatory course for mentors (described below) and maintain ongoing contact with the college for the purposes of enrichment and updating. The students stay there one day a week as observers, but are also expected to carry out minor managerial tasks under the principal's guidance. In addition they are expected to participate in meetings and take an active part in the life of the school in coordination with the principal. In order to encourage a positive atmosphere in the learning process, the principal is not expected to report to the course leaders on his personal impression of the students.

In the framework of the fourth semester studies a workshop is held in the college in which the students present their projects to the entire cohort. The students generally invite the principal with whom they carried out the project to this exposition, having generally developed a relationship with him based on mutual trust and esteem. The exposition is looked back on by the students as having been the highlight of the course.

As part of the training process, the internship is the source of much satisfaction and appreciation. It has been held for the past five years and was preceded by attempts at various formats until it was crystallized in its present state.

College lecturers who have taught the students before and after the internship have referred to the change they observe in their behaviour as a result of the internship and feel they have become more understanding and serious. The students, as stated, express satisfaction from the internship, claiming that even the theories they had learned were now more meaningful for them. The mentoring principals also stated that the process was a launching pad for personal and professional development.

Stage II: mentoring – professional support and assistance from a veteran principal who serves as a mentor to a new principal in his/her first year on the job

The complexity of the school headship makes the entry into the position difficult, threatening and anxiety-ridden. And the principal's isolation makes it even more difficult for him or her to adapt to his or her new role. At this stage an experienced senior colleague who has undergone this process successfully can lend invaluable support and assistance, for without this the novice principal finds himself/herself lacking a secure framework for consultation and interaction.

The college provides a mentor in the form of an experienced principal who offers professional as well as emotional support. His or her role is to help the new principal make his/her first proper moves, reducing his/her anxiety and restoring confidence. The new principal is free to accept or reject the mentor's consultation: the mentor is there to offer support and facilitate growth – not tips or advice – and to help the new principal find his/her own way. Clearly, the mentor has to be non-judgemental – more like an elder brother or sister than a traditional instructor. The new principal and mentor are expected to build a dialogic relationship based on confidentiality and trust, for without trust the entire process is unworkable. At the end of the first year of principalship, expectations are that the new principal has gained enough confidence to move on on his/her own.

For about ten years this phase, as an optional one, was carried out by the college on a rather small scale, although it proved to be very successful. It was adopted by the National Mission Force (Dovrat Committee) and later by the Ministry of Education, but is yet to be implemented on a larger scale.

Stage III: mentoring – principals' club for the serving principal

Meant for serving principals, this club is a framework for support, broadening horizons and enrichment. Its aim is to provide the principal with knowledge and tools for coping daily with an environment that is constantly springing surprises on him, is demanding, and often makes him/her feel isolated and helpless. The club offers a variety of activities, including meetings, seminars, courses in relevant subjects, continuing education programmes, and information on developments in the field in Israel and abroad. It also organizes delegations of principals in the framework of its overseas contact activities.

The club's activities are intended to strengthen and 'immunize' the principals, and expose them to the many others who are in the same boat, deliberating and struggling, leading them to understand that the problems they encounter are not theirs alone.

The club has about 600 active members. Its activities do not generally involve payment and any interested principal can join.

Stage IV: preparing and developing the mentors

Experienced principals who are chosen by the college or by the Ministry of Education are trained as mentors. This stage can be considered a further step in their career, in which they gain recognition and status.

The principals are offered workshops and later professional meetings during the school year. The workshop is based mainly on experiential learning: role playing, simulations and case analyses. Towards the end of the workshop, principals can start working as mentors and get the supervision they need from the college faculty.

The supervision process is also long-term. The mentors become part of a mentors' forum and are offered supervision on a continuing basis. Data gathered over the years show that the mentors themselves have become empowered during the process of mentoring.

The four-stage programme offers not only lifelong learning but also, as stated, a career path for the principal – from the time he/she is a student in a principals' training course, through the novice stage, to serving principal and later, based on proven successful performance in his job, to the status of mentor, in which his maturity and seniority are recognized.

The college ran the programme during the period 1994–2004, initially on a small scale and subsequently on a larger scale up to the establishment of the Dovrat Committee, which adopted the idea of mentoring and intended to make it a project of national scope. However, the political changes taking place in Israel upset the cards, so that committees are now deliberating once again over methods for training and development of principals.

Concluding remarks

Meanwhile, training continues in universities and colleges as in the past – mostly in the form of diploma courses but also, in the minority of cases, as master's degree courses. It is nevertheless expected that in the near future courses will be in a master's degree format, and universities and colleges are investing great efforts towards this end. The subject of principal development (in-service) has been suspended at this stage and will apparently be given over to an institute whose establishment is currently under discussion.

It may be concluded without a doubt that the question of training and development of school principals in Israel is not a passing phenomenon but is here to stay, and that an understanding exists regarding its importance for the advancement and development of the educational system.

References

Anderson, M. (1999). Training and Selecting School Leaders. In S. Smith and P. Piele (eds) *School Leadership. Handbook for Excellence*, Oregon: University Publications (pp. 53–84).

Barkol, R. (1996). Israel: Retraining Military Officer as Principals. *International Journal of Educational Reform*, Vol. 5, No. 3/July (pp. 305–310).

Barkol, R. (2003). A Mentoring Project as an Essential Stage in a Program of Lifelong Learning for Principals. Paper presented at the 6th World Convention of the International Conference of Principals, Edinburgh, July.

Barkol, R. (2005a). An Experienced Principal Escorts a New One: A Mentoring Project as a Stage in a Lifelong Learning Program for Principals. In E. Paldi (ed.) *Education and Challenge of Time 2*. Tel Aviv: Reches Educational Projects (Hebrew) (pp. 228–241).

Barkol, R. (2005b). Principalship as a Second Career: The Case of Retired Military Officers Who Were Retrained for Principalship. In I. Kuppferberg and E. Olshtain (eds) *Discourse in Education: Researching Educational Events*. Tel Aviv: Mofet (Hebrew) (pp. 306–332).

Barkol, R. (2006). She Made Us Principals: A Case Study of One Woman Who Pushed Twelve Teachers to Principalship. *International Journal of Educational Reform*, Summer.

Barth, R.S. (2002). The Culture Builder. *Educational Leadership*, Vol. 59, No. 8 (pp. 6–12).

Bush, T. (1995). *Theories of Educational Management* (Second Edition). London: Paul Chapman Publishing.

Caldwell, B.J. (2003). Mission Impossible? A Strategic View of Efforts to Lead Transformation of Schools. Paper presented at the International Conference of Principals. Edinburgh, July.

Chen, M. (1995). Training of Principals and Inspectors to Lead the Independent Community School. Paper presented to the Permanent Committee affiliated with the Pedagogic Secretariat, Ministry of Education, Culture and Sport. Jerusalem, Iyar, 5755 – May 1995 (Hebrew).

Chen, M. (1996). Academic Preparation of Principals in Israel: Empowering

Dynamic School Leadership. *International Journal of Educational Reform*, Vol. 5, No. 3, July (pp. 287–296).
Clark, D.C. and Clark, S.N. (1996). Better Preparation of Educational Leaders. *Educational Researcher*, Vol. 25, No. 8 (pp. 18–20).
Daresh, J.C. and Playko, M.A. (1992). Mentoring for Head Teachers: A Review of Major Issues. *School Organization*, 12(2), (pp. 145–152).
Deal, T.E. and Peterson, K.D. (1999). *Shaping School Culture*. San Francisco: Jossey Bass Publishers.
De Roche, E.F. (1985). *How School Administrators Solve Problems*. Englewood Cliffs: Prentice Hall.
Dovrat, S. (2005). The National Mission Force for Advancement of Education in Israel. Presented to the Prime Minister and Minister of Education, 5 January (Hebrew).
Friedman, I. (1999). *Training for Qualification as Headteachers – a Proposal for a New Process*, Jerusalem: Ministry of Education, Culture and Sports, Deputy Managing Director Bureau (Hebrew).
Friedman, I. (2000). *Headteachers Training Curriculum: Principles, Topics and Processes*, Jerusalem: Ministry of Education, Teachers Training Administration (Hebrew).
Fullan, M. (1999). *Change Forces: The Sequel*. London: Falmer Press.
Fullan, M. (2002). The Change Leader. *Educational Leadership*, Vol. 54, No. 8 (pp. 16–22).
Gibton, D. and Chen, M. (2003). Training of Principals as Public and Moral Leaders. In I. Dror, D. Nevo and R. Shapiro (eds) *Changes in Education: Profile of Education Policy in Israel for the 2000s*. Tel Aviv: Ramot. Tel Aviv University (pp. 391–406).
Gotterman, I. (2004). On the Way to Desirable Training – Trends and Changes in Head Teachers Training. Education and Its Environment. Tel Aviv. Kibbutzim Colleges Yearbook (Hebrew).
Gotterman, I. (2005). Training of Principals for Schools in Israel – Trends, Changes and Directions. In E. Paldi (ed.) *Education and Challenge of Time 2*. Tel Aviv: Reches Educational Projects (Hebrew) (pp. 211–227).
Greenleaf, R.K. (1977). *Servant Leadership*. New York: Paulist.
Hallinger, P. (2003). Leading Educational Change: Reflections on the Practice of Instructional and Transformational Leadership. *Cambridge Journal of Education*, Vol. 33, No. 3 (pp. 329–352).
Israeli, E. (1977). *A Plan for Developing a Preparation Program for Senior Administrators in the Israeli Educational System*. Jerusalem: The Ministry of Education and Culture, 36P (Mimeo, Hebrew).
Leithwood, K. and Jantzi, D. (1996). Transformational Leadership Effects: A Replication. *School Effectiveness and School Improvement*, Vol. 4, No. 10 (pp. 451–479).
Leithwood, K., Jantzi, D. and Steinbach, R. (1996). *Changing Leadership for Changing Times*. Buckingham: Open University Press.
Lev-Chaim, E. and Gaziel, C. (2005). Principals on Self-Management – Role Pressures and Burnout. In E. Paldi (ed.) *Education and Challenge of Time 2*. Tel Aviv: Reches Educational Projects (Hebrew) (pp. 198–211).
MacBeath, J. (2003). Editorial. *Cambridge Journal of Education*, Vol. 33, No. 3 (pp. 323–327).
Moos, L. and Moller, J. (2003). Schools and Leadership in Transition: the Case of

Scandinavia. *Cambridge Journal of Education*, Vol. 33, No. 3 (pp. 353–370).
Murphy, J. and Beck, L.G. (1994). Reconstructing the Principalship: Challenges and Possibilities. In J. Murphy and K. Seashore-Louis (eds) *Reshaping the Principalship*. Thousand Oaks: Corwin Press, Inc. (pp. 3–19).
OECD (2001). *What Schools for the Future?* Paris: OECD (Chapter 3).
Sarason, S.B. (1982). *The Culture of School and the Problem of Change.* Boston: Allyn & Bacon.
Seashore-Louis, K. (2003). School Leaders Facing Real Change: Shifting Geography, Uncertain Paths. *Cambridge Journal of Education*, Vol. 33, No. 3 (pp. 371–382).
Sergiovanni, T.J. (1995). *The Principalship: A Reflective Practice Perspective* (Third Edition), Needham Heights: Allyn & Bacon.
Sergiovanni, T.J. (1996). *Leadership for the Schoolhouse.* San Francisco: Jossey Bass, Inc.

Chapter 8

Preparing leaders, preparing learners

The Hong Kong experience

Allan Walker and Clive Dimmock

Introduction

Trainers and developers of school leaders across the globe are currently searching for models of best practice leadership development programmes. Are there generic features and principles of design underpinning such programmes? This chapter argues that corroborative evidence of what works – in leadership training and development – to influence principals' knowledge, skills, values and behaviours – is now emerging. It describes a model of best practice in Hong Kong – called 'Blue Skies' – founded on, and derived from, a body of international research-based evidence from successful principal leadership programmes, together with evaluation evidence from another recent Hong Kong leadership programme. First, however, the policy background to leadership preparation in Hong Kong since 1990 is outlined. This is followed by an explanation of the structure for school leader training and development established by the Hong Kong government since 2000. It is argued that with the structure in place, attention has been able to shift to the design principles of effective leadership programmes that maximise leader learning. Designs based on research evidence of what works emphasise, inter alia, learning linked to real school contexts, substantial involvement of trained and experienced principals as mentors, flexibility to meet diverse needs, multiple opportunities for reflection, and cohort bonding and networking – all of which form the platform for 'Blue Skies'.

This chapter addresses the preparation and ongoing learning of school leaders in Hong Kong. While acknowledging the positive effects of recent policy in framing a more holistic and coherent approach to school leadership development, it is suggested that attention now turn from the structures needed to build worthwhile programmes to the form and effectiveness of the programmes themselves. In other words, as policy structures for preparing and upgrading principals become more accepted and embedded within the leadership community, energy can be redirected towards processes and participants' experiences in programmes, and how school leaders best learn. While recognising a broad range of meanings for the term 'leadership preparation', we use the term here to include formal policy intent, structures, frameworks and programmes designed and implemented to provide an articulated set of activities for both the preparation and ongoing development of potential and serving school leaders. 'Leadership learning' is conceptualised as the processes, contexts and mechanisms within particular courses or programmes which target how school leaders best learn. The chapter tracks the following path:

- Policies governing school leadership preparation and development in Hong Kong have evolved rapidly over the last five years. These policies mandate a considered structure which provides a coherence heretofore missing from leadership development. The structures have now been implemented, and are firmly rooted within the leadership landscape. This is no mean feat given the scattered and fragmented nature of school governance in Hong Kong. The chapter outlines the evolution of relevant policy and programmes targeting school leadership preparation in Hong Kong since the late 1990s.
- With the increasingly ingrained status of the new leadership development structures it is argued that energy can be turned to improving the efficacy of the programmes and focusing on ways to improve avenues for learning. One way to start this process is to study an established leadership development programme formed as part of the recent policy framework. This chapter therefore outlines a number of evaluation studies of one designated programme for Newly Appointed Principals (NAPs) in Hong Kong, which ran for over a four-year period. A synthesis of the findings from these studies provides useful information in identifying features which the NAPs believed enhanced their leadership learning.
- Key recommendations from effective leadership learning programmes have also recently emerged from across a number of other systems. These features are juxtaposed with those found in Hong Kong. When brought together they inform the development of a new, more learning-focused, leadership development programme for beginning principals in Hong Kong. The chapter discusses the overseas literature in relation to the Hong Kong findings, displays the combined set of key learning features arrived at and then outlines a new programme – 'Blue Skies' – which has been developed on the back of these findings.

More specifically, the chapter is divided into five sections. The first section provides a brief description of the leadership development context of Hong Kong. Discussion focuses on the development, requirements and implementation of the landmark policy 'Continuing Professional Development for School Excellence' which has substantially changed the official, structured face of principal preparation and development in Hong Kong. Sections two to four recount the process followed, focusing on the research consulted in identifying the key features of programmes which appear to promote leadership learning. In particular, the second section focuses on what was the longest running programme associated with the new policy – that targeting the development of NAPs. Drawing on evaluation reports and other studies, it discerns the key features which principals believed provided their most valuable learning experiences. Pre-eminent among these was a desire to work more closely with some type of experienced mentor. The third section reviews selected international literature intended to identify mechanisms and processes found to promote worthwhile leadership learning outside of Hong Kong. Among the key features identified were opportunities for reflection, intense involvement of experienced colleagues and a context-based emphasis. The fourth section displays the juxtaposition of the findings from the Hong Kong NAP programme and the international literature and, in the process, identifies the processes and mechanisms that appeared more effective for leadership learning. The final section briefly introduces a new programme for NAPs – 'Blue Skies' – which was built around the findings.

Interest in leadership development and learning programmes is presently an international phenomenon. Perhaps the most visible manifestation of this interest is the National College for School Leadership (NCSL) in the UK (Southworth, 2004). Markers of the NCSL's productivity and influence can be found in its innovative programmes and wide-ranging, action-centred research agendas (Bush, 2004, 2005). Widespread interest across and within many other national boundaries shows that debate on leadership development philosophies and programmes is not peculiar to Hong Kong, or any other context (for example, see Björk and Murphy, 2005; Bush and Jackson, 2002; Hallinger, 2003; Huber, 2004; Wales and Welle-Strand, 2005). It should also be noted that many of the development programmes emerging from centralised initiatives are not without their problems or critics. They are often contested at formulation, implementation and evaluation stages – this is certainly true in Hong Kong where formal requirements for serving principals were somewhat 'loosened' in response to practitioner concerns. Earley and Evans's (2004) critique of some of the NCSL's work provides an example of some of the tensions accompanying ongoing leadership development in the UK.

The leadership preparation and development context

In the decades prior to 2000 leadership preparation and development in Hong Kong tracked an incoherent and scattered course. New principals were required to attend a basic course focusing on administrative matters only. Other opportunities for potential, newly appointed and serving principals were diffuse and organised on an ad hoc basis by the Education Department (ED), different School Sponsoring Bodies,[1] higher education providers and their associated specialised centres, and some professional associations (Lam, 2003; Walker, 2004). Preparation was linked only loosely to major education reform initiatives[2] and rarely touched 'real' leadership life in schools. The focus of preparation and 'upgrading' courses was determined by the formal system (at its various levels), by the preferences and/or expertise of local academics or their visiting colleagues from overseas. The characteristics of principal professional development mirrored those of Continuous Teacher Education (CTE) in Hong Kong which was accurately described by Ng (2003), as peripheral, ad hoc, policy- and provider-led, competency based and built predominately around perceived deficits. In terms of methodology, the few centrally supported programmes for education leaders pre-2000 appeared overwhelmingly classroom-based, were tendered out to universities, rarely involved practicing leaders in more than 'legitimising roles' and, with few exceptions, were largely detached from school life (Walker and Dimmock, 2005).

Prompted by the Hong Kong government's increasingly invasive reform agenda, particularly related to changes in school governance structures, and increased grumblings within the school leadership community, in 1999, the ED, established a Task Group to look into the training and development of school heads (Task Group on the Training and Development of School Headers, 1999). The group developed for broader consultation a draft programme and framework 'to equip and develop school principals with the necessary knowledge, skills and attributes to become competent leaders to lead schools into the new millennium' (Cheng, 2000, p. 68). While the consultation document was quite positively received, some interest groups expressed reservations about certain recommendations. These reservations included the difficulty of instituting a 'uniform' programme for all principals (and potential principals) and the requirement that serving principals obtain a 'certificate of principalship'. In reaction to these and other concerns, a second consultation document was released and then adopted as policy in 2002. The policy 'Continuing Professional Development for School Excellence' (Education Department, 2002) presented a more coherent framework for principal development – one that aimed to meet the needs of Hong Kong's practicing and aspiring principals at various stages of development. The framework underpinning the policy was drawn from *The Key Qualities of the Principalship in Hong Kong* (Walker *et al.*, 2000; Walker *et al.*, 2002) – a document developed to form the basis of needs assessment for newly appointed principals.

The landmark policy that emerged for the first time differentiated levels of leadership, mandated pre-principalship certification, introduced a set of principalship beliefs and 'standards', and a time-regulated structure for development. Requirements were differentiated for Aspiring Principals (APs) – deputy principals and department heads, Newly Appointed Principals (NAPs) – for principals during their first two years in post, and Serving

Principals (SPs) – principals with over two years experience. The standards organised clustered sets of values, knowledge, skills and attributes around six core areas of school leadership: strategic direction and policy environment; teaching, learning and curriculum; leader and teacher growth and development; staff and resource management; quality assurance and management; external communication and connection (Education Department, 2002; Walker *et al.*, 2000).

Under the new policy, aspiring, newly appointed and serving principals faced different requirements. Aspiring principals were to attain, within a two-year period, a Certification for Principalship (CFP) involving three components:

1 a needs analysis;
2 a designated Preparation for Principalship course;
3 submission of a portfolio.

APs are given a maximum of two years to complete the CFP which then holds validity for five years from the date of conferment. NAPs were to undergo a needs assessment, an induction programme, and what were called the School Leadership Development Programme and the Extended Programme. They were also required to engage in activities relevant to their personal and school needs, and submit annually a professional portfolio to their School Management Committees (SMCs). SPs were to engage in a self-selected range of professional activities clustered under the headings of structured learning, action learning and service to education and the community for a minimum of 150 hours over three years. They could also undertake a needs analysis and were asked to develop a personal development plan as part of the overall school plan. Table 8.1 summarises some of the key points in the development and implementation of the continuing leadership development policy.

Although certainly not without difficulty or sometimes heated dialogue, and perhaps unapparent to educators outside Hong Kong, the ED/EMB's policy constituted a substantial shift from the status quo in that it delineated levels of leadership development, introduced mandatory requirements, including certification, for principal positions, demanded that (at least) APs had to pay for their own certification, adopted a set of 'local' leadership competencies or standards developed in Hong Kong, asked school leaders to take responsibility for their own and their colleagues learning and aimed to significantly elevate the value of formal, non-university accredited development programmes. Within a five to six-year period since their launch, the reforms have embedded professional structures, frameworks, requirements and programmes into the psyche and career planning of school leaders. The process associated with policy implementation has certainly begun to shift beliefs about the importance of different forms of preparation. Given the secure anchoring of structures provided by the policy, the obvious next step was to look more deeply into the programmes comprising the policy. The main purpose for this is to move beyond the formal policy structures legitimising leadership preparation to ways the programmes can build a meaningful and enduring learning culture among the school leadership community. In other words, the next stage in the evolution of leadership learning is identifying how programmes can best help school leaders learn. The following section reports a synthesis of studies recently undertaken into the success and efficacy of the most established programmes with an eye to identifying key learning features.

Informative research on school leadership development from Hong Kong

In 2003, with the policy framework in place, the Education and Manpower Bureau (EMB) commissioned a review of the four-year-old NAP programme (EMB, 2004). Data were collected through a survey of participants who had completed the entire programme during the 2000–2003 school years and focus group interviews with, first, selected participants who had completed the programme, and second, another group who had completed the PfP and the NAP programme. This was an important review in that it explored principals' perceptions *after* they had finished the programme and were back, well-ensconced in their schools. The programme was generally favourably reviewed and was believed to have had a positive impact on work in schools. Participants believed the following elements had a significant (positive) impact on their learning:

- Professional exchanges and interaction that provided opportunities to raise questions and discuss solutions.
- Opportunities to see good practices and to reflect on situations that pertained to themselves and their schools – through visits to other schools and interviews with experienced principals.
- Networking of NAPs for professional exchanges, building interpersonal relationships, sharing of experience and mutual support.
- Liaison with experienced principals who could provide concrete help in dealing with problems.

This was supported by the conclusion stating that:

> As regards the mode of delivery, opportunities for interaction, especially with veteran school leaders, were highly prized. In the survey, 'interviews with experienced principals' received a mean score of 5.41 on the 6-point scale as against 4.75 for 'structured learning'. Both in the survey and focus group discussions, a number of interactive activities were sug-

Table 8.1 Key points in the recent development of the principalship development in Hong Kong[a]

Year	*Policy/Programme*	*Notes*
1999	Consultation paper *Leadership training programme for principals* (Task Group on the Training and Development of School Headers, 1999)	First formal attempt to explore leadership development and preparation needs in Hong Kong.
2000	*School leadership in Hong Kong – A profile for a new for a New Century* (Walker et *al.*, 2000)	Intensive work with experienced principals to identify 'the principalship' in Hong Kong.
2000	*Key Qualities of the Principalship in Hong Kong* (Walker et *al.*, 2000)	Development of guiding leadership standards or guiding development programmes.
2000–2004	*Needs Assessment for Newly Appointed Principals in Hong Kong* (Walker and Dimmock, 2000)	The Needs Analysis and extended programme for NAPs began as a pilot in 2000. Lessons learned through this helped inform the 2002 policy.
2000–2004	*School Leadership Development Programme* (LDP) and *Extended Programme* (EP) for NAPs	LDP run by ED/EMB[b] with overseas scholars. EP tendered to Higher Education Institutions. Three components (with NA) labelled Designated Programme.[c]
2002	*Continuing Professional Development for School Excellence: consultation paper on the continuing professional development of principals* (ED, 2002, Feb.)	This became the formal policy in September, 2002.
2003–ongoing	*Developmental needs analysis for aspiring principals in Hong Kong* (Walker and Dimmock, 2003)	The PfP was written by local academics and is tendered to Higher Education Institutions.
	72 hour *Preparation for Principalship* (PfP) Course (APs) (The Chinese University of Hong Kong, 2003)	Practitioners must be involved in the offer of the programme.
	Portfolio construction and submission	Portfolios are assessed through the EMB by practicing principals.

Table 8.1 Continued

Year	*Policy/Programme*	*Notes*
2004	*Review of the Designated Programme for Newly Appointed Principals* (EMB, 2004)	As a result of this review and implementation of the Principal Development Framework the programme for NAPs was altered.
2004–ongoing	*Serving principals Needs Analysis Programme* (SpNAP) (Walker and Quong, 2004)	Self-regulated optional learning programme (for SPs) based on lessons learned through previous programmes.
2005	*Blue Skies: A Professional Learning Programme for Beginning Principals* (Walker and Quong, 2005a)	New programme for beginning principals based on lessons learned through the first NAP programme.

Notes

a This is not a complete list. During the given timeframe there were plenty of other worthwhile (although often disconnected) leadership development programmes in various stages of development and implementation. These were run by Institutes of Higher Education, specific units in the ED/EMB, individual or groups of SSBs, Education interest groups and Professional Associations or even specific schools. Programmes included conferences, short courses, overseas visits, professional upgrading courses, Quality Education Fund (QEF) projects and, increasingly, programmes offered by school–university partnership centres.

b In 2002 the Education and Manpower Bureau (EMB) and the Education Department (ed.) were amalgamated to form an overarching educational body, adopting the title of the former. There is no longer a Director of Education; rather, there is a politically-appointed Secretary for Education and Manpower and a Permanent Secretary for Education and Manpower drawn from the ranks of the Public Service bureaucracy.

c The aims of the NAP designated programme can be found in EMB (2002) which in turn can be found at EMB's website: http://www.emb.gov.hk/index.aspx?langno=1&nodeid=264.

> gested revealing a preference for active participation in the programme ... (and) an experienced principal as mentor.
>
> (Education and Manpower Bureau, 2004, pp. 8, 21)

Review recommendations called for greater coherence between components and providers, a more applied, contextually relevant focus and the greater involvement of experienced principals (mentors). This was moderated by suggestions that mentors be trained, have clear role descriptions and come from schools outside the new principals' spheres of influence and involvement. In an in-depth study of beginning principals who had also participated in the NAP programme, Cheung (2004) found that new principals preferred that their mentors be experienced practitioners and that they be supported by academics (also see Cheung and Walker, 2006). In the EMB review, participants also suggested more practical information and references to key literature could be provided (and that this need not be delivered face-to-face), and that programmes encourage more discussion, case studies, problem-based learning and sharing by principals. In sum, the strongest suggestions were for increased and more focused practitioner involvement as well as contextual sensitivity and relevance.

The value of greater practitioner involvement in the NAP programme was supported by evaluations of the needs analysis component of the NAP programme conducted from 2000 to 2004 (Walker and Dimmock, various years; Walker, various years). Evaluations were done immediately following the needs analysis exercises which ran over a six-week period and involved between eight and ten analysis mechanisms. Approximately 95 per cent of all principals taking up their first appointment from September 2000 to September 2003 went through the programme. Tables 8.2 and 8.3 report (primary, secondary and special school) participants' perceptions of the relevance and usefulness of the mechanisms for preparing them for the principalship (Table 8.2); and the quality of feedback for 'leadership development' they provided (Table 8.3).

During the needs analysis process, each participant was matched (one-on-one) with an experienced principal, called an assessor. Assessors were intensely involved through the mechanism 'personal discussion and plan' where they discussed the outcomes of the other mechanisms (except the psychometric instrument – 16 Personality Factors) and helped the new principals put together a personal development plan. Depending on the relationship formed, the time was also used to discuss issues faced by the new principals in their schools. Overall, participants found the personal discussion to be the most relevant and useful mechanism, and that it provided the highest quality feedback. This perception was even more strongly reported in assessor evaluations, echoed in evaluations of a similar programme for aspiring principals (for example, see Walker, 2004a) and backed-up by participant responses when asked separately to nominate the most valued aspects of the programme. 'It's a real conversation between Assessors and Principals not only based on document assessment but with more understanding of the group's real situation' (Cohort 4). 'Being forced to face discussion and probing questions can really stimulate thoughts' (Cohort 4). 'NAPs need time and guidance in self-reflection. Experienced principals not only share their management experiences, but also show strong support towards the NAPs' (Cohort 5). 'The Assessor's experience and advice throw some insight on what I am doing now as a principal' (Cohort 5). 'I found the Personal Discussion of most value because (1) helpful and valuable comments from, and sharing of experiences with, the assessors; (2) know more about myself from other people's point of view and (3) possible solutions for my school problems can be given' (Cohort 6).

Table 8.2 Relevance and usefulness of needs assessment mechanisms for principalship preparation (2000 to 2004)

Activity	*Cohort 1 (Valid N = 41 in Oct. 2000)*		*Cohort 2 (Valid N = 58 in Jun. 2001)*		*Cohort 3 (Valid N = 62; Nov. 2001)*		*Cohort 4 (Valid N = 91; Nov. 2002)*		*Cohort 5 (Valid N = 88; Nov. 2003)*		*Cohort 6 (Valid N = 16, Nov. 2004)*	
	Valid %	*Rank*	*Valid %*	*Rank*	*Valid %*	*Rank*	*Valid %*	*Rank*	*Valid %*	*Rank*	*Valid %*	*Rank*
Personal Belief Statement	34.1	7	63.8	3	51.6	4	47.3	7	40.9	6	50.0	4
Principal Feedback Quest.	36.6	6	51.7	5	54.8	3	48.4	6	60.9	3	37.5	5
Teacher Feedback Quest.	46.3	4	50.0	6	46.8	5	50.5	5	62.5	2	68.8	3
Written In-Tray Exercise	48.8	3	60.3	4	46.8	5	31.9	7	30.7	8	68.8	3
Personality Profile (16PF)	65.9	1	77.6	2	71.0	1	56.0	4	55.7	4	68.8	3
Group Interaction Exercise	48.8	3	84.5	1	69.4	2	59.3	3	53.4	5	81.3	2
Prof. Develop. Record	39.0	5	60.3	4	45.2	6	NA	NA	NA	NA	NA	NA
Personal SWOP Audit	NA	NA	NA	NA	NA	NA	27.5	8	37.5	7	50.0	4
Personal Discussion and Plan	58.5	2	77.6	2	71.0	1	73.6	1	64.8	1	93.8	1
Prof. Develop. Plan	NA	NA	NA	NA	NA	NA	61.5	2	53.4	5	68.8	3

Table 8.3 Quality of feedback for 'leadership development' provided by mechanisms (2000 to 2004)

Activity	*Cohort 1 (Valid N = 41 in Oct. 2000)*		*Cohort 2 (Valid N = 36 in Jun. 2001)*		*Cohort 3 (Valid N = 62; Nov. 2001)*		*Cohort 4 (Valid N = 91; Nov. 2002)*		*Cohort 5 (Valid N = 88; Nov. 2003)*		*Cohort 6 (Valid N = 16, Nov. 2004)*	
	Valid %	*Rank*	*Valid %*	*Rank*	*Valid %*	*Rank*	*Valid %*	*Rank*	*Valid %*	*Rank*	*Valid %*	*Rank*
Personal Belief Statement	31.7	7	44.8	7	37.1	5	40.0	8	36.4	7	62.5	5
Principal Feedback Quest.	29.3	8	44.8	7	32.3	6	47.3	6	48.3	6	50.0	7
Teacher Feedback Quest.	41.5	6	50.0	6	32.3	6	52.7	5	54.5	3	75.0	3
Written In-Tray Exercise	56.1	3	67.2	4	48.4	3	40.7	7	35.2	8	56.3	6
Personality Profile (16PF)	63.4	1	74.1	2	64.5	2	58.2	4	53.4	4	68.8	4
Group Interaction Exercise	53.7	4	81.0	1	66.1	1	60.4	3	52.3	5	81.3	2
Prof. Develop. Record	46.3	5	58.6	5	46.8	4	NA	NA	NA	NA	NA	NA
Personal SWOP Audit	NA	NA	NA	NA	NA	NA	34.1	9	36.4	7	68.8	4
Personal Discussion and Plan	58.5	2	70.7	3	64.5	2	73.6	1	59.1	1	100.0	1
Prof. Develop. Plan	NA	NA	NA	NA	NA	NA	65.9	2	58.0	2	75.0	3

Wong's (2005) focused study of the overall NAP programme with a small sample of female principals (as part of a comparative study with UK principals) also provides insights into the NAP programme. Despite its limitations (see Wong, 2005), as with the EMB review, her study is particularly valuable in that the sample was drawn from principals who had completed the NAP programme and had thus had a chance to reflect upon its impact on their leadership in school. Wong asked participants to describe the impact of the programme on their knowledge, skills, values and attributes and to illustrate this impact with evidence. Such evidence included impact on school programmes, changes in behaviour toward staff, 'new' ways of doing things and involvement in leadership networks.

Although admittedly based on a small sample, Wong's findings provide a number of critical insights into the NAP programme. First, she found it difficult to determine the impact of the programme on knowledge and skills because of the possible influence of previous training and experience, and differing school contexts. In other words, the subsequent impact on knowledge and skills related to the individual contexts of the principals. Second, the principals were quite positive about the programme's impact on their values and attributes. The impact appeared to permeate the structures and processes of the programme such that it activated participants' reflection, exposure to diverse values and entry to broader leadership networks. One principal explained thus:

> I think the training has a greater impact on the attributes. Throughout the course, there were opportunities for me to meet a variety of different types of principals. It allowed me to observe the type of principal I would like to be and I paid close attention to the style and characteristics of that particular type.
>
> (Principal B, H.K; in Wong, 2005, p. 19)

The principals in Wong's study believed the programme made a difference to their leadership through providing, sometimes serendipitously, an entrée to existing and newly formed networks of new and experienced principals. This appears in line with Wong and Ng's (2003) finding that new principals perceived learning on the job, learning from supervisors (who served as mentors), and sharing with fellow principals as more effective than taking principalship training courses or M.Ed. courses; and with Pang and Gamage's (2005) finding that Hong Kong principals wanted development mechanisms which placed increased emphasis on the 'observation of exemplary educational leaders and group work' (p. 34). Wong's (2005) findings also suggested that membership in informal learning networks provide opportunities for open sharing as well as for emotional and practical support. The new principals in the study, overall, felt that interaction with experienced colleagues had a positive impact on their leadership learning, mainly through exposure to new ideas, role modelling, practical advice and physiological support. It should be noted, however, that mentorship was of little value if it did not relate to the realities of the NAPs' leadership and school life.

In summarising the study Wong (2005) identified a number of factors which appeared to determine how NAPs (in Hong Kong and the UK) perceived the impact of their development programmes. These included, the NAPs' previous experiences, the immediate applicability of the learning to real life in schools, the mode of delivery (sharing, reflection and ownership were seen as important), the timescale, opportunities for professional socialisation, and the performance and commitment of experienced principals. While identifying these general factors, Wong stressed that it was often difficult for principals to articulate or 'know' whether training of any type or form had made an impact on their learning. It should also be noted that little mention was made by principals in the study about the (direct or indirect) impact of the programme on student learning.

Findings of the studies were synthesised and, when taken together, eight key (closely related) features were distinguished:

- learning linked to school and leadership context;
- an ongoing focus on real-time, real life issues as the basis for learning;
- substantial involvement by experienced principals (mentoring, sharing, observing, questioning);
- adequate training and role definition for experienced principals involved;
- a structure flexible enough to meet diverse needs (learning methods and content);
- multiple opportunities for reflection, sharing and questioning;
- respect for existing skills, values and knowledge (experience);
- cohort bonding (and collaboration) and opportunities for sideways and hierarchical networking.

The following section turns from Hong Kong specific studies to writings and research conducted in other contexts.

Informative literature on school leadership development from outside Hong Kong

A growing body of literature is accumulating on school leadership development. To the extent that this literature is corroborative, it provides valuable advice on how to shape worthwhile leadership learning programmes. This section spotlights selected research in order to identify emerging practice internationally. International findings are then juxtaposed with research on the Hong Kong NAP programme and, finally, a new programme currently being piloted in Hong Kong is outlined. This programme was informed by the outcomes of both local and overseas insights and is included to illustrate the process of translation of emergent findings into a leadership learning programme.

Perspectives on leadership learning taken from writers such as Eraut (2000), Goleman (2002) and Kotter (1996) highlight self-awareness and self-learning as an essential path to improved leadership practice. Kotter (1996), for example, claims that leadership learning is sustained through the development of five mental habits. These include, risk-taking, or a willingness to push oneself outside of comfort zones; humble self-reflection, or an honest assessment of success and failure, particularly the latter; solicitation of opinions, or the aggressive collection of information and ideas from others; a propensity to listen to others and openness to new ideas – a willingness to view life with an open mind (p. 183). Goleman (2002, p. 107) claims that: 'The crux of leadership development that works is self-directed learning: intentionally developing or strengthening an aspect of who you are and who you want to be, or both'.

Leaders learn from insights which emerge and accumulate through simultaneously applying intuition and collecting and analysing knowledge and evidence in specific leadership situations (Dimmock, 2000). Likewise, Eraut (2000) holds that leaders aspire to what he calls 'a maturity of judgement' – and that this results from meaningful learning. He suggests that leadership maturity is neither purely analytic nor purely intuitive, but involves the ability to reflect upon issues in order to explore how others might perceive them and how they might impact the future. The exercise of professional learning therefore involves the process of applying personal knowledge (often informed by codified knowledge) to a unique set of circumstances while taking into account a 'range of implications and conflicting perspectives' (Glatter and Kydd, 2003, p. 239).

It should be noted that research and comment on leadership learning does not stand apart from similar work into teacher or more general professional development – there are obvious reciprocal linkages between the two closely related bodies of knowledge. For example, the general design themes suggested by Bredeson (2003) appear to hold considerable currency for conceptualising and constructing leadership development programmes. Bredeson's (2003, p. 8) themes are: professional development is about learning; professional development is work; professional expertise is a journey not a credential; opportunities for professional learning and improved practice are unbounded; student learning, professional development and organisational mission are intimately related; and professional development is about people, not programmes. Such themes are apparent throughout the leadership development literature.

Reporting a 15-country international comparative study into development programmes specifically for school leaders, Huber (2004) found that the most effective programmes had centralised guidelines for quality assurance, but decentralised implementation to allow greater flexibility and contextualisation. He also found that effective programmes focused on long-term skill development, not just on-the-job training, and actively involved participants through stressing the central role of collaboration (so that collaborative learning networks can continue beyond the bounds of the programme). Huber also emphasised the importance of relating learning opportunities to school context, finding a balance between theory and practice, and involving trainers and facilitators with appropriate backgrounds. He decried the lack of systematic evaluation of programmes. This point appears paramount, as few studies have adequately explored whether the programmes really make a difference to improving leadership and student learning outcomes.

In a similar review of school leadership programmes internationally, Hallinger (2003) identified a number of themes describing current best practice in 12 (East Asian, European and North American) societies. The themes included the movement from passive to active learning, creating mechanisms and learning processes that connect training to practice, crafting an appropriate role and tools for using performance standards, supporting effective transitions into the leadership role, evaluating leadership development programmes and developing and validating an indigenous knowledge base across cultures. Bolam (2003) and Walker and Dimmock (2005) also stress the importance of contextual relevance. Bolam insists that leadership development models be grounded in a particular context. While specifically discussing the place of experienced practitioners within the context of such programmes Walker and Dimmock (2005) couch increased practitioner involvement within a framework of intentionality, strategic thinking and formal design.

Synthesising more than 20 years of their work into headship and leadership development in the UK, Earley and Weindling (2004) found that heads believed the most valuable 'on-the-job' learning activity was working with others, especially effective head teachers. The most useful off-the-job activities included attending courses, visiting other schools, networking with other head teachers, working on specialist tasks and meetings/contacts with non-educationalists. They also expressed heads' concerns about finding the best ways to deal with leadership development in a coherent manner. Head teachers supported further development of the roles of experienced heads as mentors/coaches. Weindling (2004) identified more explicitly the key features and principles of leadership development programmes as the adoption of suitable learning theories, mentoring and coaching, opportunities for reflection, problem-based learning and case studies, action learning, storytelling and drama, journals and portfolios, e-learning and computer simulations, cohorts, groups and learning communities. These generally cohere with the research-based suggestions of Huber (2004), Hallinger (2003) and Hallinger and Snidvongs (2005).

In their recently published review of school leadership development in both the business and educator sectors, Hallinger and Snidvongs (2005) distil a number of conclusions and recommendations about the desired future state of such programmes. Among these is that the shifting knowledge base and context of school leadership makes a commitment to lifelong learning inescapable; that the development of lifelong learning capacity calls for 'blended learning ... that maximise(s) the impact of on-line and face-to-face, as well as synchronous and asynchronous experiences' (p. 8). They also reinforce that leadership development must engage actively with the real problems school leaders face in their schools; and that the learning of new knowledge and skills calls for flexibly combining on-site coaching and networks of professional support. Likewise, Glatter (1991) suggested that school leadership development policies:

> must be closely related to the actual work and functioning of the school; ... need to extend over a considerable period of time; (that) preparation and follow-up are crucially important; (that) they should foster a 'team development' approach and make considerable use of experience-based methods, rather than simply relying on formal 'courses'.
>
> (p. 226)

Like Weindling (2004), Glatter also called for programmes to provide scope for reflective learning and focus on concrete situations and application of learning in collaboration with colleagues.

Findings from the evaluation and study of the NAP programme in Hong Kong and recommendations drawn from research internationally come together at a number of interrelated points. A rough mapping of these interrelated features and examples of possible associated structures and processes are shown in Table 8.4.

Applying the key features of leadership learning programmes – 'Blue Skies'

This section outlines a programme funded by the EMB and implemented, on a trial basis, for beginning principals in Hong Kong in mid-2005. The programme is called 'Blue Skies – a Professional Learning Programme for Beginning Principals'[3] (Walker and Quong, 2005a) and is loosely guided by the *Key Qualities of the Principalship in Hong Kong*. It is designed to fit coherently with programmes for aspiring and serving principals and a centralised induction programme. 'Blue Skies' was designed after ongoing evaluations, formal review and other studies into the original NAP programme summarised earlier in this chapter. It was also informed by international research

Table 8.4 Key features of school leadership learning programmes

Key features of school leadership learning programmes identified in both Hong Kong and internationally	*Examples of micro-structures and processes associated with successful school leadership programmes*
• Mechanisms/content to maximise contextual- and cultural sensitivity	• Action learning • Policy/reform components • Differentiated expectations • Cultural consideration
• Linkage to leadership reality and school life and outcomes	• 'Real' problem-based focus • Opportunities for acknowledging diverse views • Opportunities for increasing personal awareness • Action Learning
• Opportunities for reflection	• Small group structure (within larger cohort) • Extended time frame • Relationship building • Use of journals and records (or portfolios)
• Intense involvement of experienced practitioners as mentors and/or coaches	• Involvement from design to implementation to review • The training of mentors and/or coaches • Defined role (flexibility within structure) • Focus on reality
• Multiple learning gateways[a]	• Multiple delivery modes • Suitable for different learning styles • Flexible content to address both basics and variable situations • In and outside of school (and education)
• Intentional design	• Flexibility within structure • Internal and external quality assurance • Cultural setting and expectations

• Formal and informal grouping and networking	• Formal networking through purposefully constructed learning sets • User-friendly structures for electronic networking • Encouragement of informal, self-driven networks (within and beyond education)
• Meaningful evaluation	• Formative and summative evaluation; • Self-evaluation • Focus on impact on practice and student learning
• Participant control	• Flexible time/involvement schedule • Self-paced (within structure) • Focus areas

Note

a For example, Walker and Quong (2004) developed an electronic programme for serving principals based around what they call the four leadership learning gateways – *what is important to me* (Gateway 1), *what others think about me* (Gateway 2), *what's happening now* (Gateway 3) and *what else is out there* (Gateway 4). Also see Walker and Quong (2005c). Further additional information can be obtained from: http://www3.fed.cuhk.edu.hk/eldevnet/NAFPhk_SP.asp.

and insights, particularly as reported in Weindling (2004). The research outcomes and recommendations are apparent in the shape and content of the programme.

'Blue Skies' is a 12-month learning programme for beginning principals which starts at the end of their first year in post. The programme was developed by a group of academics and practising principals, all of whom had been heavily involved in the design and implementation of the previous NAP programme. The stated purpose of 'Blue Skies' is that:

> Beginning Principals (will) leave the programme with increased confidence in themselves as leaders ... (and) be better equipped to both lead and manage their schools. Following their involvement they will be more knowledgeable and resilient, and more connected to learning networks.
>
> (Walker and Quong, 2005b, p. 3)

The programme presents an integrated approach to ongoing professional learning for beginning principals and is designed to help them start their principalship on a positive note. It also helps them clarify what is important in their principalship and engages them in ongoing professional learning – all within a supportive collegial environment. The learning principles underpinning 'Blue Skies' are listed below.

Beginning principals:

- Are self-directed learners;
- cannot learn effectively without a solid knowledge of themselves – including their strengths and weaknesses – as people and as leaders;
- learn through personal reflection, asking hard questions and receiving feedback and new ideas from peers and others;
- need an intentional and personalised design to guide their learning;
- have many commitments and demands on their time. As a result, they are more likely to commit to learning when the goals and objectives are realistic, and perceived as being immediately useful;
- bring with them a wide range of experiences, knowledge, skills, interests, and competencies to all learning situations;
- sometimes fear external judgment and that this can produce anxiety during new learning situations;
- need to see results from their efforts and receive accurate feedback about their progress;
- need ample opportunity to share with, and learn from, each other, and other principals and professionals;
- relate most strongly to learning which connects directly with their school context.

At the heart of 'Blue Skies' learning are a group or carefully selected sponsors and approximately 17 learning sets called Learning Squares. A 'Blue Skies' sponsor is a recognised (effective) experienced principal who formally agrees to 'sponsor' one or more beginning principals for the duration of the 'Blue Skies' programme. A sponsor agrees to take shared responsibility for a beginning principals' learning and professional welfare during the first years of their principalship (and hopefully, following the completion of the formal programme). A sponsor has three interrelated roles: peer mentor, principal coach and professional counsel. Each sponsor is carefully matched with three beginning principals to form a Learning Square. This configuration was designed to spread the support, learning and responsibility so that the sponsor supported each beginning principal, and they supported each other. Although each sponsor takes a greater 'driving' role, the four corners of the square symbolically represent the four partners each holding up an equal corner of learning.

The programme works through four major stages:

1 welcome and briefing (beginning principals) and formal training for Sponsors;
2 stocktake;
3 leaders' forum;
4 the partnership programme.

The first stage for sponsors involves initial programme familiarisation and two dedicated training occasions – one specifically targeting the programme philosophy, justification and mechanisms, as well as strategies for initial group formation; and the other explicitly targets the skills and knowledge necessary to be a successful sponsor. The first stage for participants, the 'welcome and briefing', is run by a small group of experienced principals who outline the programme rationale and structure, introduce Learning Square members, clearly explain expectations and distribute Stocktake tasks. At the conclusion of the briefing, beginning principals are asked to set an initial behavioural learning goal and, given the voluntary nature of the programme, they are asked to formally commit to it, or elect otherwise.

The second stage of 'Blue Skies', 'Stocktake', asks beginning principals to carry out a set of tasks within their schools over a one month period. The tasks include a brief school capacity audit, core values scan, perceptions and expectations, icons, rules and resources – and to set a small number of initial learning goals. The tasks are designed to firmly ground the programme in the reality of school life and leadership from the outset and to kick start the processes of reflection, curiosity and analysis. The third stage involves the entire cohort of sponsors and beginning principals (in Learning Squares) in a focused 'leadership forum'. The forum has two major and closely interwoven purposes. The first is to begin in earnest the building and bonding of professional and learning relationships in and between Learning Squares. The second is to reinforce the school-based focus of the programme – this is done through using the completed stocktake tasks as the basis for group activity and interaction. In other words, the information collected in the beginning principals' schools underpins Learning Square activities during the forum (other activities, such as dilemma identification and analysis are also included). The sponsor's job during the forum is to build group relationships, focus learning on school leadership and improvement and work with their Learning Squares to set initial learning goals and plan a meeting schedule and framework for the duration of the programme.

The fourth stage – the 'partnership programme' – forms the core of 'Blue Skies' in terms of purpose, intent and time commitment and centres on individual school, principal and Learning Square needs. The stage is about ongoing collaborative learning and support, and seeks to build a unique and flexible learning partnership over a period of approximately 12 months. The partnership also draws on other expertise, opinion and research as necessary.

In designing the 'partnership programme' the development group recognised that principals are busy people who face severe time limitations that restrict formal professional learning. On the other hand, however, there was acknowledgment that if a concerted effort was not made to design or intentionally structure professional learning, then it may be less effective and, as a result, beginning principals could find themselves becoming professionally isolated. The partnership programme, therefore, is based on a balanced mixture of structure and flexibility, or what we labelled 'flexibility within structure' or 'bounded flexibility'. There are some components which everyone does together as a cohort, and others which are done in Learning Squares. For Learning Squares, the principals themselves decide the 'how', 'why' and 'when' of their learning. Subsequently, it is hoped that 'Blue Skies' will evolve through individual/contextualised learning agendas and recognise that the key to making the 'partnership programme' work are the relationships formed within the Learning Squares. The required and elective components of 'Blue Skies' are listed and very briefly described in Table 8.5 (also see: http://www3.fed.cuhk.edu.hk/eldevnet/blue_skies.asp.

The programme, including in its early stages, is being evaluated on an ongoing basis both internally and externally. A rigorous quality assurance (QA) scheme has been planned and an external consultant engaged. However, at this very early stage of implementation it is not possible to make any definitive judgements about the programme's success; in fact, these may not be clear until well after the formal programme is completed. The programme, based on clear research findings both locally and internationally, is designed to build on and extend the existing culture of leadership learning and turn it toward a more realistically grounded, collaborative process. Whether this will suit the unique Hong Kong context is yet to be seen.

Table 8.5 Blue Skies partnership programme: required and elective components

Required components	
Component	*Structure/focus/purpose*
• Learning Square Breakfast Meetings	• At least five Learning Square meetings (every other month) scheduled by members in schools on rotational basis. • Focused on school and leadership issues faced by beginning principals. • Regular contact, learning and support focused on real issues.
• Breakfast Inspiration Series	• Five centrally scheduled meeting for entire cohort every other month. Presentation by high profile speakers (from in or outside of education). • Focused on challenge, excitement, 'difference' and 'new ideas'. • Whole group connection, valuing of principals, infuse new and socially-responsive mindsets.
• Peer Learning	• Total of two days (any configuration) in Learning Squares engaging in activities negotiated to provide maximum benefit to beginning principals (e.g. principal or student shadowing, seminars, targeted visits etc.). • Focused on school and leadership issues faced by beginning principals. • Encourage sharing, openness, learning and support of real issues
• Individual Learning Plan	• Basic Individual Learning Plan to set and work through personal/Learning Square Learning goals (includes goals, link to school development and review etc.) • Focuses on individual/school-based learning organised around the six core areas of learning. • Encourage strategic intent, individual planning and accountability. Ground learning in school and individual context.
Elective components	
Component	*Description*
• Sharing the Knowledge	• Dedicated email system for discussion, questions and networking.
• Memorable Messages – ACT	• Collection of 'rear mirror' advice from experienced principals which AFFIRMs something positive they did as a BP; something they would certainly CHANGE if they could go back, and something they wished they had TRIED.
• Mini-Modules	• A set of 12 purpose-written booklets (in electronic form) targeting areas identified as important to BPs. Distributed each month to entire cohort. For example, BPs and the Law, Enquiry Learning, 'Getting out of the Engine Room', Performance Management, 'Asking Hard Questions'.
• On-Time Advice	• A register of expertise available to BPs.
• Additional Self-Appraisal and Insight	• A collection of psychometric and other mechanisms which principal can choose to access. Other opportunities are disseminated and offered.
• Other Learning Opportunities	• Blue skies does not intend to be restrictive or self-contained. It is designed to meld with other programmes
• Additional Resources	• List of websites and other resources which may be useful to schools

Conclusion

This chapter has attempted to highlight the important elements of the school leadership development landscape in Hong Kong over the last five years. There is little doubt that the EMB's targeted policy initiatives have successfully challenged the thinly spread and largely incoherent approach to leadership development that typified Hong Kong throughout the 1990s. Within a relatively short time the reforms have embedded forward-looking structures, frameworks and programmes into the psyche and plans of future and serving school leaders. The reform polices set requirements to guide leadership preparation outside of academic qualifications and in doing so has begun to shift beliefs about the importance of different forms of preparation. Given the consolidation of more imaginative and flexible structures necessary to entrench the concept of leadership development in the professional community, the argument suggested it was time to turn attention towards how programmes can better help leaders learn.

Using data collected during and after the most established existing programme – that for newly appointed principals – the chapter identified a number of features which the principals suggested would make the programme more useful to their learning. Salient features of leader learning to emerge from the Hong Kong programme evaluations were juxtaposed with findings and recommendations from successful leadership learning programmes internationally. This resulted in the identification of a set of key features which were regarded as offering the potential to inform the design of a new generation of leadership learning programmes in Hong Kong – programmes more geared toward learning processes and relationships rather than structures and frameworks. The identified features were used to inform the development of a new learning-centred, school-focused programme for beginning principals. The programme introduced and outlined is only very recently implemented and is, as yet, untested. As such, it can be seen as another small step towards the evolution of worthwhile learning programmes for school leaders in Hong Kong – one which focuses firmly on improving and implanting collaborative learning habits.

Notes

1 For an explanation of the history and role of School Sponsoring Bodies (SSBs) see Walker (2004).
2 As in many other settings, Hong Kong has been beset by a broad range of education reforms. These moved into full swing in 1997. Reforms have targeted areas including curriculum, teacher language proficiency, information literacy, medium of instruction, school governance (through school-based management); all within an overall priority to overhaul the entire education system (Education Commission, 1996). Some bodies attempted to provide reform-targeted leadership development. For example, following the launch of the devolution-oriented School Management Initiative (SMI) in 1991 ED instituted a series of 30-hour training

course for schools joining the scheme. See Wong (2004) for another example.

3 Given space restrictions the programme can only be very briefly outlined here. Further information can be obtained from the author or from visiting the programme website at: http://www3.fed.cuhk.edu.hk/eldevnet/blue_skies.asp.

References

Björk, L. and Murphy, J. (2005) School management training country report: the United States of America, *Studies in Education Management Research*, No 13, Norway: CEM Centre for Education Management Research, Norwegian School of Management and University of Oslo Institute of Educational Research.

Bolam, R. (2003) Models of leadership development: learning from international experience and research, in: M. Brundrett, N. Burton and R. Smith (eds) *Leadership in Education* (London, Sage).

Bredeson, P. V. (2003) *Designs for learning: a new architecture for professional development in schools* (Thousand Oaks, Corwin Press).

Bush, T. (2004) Editorial: the National College for School Leadership, *Educational Management Administration and Leadership*, 32(3), 243–350.

Bush, T. (2005) School management training country report: England, *Studies in Education Management Research*, No 14, Norway: CEM Centre for Education Management Research, Norwegian School of Management and University of Oslo Institute of Educational Research.

Bush, T. and Jackson, D. (2002) A preparation for school leadership international perspectives, *Educational Management and Administration*, 30(4), 417–429.

Cheng, Y. C. (2000) The characteristics of Hong Kong school principals' leadership: the influence of societal culture, *Asia Pacific Journal of Education*, 20(2), 68–86.

Cheung, M. B. (2004) A qualitative study of beginning principals in Hong Kong secondary schools operating within an educational reform environment. A EdD thesis. The Chinese University of Hong Kong, Hong Kong.

Cheung, M. B. and Walker, A. (2006) Inner worlds and outer limits: the formation of beginning principals in Hong Kong, *Journal of Educational Administration*, 44(4), 389–407.

Chinese University of Hong Kong, The (2003) *Preparation for Principalship Course* (Hong Kong, Department of Educational Administration and Policy, The Chinese University of Hong Kong).

Dimmock, C. (2000) *Designing the learning-centred school: a cross-cultural perspective* (London and New York, Falmer Press).

Earley, P. and Evans (2004) Making a difference? Leadership development for headteachers and deputies – ascertaining the impact of the National College for School Leadership, *Educational Management Administration and Leadership*, 32(3), 325–338.

Earley, P. and Weindling, D. (2004) *Understanding school leadership* (London, Paul Chapman).

Education and Manpower Bureau (EMB) (2004) *Report of the panel for the review of the designated programme for newly appointed principals* (Hong Kong, Education and Manpower Bureau, HKSAR).

Education Department (2002, February and September) *Continuing professional development for school excellence consultation paper on continuing development of principals* (Hong Kong, Education Department, Hong Kong Government).

Eraut, M. (2000) Non-formal learning and tacit knowledge in professional work, *British Journal of Educational Psychology*, 70(1), 113–136.

Glatter, R. (1991) Developing educational leaders: an international perspective, in: P. Ribbins, R. Glatter, T. Simkins and L. Watson (eds) *Developing educational leaders – international intervention programme 1990* (Glasgow, Longman).

Glatter, R. and Kydd, L. (2003) 'Best Practice' in educational leadership and management: can we identify if and learn from it, *Educational Management & Administration*, 31(3), 231–243.

Goleman, D. (2002) *The new leaders: transforming the art of leadership into the science of results* (London: Little Brown).

Hallinger, P. (2003) The emergence of school leadership development in an era of globalization: 1980–2002, in: P. Hallinger (ed.) *Reshaping the landscape of school leadership development: a global perspective* (Netherlands, Swets & Zeitlinger), 3–23.

Hallinger, P. and Snidvongs, K. (2005) *Adding value to school leadership and management: a review of trends in the development of managers in the education and business sectors* (Nottingham, National College for School Leadership).

Huber, S. G. (2004) *Preparing school leaders for the 21st century* (London: Routledge).

Kotter, J. P. (1996) *Leading change* (Boston: Harvard Business School Press).

Lam, Y. L. J. (2003) Balancing stability and change: implications for professional preparation and development of principals in Hong Kong, in: P. Hallinger (ed.) *Reshaping the landscape of school leadership development* (Netherlands, Swets & Zeitlinger), 175–190.

Ng, H. M. (2003) An analysis of continuous teacher development in Hong Kong, *Journal of Education Policy*, 18(6), 657–672.

Pang, N. S. K. and Gamage, D. (2005) A comparative study of continuing professional development of school principals in New South Wales, Australia and Hong Kong, *Comparative Education Bulletin*, 8, 29–35.

Southworth, G. (2004) A response from the National College for School Leadership, *Educational Management Administration and Leadership*, 32(3), 339–354.

Task Group on the Training and Development of School Headers (1999) *Leadership training programme for principals consultation paper* (Hong Kong, Education Department, Hong Kong Government).

Wales, C. and Welle-Strand, A. (2005) School management training country report: Norway, *Studies in Education Management Research*, No 16, Norway: CEM Centre for Education Management Research, Norwegian School of Management and University of Oslo Institute of Educational Research.

Walker, A. (2004) Constitution and culture: exploring the deep leadership structures of Hong Kong schools, *Discourse: Studies in the Cultural Politics of Education*, 25(1), 75–94.

Walker, A. (2004a) *Evaluation of developmental needs analysis for aspiring principals in Hong Kong* (Jan. 2003–Apr. 2004) (Hong Kong, Hong Kong Centre for the Development of Educational Leadership).

Walker, A. (various years) *The developmental assessment of newly-appointed principals in Hong Kong – final reports, 2003 & 2004* (Hong Kong, Hong Kong Centre for the Development of Educational Leadership).

Walker, A. and Dimmock, C. (2000) *Needs assessment for newly appointed principals programme (package) in Hong Kong* (Hong Kong, Hong Kong Centre for the Development of Educational Leadership).

Walker, A. and Dimmock, C. (2005) Developing leadership in context, in: M. Coles and G. Southworth (eds) *Developing leadership: creating the schools of tomorrow* (Milton Keyes: Open University Press), 88–94.
Walker, A. and Dimmock, C. (various years) *Needs assessment for (Newly-Appointed) principals in Hong Kong (NAFPhk) – final reports 2000, 2001, 2002* (Hong Kong, Hong Kong Centre for the Development of Educational Leadership).
Walker, A. and Quong, T. (2004) *Serving principal needs analysis programme – a professional learning package developed for serving principals in Hong Kong* (Hong Kong, Hong Kong Centre for the Development of Educational Leadership).
Walker, A. and Quong, T. (2005a) *Blue skies: a professional learning programme (package) for beginning principals in Hong Kong* (Hong Kong, Hong Kong Centre for the Development of Educational Leadership).
Walker, A. and Quong, T. (2005b) *Overview booklet, in Blue skies: a professional learning programme (package) for beginning principals in Hong Kong* (Hong Kong, Hong Kong Centre for the Development of Educational Leadership), 3.
Walker, A. and Quong, T. (2005c) Gateways to international leadership learning: beyond best practice, *Educational Research and Perspectives*, 32(2), 97–121.
Walker, A., Begley, P. and Dimmock, C. (2000) *School leadership in Hong Kong: a profile for a new century* (Hong Kong, Hong Kong Centre for the Development of Educational Leadership).
Walker, A., Dimmock, C., Chan, A., Chan, W. K., Chueng, M. B. and Wong Y. H. (2002) *Key qualities of the principalship in Hong Kong* (Hong Kong, Hong Kong Centre for the Development of Educational Leadership).
Weindling, D. (2004) *Innovation in headteacher induction* (Nottingham, National College for School Leadership).
Wong, K. C. and Ng, H. M. (2003) On Hong Kong: the making of secondary school principals, *International Studies in Educational Administration*, 31(2), 35–53.
Wong, P. M. (2004) The professional development of school principals: insights from evaluating a programme in Hong Kong, *School Leadership & Management*, 24(2), 139–162.
Wong, S. L. (2005) *Impact of leadership training on newly-appointed female principals in middle/secondary schools in England and Hong Kong* (Nottingham, National College for School Leadership).

Chapter 9

Only connect

Australia's recent attempts to forge a national agenda for quality school leadership

Simon Clarke

Introduction

This chapter examines recent Australian progress in the advancement of a national agenda for developing the quality of school leadership. The scope and complexity of this task means that the chapter is necessarily selective and that it is also confined to circumstances occurring over the last five years or so. The chapter falls into three main sections. The first section provides a background to the unprecedented attention that has been devoted to the quality of school leadership in this country. To comprehend the logistics of promoting a national approach to quality of school leadership, the second section examines the complex sharing of responsibilities for education that exists between the Commonwealth or Federal level of government and the States and Territories in Australia and the third section reports some promising initiatives in shaping a national agenda for enhancing school leadership as the customary fragmentation of arrangements shifts towards convergence.

The ascendancy of school leadership

In common with international trends, attention devoted to the quality of school leadership in Australia has been galvanised by the discourse of school effectiveness. Lists of characteristics of effective schools and associated quality indicators have been convincing in their endorsement of the importance of leadership (Christie and Lingard, 2001) and its positive impact on student achievement. A particular linkage between leadership and school effectiveness that has been stressed in the Australian context is the relationship between the quality of educational leadership and the quality of teaching (Ramsey, 2000). Certainly, there is an acceptance that different styles of leadership have a profound influence on the motivation and effectiveness of teachers (DEST, 2003).

Again, in common with international trends, the complexity of exercising school leadership in Australia has increased substantially over recent years.

The shift towards greater autonomy, efficiency and accountability that has characterised school-based management has placed new demands on the principal (Wildy and Louden, 2000). In particular, responsibilities have been introduced not only for finance and staffing, but also for school development (Christie and Lingard, 2001). Add to these extra responsibilities the challenges presented by the changing nature of student learners, the expansion of new technologies, the need for appropriate pedagogy and the additional demands made of teachers in a turbulent educational environment and the complexity of school leadership is indisputable (Australian College of Education, 2001).

One useful way of conceptualising the enormous complexity and ambiguity of contemporary school leadership is according to dilemmas. For example, principals are confronted regularly with the dilemmas of providing both strong and shared leadership; using resources effectively while working collaboratively; being responsible for decisions made by or with others; and being responsive to local needs within a framework of system priorities (Wildy and Louden, 2000). Likewise, Dempster *et al.* (2001) refer to 'values dualities' that principals need to contend with such as the rights of the individual vs. the rights of the majority; self-determination vs. social responsibility; loyalty to teachers vs. loyalty to parents; compliance vs. professional autonomy and local needs vs. system priority. Dealing with these dilemmas and tensions entails considerable 'emotional labour' on the part of leaders (Duignan, 1997); consequently, self-knowledge and an ability to contexualise, understand, accept and develop the emotional character of their school experience is vital (O'Brien *et al.*, 2003).

Given the increasing complexity and demands of school leadership, it might be questioned whether leaders and aspiring leaders are currently equipped to tackle such a formidable undertaking. Indeed, the nature of the challenges facing schools means that it is unlikely that principals are able to act single-handedly (Christie and Lingard, 2001). Rather, it is now seen as desirable that leadership should be distributed as widely as possible across the school engendering dispersed responsibility for tasks (Crowther, 2002). This distributed approach to leadership is especially important if innovation is to become the dominant motif of schooling (DEST, 2003, p. 221) because it builds the capacity of a school to move forward.

Hence, the unprecedented complexity of school leadership in Australia as well as new conceptions of leadership that this complexity has engendered have important implications for the ways in which school leaders are prepared and developed for their roles. The significance of this observation is heightened when it is considered that in Australia there continues to be a heavy dependence on the traditional apprenticeship model according to which future school leaders have been prepared mostly by moving up the ranks from classroom teachers to master teachers to heads of departments and to school principalship (Su *et al.*, 2003). There has been, in other words, an assumption that capable teachers will morph into effective leaders without specific or mandatory preparation. It might be questioned whether this 'on the job' approach to nurturing school leaders is sufficient in itself for acquiring the level of leadership acumen that is needed to deal with the circumstances that are integral to the contemporary educational environment.

The imperative to develop strategies for recruiting and retaining high-quality school leaders is accentuated even further by the increasing difficulty of attracting leaders to the principalship, especially given the increased complexity and demands associated with the position. As d'Arbon *et al.* have commented (2002) on this issue:

> the role of, and expectations for, the principalship are increasing in intensity and complexity and are causing many principals to reflect on why they should continue to do the job or why aspiring principals might be discouraged from applying.
>
> (p. 469)

An added complication is that principals are inevitably drawn from teachers (d'Arbon *et al.*, 2002). Preston (2005), however, has highlighted projected shortfalls in numbers of teachers across Australia, a trend that is likely to diminish the pool of future school leaders even further. This is a disconcerting trend, given that the teaching workforce in Australia is also ageing which is another issue affecting school principal positions with a high proportion of principals expected to retire in the next decade (Allen Consulting Group, 2004). The New South Wales Department of Education and Training is representative of educational systems throughout Australia in facing the spectre of a leadership vacuum in the next ten years. According to Scott (2003, p. 1), the current mean age of NSW Education Department secondary principals is 52 and for deputy principals it is 49, with the mean age of primary principals being 50 and deputy principals 48. Retirement projections indicate that 74 per cent of secondary principals and 59 per cent of primary principals will retire within the decade. Clearly, these demographic circumstances demand that school leadership succession and development cannot be left to chance.

For a number of reasons then, policy makers, system administrators, practitioners and the community in Australia have devoted much scrutiny to the quality of school leadership. This attention has been created by the connection that has been established between good leadership and school effectiveness and improvement, the perceived complexity of school leadership in the contemporary educational environment and a lack of succession planning for sustaining leadership in schools. These circumstances have led to considerations of how it might be possible to solicit, improve and assure the quality of school leaders according to a national coordinated approach (APPA *et al.*, 2003). To comprehend the logistics of promoting a national approach to quality of school leadership, the next section of this chapter examines the complex sharing of responsibilities for education that exists between the Commonwealth or Federal level of government and the States and Territories in Australia.

Education policy making

Under the Australian Constitution, education remains a residual constitutional power of six States and two Territories. As such, it is the responsibility of States and Territories' Ministers for Education to provide schooling for all young people between the ages of six and 15 years (with some State variations in the compulsory leaving age). Whereas States and Territories are responsible for delivering education within their borders, the Commonwealth Government is mainly concerned with the development of national policies and strategies for education. For this purpose, the Commonwealth Government provides significant funding for education and administers some national programmes.

The 'complex and interwoven' policy situation in education (Lingard and Porter, 1997, p. 3) has not constrained the development of national policies relating to Australian schooling. In recent years, national moves relevant to school improvement and more specifically the quality of school leadership have been pursued according to the rhetoric of collaboration and partnership (Lingard and Porter, 1997) between the Commonwealth Government and the States and Territories through the Ministerial Council on Education, Employment, Training and Youth Affairs (MCEETYA). This Council consists of the Commonwealth, State and Territory Ministers for Education and its responsibilities cover national coordination and policy development involving all levels and sectors of education.

In April 1999 MCEETYA signed *The Adelaide Declaration on the National Goals of Schooling for the 21st Century* for the purposes of:

- further strengthening schools as learning communities where teachers, students and their families work in partnership with business, industry and the wider community;
- enhancing the status and quality of the teaching profession;
- continuing to develop curriculum and related systems of assessment, accreditation and credentialling that promote quality and are nationally recognised and valued;
- increasing public confidence in school education through explicit and defensible standards that guide improvement in students' levels of educational achievement and through which the effectiveness, efficiency and equity of schooling can be measured and evaluated (MCEETYA, 1999).

The Adelaide Declaration represents a resolve by ministers for education to promote policies that safeguard the entitlement of all young people to high-quality schooling (Caldwell, 2002). As such, it provides an important framework within which the Commonwealth level of government in cooperation with States and Territories have conceived school improvement initiatives including the development of a national agenda for enhancing quality in school leadership. It might also be argued that the democratic purposes of schools that are evident in the national goals have significant implications for ways in which school leadership is understood and the ways in which school leaders are developed (Mulford, 2004).

One of MCEETYA's taskforces is devoted to promoting Teacher Quality and Educational Leadership for achieving the national goals of schooling. In particular, this taskforce provides advice on:

- teacher preparation and ongoing development aimed at improving the quality and standard of teaching and learning;
- the establishment of a fully integrated professional development regime involving preservice education and training, skill maintenance and upgrading, in service professional upgrading;
- professional standards for teachers and principals, both for entry to the profession and to meet the ongoing needs of students over time;
- issues around the supply and demand for teachers; and
  encouraging professional leadership in schooling (MCEETYA, 2001).

In May 2005 this taskforce evolved into the Improving Teacher and School Leadership Capacity Working Group with a brief to:

- assure the quality of teachers and teaching by ensuring that nationally consistent standards for graduate teachers are developed and embedded in requirements for teaching in all Australian schools;
- coordinate national collaboration to develop a consistent view of school leadership capabilities, and support the sharing of strategies and programmes to develop those capabilities;
- consider how the relationship between the work of the national working group and the work of Teaching Australia (a national organisation examined later in this chapter) can best be managed (MCEETYA, 2007).

Fragmentation

Notwithstanding recent progress towards cooperative activity in education policy making, traditionally in Australia, there has been a distinct absence of a national sense of collaboration in preparing, developing and supporting school leaders. Until very recently, the ways in which interest and capacity in school leadership were enhanced were dependent entirely on location; there was, in effect, no coherent and comprehensive strategy in place either across the nation as a whole or within a single system (Caldwell *et al.*, 2003). Arrangements for the preparation, development and support of school leaders continue to vary considerably from one state to another as well as between educational jurisdictions. Some states, such as Western Australia and South Australia have leadership centres. Some educational jurisdictions provide courses related to preparation for leadership, some have induction processes, some have programmes of support for specific issues (APPA *et al.*, 2003). Most school authorities across the country have now produced standards and competencies frameworks used to inform professional development of principals and in some cases for their selection and promotion as well (Dempster, 2001).

It might be argued that this fragmented approach to developing capacity in school leadership is problematic. According to current disjointed arrangements, school leadership development cannot be based on any consensus about what it means to be a school leader. There is also a danger that the learning and development of school leaders will be drawn toward system initiatives, priorities and policies, rather than concentrating on what practising professionals require of themselves and their colleagues (Dempster, 2001). In other words, there is a danger that leadership programmes will lean towards a focus on system priorities rather than a people focus that promotes professional sustenance (Dempster, 2001).

Furthermore, in his critique of school leadership development in New South Wales, Ramsey (2000, p. 87) observes that although leadership programmes are open to all who are interested, they do not discriminate sufficiently between participants on the basis of contexts, prior knowledge and skills and readiness to undertake further learning. The importance of differentiating participants according to context may be illustrated with reference to the distinctiveness of leadership in small schools, especially given their numerical significance in the Australian setting. In most states about 25 per cent of government primary schools cater for fewer than 100 students with a principal who also has a substantial teaching commitment (Clarke and Wildy, 2004).

Principals of small schools tend to be more immediately important to the day-to-day running of their schools than their counterparts in larger schools because of the different ways that small school communities relate to their leaders (Mohr, 2000). These principals, however, have to contend with a number of challenges that make leadership of small schools distinctive. In particular, they often have to contend with a 'double load' that may cause tensions between the professional concerns of teaching and the demands of management and leadership. This double load can appear all the more daunting for the relatively young and inexperienced principals often appointed to small schools.

In addition, the isolation of many small schools can present a challenge insofar as the remote location restricts opportunities for teaching principals to exchange views and practice. The tyranny of distance restricts opportunities for District Office personnel to visit remote schools and can make it difficult for principals to attend meetings and professional development activities.

Isolation can also lead to conservative communities that compound the difficulties of initiating, establishing and sustaining school improvement. Conservatism is likely to influence the culture of the school because staff in small, rural and isolated schools are often drawn from the community itself and may also be long serving. Hence, a principal might encounter existing ways of operating in the school that are shaped by unspoken rules and expectations as well as activities which evolve into a culture of solidarity and comfortable coexistence. The change process in these circumstances can be complex and slow. People who are accustomed to doing things in a certain way may need some convincing before they are willing to embrace different arrangements.

There is, in fact, a wide range of problems related to poverty and disadvantage often occurring in small, isolated communities. Many rural communities in Australia are considered to be in a state of crisis (Kilpatrick *et al.*, 2002) because economic developments have brought about a decline in traditional industries such as agriculture, mining and manufacturing. This downturn has been associated with unemployment and a declining population that pose significant challenges for building and sustaining robust school–community partnerships. Indeed, the expectation of system administrators that teaching principals will use the centrality of the school to develop productive relationships with the community may underestimate the difficulties that are likely to be encountered by rural principals in this dimension of their work.

These difficulties might be compounded further within indigenous communities necessitating approaches to school leadership that engage the community in ways that enable specific and local needs to be identified and educational provision designed accordingly (Boston, 1999).

In spite of the distinctive nature of small school leadership and the inexperience of many teaching principals on their first appointment, a recent survey (Clarke, 2003) portrays a picture of under-prepared staff being expected to improve and sustain schools with little induction and support. The survey of 119 Queensland teaching principals revealed that most of them consider their most significant professional learning to have occurred on-the-job and by trial and error rather than through formal professional development activities. Only 29 per cent of teaching principals located in isolated areas had participated in an induction process compared with 42 per cent of principals in rural locations and 35 per cent in an urban setting. Furthermore, 68 per cent of the teaching principals surveyed considered their induction to be insufficient in preparing them for the complexities of the role.

The example of principals of small schools is especially pronounced in Australia and also highlights that ideally, the preparation, development and support of school leaders should address the needs of all those in leadership roles through its connection with context, settings and relationships (DEST, 2003).

It is evident, therefore, that a national agenda for promoting the quality of school leadership in Australia represents a break with the past as well as a perception amongst many key groups in the education community that traditional arrangements are not preparing, developing and supporting school leaders adequately for the complexity of their roles.

Towards convergence

The Commonwealth Government has made a commitment to a national agenda by pursuing a strategy of facilitating national discussions and projects dealing with the process of change and the development of priorities for advancing quality teaching that also embraces considerations of school leadership. This strategy was especially apparent in the package of measures included in the Commonwealth Government's initiative, *Teachers for the 21st Century: Making the Difference* (DETYA, 2000). One key element of this initiative was the promotion of 'Quality Leaders'. Since 2001 the Commonwealth has supported professional dialogue amongst principals' peak organisations to explore issues, challenges and opportunities associated with school leadership. The Commonwealth envisaged that the debate generated would promote a commitment to the advancement of an 'excellence in school leadership' agenda incorporating the following goals:

- national commitment for continuing the discussion about a united professional voice;
- a national cooperative activity to facilitate national communication/coordination;
- a common conceptual framework for the development and support of school principals and leaders; and
- new forms of partnership, alliances, networks to progress the pivotal role of the principal in improving student outcomes (Australian College of Education, 2001).

The achievement of these goals has been met to some extent through two important initiatives in the last five years. First, through the projects of The Australian Principals Associations Professional Development Council (APAPDC). Second, through the recent establishment of a National Institute for Quality Teaching and School Leadership (NIQTSL).

In regard to the first initiative, the national peak organisation, APAPDC has been funded by the Commonwealth to provide professional development for school leaders. This body is driven inevitably by government priorities and the availability of funding for this purpose. Nevertheless, the APAPDC brings together principals' associations across all education sectors and represents a powerful voice in the advocacy of school leadership throughout the nation. Certainly, the conversation about school leadership development that has been generated within this forum, as well as some promising approaches and practices resulting from the initiative, demonstrate the value of collaborative activity at the national level.

An especially promising approach in the national conversation about school leadership has been the *Leaders Lead* project. The current APAPDC website (APAPDC, 2007) describes how the first phase of this project, *Leaders Lead: Strengthening the Australian School*, began in 2001–2002 and comprised a programme of National and State/Territory seminars and workshops that focused on what it means to be a leader and, in particular, on what it means to be a school leader. This process brought together school leaders from throughout Australia as well as from across the sectors and provided an opportunity to tackle the 'big picture' issues that individual education systems and sectors are thought to neglect. The quality leadership discourse, therefore, began to move beyond familiarisation with operational issues that are often preeminent to a consideration of the full complexity of school leadership (APAPDC, 2002). This is evidence, perhaps, for the view that leadership development programmes require a balance between a system focused approach of promoting functional knowledge and skills to carry out everyday tasks and a people focused approach that draws on individual and collective experience of people in their day-to-day experience in education (Dempster, 2001).

This first phase of the *Leaders Lead* project, then, was an effective exercise in harnessing the collective voice of school leaders from many different contexts and began a process of conceptualising a nationally agreed view of what contemporary school leadership entails. A particular coherence emerged around school leadership themes such as developing a shared vision for the school, making hard decisions, clarity and courage in initiating, enabling and sustaining change and capacity to sustain the role (APAPDC, 2002, p. 3).

These emerging themes germane to quality leadership have been integrated into the APAPDC Educational Leadership Model developed in response to the issues and concerns generated in the first phase of the project. The model identifies four domains of educational leadership (curriculum and pedagogy, organisational leadership and management, political and community leadership, cultural and wise leadership) and associated competencies and was used as the framework for the focus of the second phase of the project *Succession Planning: Building Leadership Capacity for Australian Schools*.

The model, it is argued (APAPDC, 2002), represents a change in thinking about educational leadership in two main respects. First, the model is purported to sharpen the focus from the individual school principal to what schools as a whole need from educational leadership. In doing so, there is an implicit recognition that leadership development should not be preoccupied with positional authority, 'opening the way for the principalship to be redefined and restructured' (APAPDC, 2002. p. 1). Second, the model positions students' learning and development as the main object of school leadership. Hence, the model reflects a shift from a managerial understanding of leadership to one that is more visionary and collegial and which focuses on the centrality of student learning. As such, it has potential to provide a basis to develop programmes of professional learning that engage with the complex issues integral to the experience and practice of contemporary school leadership; the accreditation process for aspiring leaders designed by the Queensland Association of Primary Principals (QASSP) is a case in point.

This potential has also been partly evident in the second phase of the *Leaders Lead* project conducted in 2002–2003, *Succession Planning: Building Leadership Capacity for Australian Schools* which is also described on the APAPDC website (APAPDC, 2007). The key aims of this phase of the project were to recognise the importance of maintaining quality leadership in schools as portrayed in the APAPDC model, in particular by developing a theoretical framework for succession planning and a practical tool that can support principals and leadership teams in building leadership capacity in their schools. To this end, a professional development resource, *Learn, Lead, Succeed*, has been developed for the use of principals and leadership teams in their schools, as well as by individual aspirant leaders. It is primarily aimed at preparing aspiring educational leaders for positional leadership in schools, though it is also claimed to be as applicable for the development of teacher leaders in schools.

The framework consists of five propositions:

1 Leadership starts from within.
2 Leadership is about influencing others.
3 Leadership develops a rich learning environment.
4 Leadership builds professionalism and management capability.
5 Leadership inspires leadership actions and aspirations in others (APAPDC, 2007).

These propositions are designed to facilitate a deeper knowledge of the components of sustainable school leadership, how it is grounded in understandings of wellbeing, and how it can be developed at individual and organisational levels; a deeper knowledge and understanding about the nexus between the professional, interpersonal and personal demands of leadership and the professional and personal capabilities that are required to ensure that quality, widespread and sustainable leadership is integral to the school culture (APAPDC, 2007). *Learn, Lead, Succeed* has been disseminated to a large number of school leaders throughout Australia.

The outcomes of this national conversation about school leadership initiated by the Commonwealth through the APAPDC have been fruitful. The opportunity for school leaders from across the country and across contexts to converge in this way has resulted in information and insights being shared, common issues debated, ideas tested, and understandings of what is meant by school leadership developed. In doing so, this experience has affirmed the high level of cooperation that exists among professional associations and has attested to the value of learning derived from individual and collective experience of practising leaders. A significant contribution has been made, therefore, to developing a coordinated national approach to soliciting, improving and assuring the quality of school leaders, as well as identifying some key elements of effective leadership development provision.

The provision of coordinated and effective leadership development is a core focus of another significant national initiative for supporting quality in school leadership, namely, the Commonwealth Government's establishment of a National Institute for Quality Teaching and School Leadership (NIQTSL). The formation of NIQTSL represented the culmination of a concerted effort by principals' associations to promote a national approach to building the capacity of school leadership and the Commonwealth provided an initial $10 million to set up the Institute that was launched officially in June 2004. NIQTSL was located in the national capital Canberra on the campus of the Australian National University, a site that promotes the Institute's intention to forge close links with the university sector.

According to the then Commonwealth Minister for Education, Science and Training, Brendan Nelson, NIQTSL would have four key functions (Nelson, 2004). First, the development and implementation of nationally agreed teaching and leadership standards for accreditation purposes. The second key function would be the facilitation and coordination of professional development courses as well as providing a quality assurance role for these courses. Third, NIQTSL would initiate and draw on research that supports the core role of providing intellectual leadership for and on behalf of the profession and, fourth, NIQTSL would provide teachers and school leaders with a national voice and an ability to influence the national education professional agenda.

In spite of NIQTSL's dependence on Commonwealth funding, Nelson argued (Nelson, 2004) that the governance structure would ensure that the Institute will be managed by the profession for the profession. There were to be 15 voting members of the interim board, of whom 11 members would be drawn from the profession. The other four were to consist of the Chair, a nomination from each of the Australian Council of Deans of Education, the Australian Forum of Teacher Registration and Accreditation Authorities, and an educational expert nominated by the Australian Government Minister for Education.

Since the launch of the interim NIQTSL in June 2004, the organisation has been established as a permanent body, Teaching Australia – the Australian Institute for Teaching and School Leadership (TA). A further $20 million has also been received from the Commonwealth Government in order to make progress with its key initiatives. The most pertinent of these initiatives to this chapter has been the selection of the Australian Council for Education Research (ACER) to provide TA with advice on standards for leadership in schools. This was to be achieved by surveying and analysing standards employed internationally; describing and analysing standards for school leadership in each Australian jurisdiction; focusing on national approaches to a set of Australian standards for leadership in schools; describing processes for the certification of school leaders who attain these standards; and discussing the impact of standards and their application on leadership practices (Australian Council of Educational Research, 2005). A process of consultation has already elicited the views of the profession on the options for a national approach to the development of standards and professional certification for prospective and established principals. It seems, however, that the process has generated some disquiet about TA's intentions regarding standards for school leaders (Teaching Australia, 2007) and raised more questions than it has answered; for example, what is meant by school leaders? What purpose would professional standards for school leaders serve? What is the value of a national system and how should standards be developed? (Teaching Australia, 2007). This hesitant response from the profession as a whole has meant that, as yet, no decision has been made about the direction a national system of standards should take.

Although a set of Australian standards for leadership in schools is still to be articulated, the management-consulting firm Hay Group, in conjunction with the University of Melbourne, were commissioned in 2005 to design and deliver a national leadership programme entitled *Leading Australia's Schools*. The national scope of this programme was a first for Australia. The programme was designed and developed in collaboration with national principals' associations and launched in 2006 with the broad aim of improving the knowledge and leadership skills of Australia's school leaders into the future. For this purpose, the programme has catered for two cohorts a year of 40 early-career principals selected from all sectors, levels of schooling, states and territories.

The three-month course consists of pre-work, a five-day residential workshop, a school-based challenge project followed by a two-day residential recall session and the development of an ongoing learning community. The course is also guided by five themes:

1 The nature and challenge of leadership.
2 Myself as leader.
3 Leading a learning organization.

4 Myself as a leader in education.
5 Myself as a leader of the future (Teaching Australia, 2007).

At this juncture, it is still relatively early to assess the impact and sustainability of TA's attempts to promote a national coordinated approach to school leadership for preparing, developing and supporting school leaders. A particular challenge for TA will be to deal with the tension inherent in presenting itself as an independent body managed by and for the profession on the one hand and being funded by the Commonwealth Government on the other (Australian College of Educators, 2004). This is certainly the view of the Australian Education Union (AEU), which sees the key functions of TA being determined by the Commonwealth Government rather than the profession itself (Byrne, 2006). It is vital that in promoting quality school leadership the focus should be placed on school leaders' needs rather than being distorted by the sometimes capricious agenda of politicians. If the profession perceives TA as a conduit for Commonwealth Government policy, it is unlikely to have a significant impact on building capacity in school leadership.

Another challenge for TA will be to demonstrate that, in its attempt to converge approaches to leadership preparation, development and support, it also complements existing arrangements in other educational jurisdictions throughout the country. The Australian College of Educators has expressed this requirement well in its comment that 'NIQTSL [now Teaching Australia] must be able to do what no other agency is doing and in ways that break new ground, foster new approaches and promote new synergies' (Australian College of Educators, 2004). A corollary of this last exhortation is that TA will need to provide practising and aspiring school leaders with the kind of leadership development they deserve. In other words, this connotes promoting professional learning and development opportunities that align with the experiences and challenges of modern school leadership. From this perspective, the results of the 2007 evaluation of the *Leading Australia's Schools* programme are likely to be instructive.

Conclusion

This chapter has outlined some of the key issues facing school leadership in Australia and described recent progress towards a national coherent approach for building capacity amongst school leaders. The process has involved a discernible shift from a customary dependence on fragmented practices in the preparation, development and support of school leaders towards a convergence of provision. This trend has been manifested in the creation of policy and organisational frameworks that have the potential to promote a collaborative approach to quality in school leadership. This is an accomplishment in itself within such a vast country that also has a complex federal system of government. Moreover, it is apparent that there is an emerging consensus within the teaching profession about what it means to be a school leader in the contemporary educational environment and what this understanding engenders for the development of school leaders.

As Fran Hinton, the Chief Executive of the then nascent NIQTSL (now Teaching Australia) observed (2005, p. 16), this is an exciting time for school leadership in Australia. First, an inaugural national body has been established with the explicit purpose of advancing school leadership. Second, a dialogue has been galvanised across the professional community that seems to be sharpening understandings of the complexity of school leadership, the knowledge, skills and dispositions required to perform the role effectively and the ways in which school leaders can best be assisted to develop the kind of leadership capacity that contemporary schools increasingly demand. On a more cautionary note, however, Bush and Jackson (2002, p. 427) have pointed out that speculation about the future of school leadership development is a risky venture at the best of times as arrangements tend to be so varied. In Australia, this is particularly the case because of the greater potential for disparate approaches to building the capacity of school leaders than might be the case in smaller countries that do not have such complex environments informing education policy. It is also fair to say that the national agenda for quality in school leadership has reached a critical juncture and has some way to go before its true shape becomes clearly defined.

References

Allen Consulting Group (2004) National Institute for Quality Teaching and School Leadership Implementation Study Report. Report to the Australian Government Department of Education, Science and Training. Available online at http://www.allenconsult.com.au/ (accessed 15 February 2005).

APAPDC (2002) Leaders Lead. Succession Planning: Building Leadership Capacity, Discussion Paper. Available online at www.apapdc.edu.au/ (accessed 19 February 2005).

APAPDC (2007) The Australian Principals Associations Professional Development Council. Available online at www.apapdc.edu.au/ (accessed 21 January 2005).

Australian College of Education (2001) Excellence in School Leadership. Background Paper. Developed by ACE for the Australian Secondary Principals Association. Available online at www.austcolled.com.au (accessed 1 February 2005).

Australian College of Educators (2004) Extracts From the ACE Response to the Issues Paper, Establishing the National Institute for Quality Teaching and School Leadership. Available online at www.austcolled.com.au (accessed 1 February 2005).

Australian Council of Educational Research (2005) Available online at http://www.acer.edu.au/ (accessed 19 February 2005).

Australian Primary Principals Association (APPA), Australian Secondary Principals Association (ASPA), Association of Principals of Catholic Secondary Schools of Australia (APCSSA), Association of Heads of Independent Schools of Australia

(AHISA) (2003) An Essential Investment Proposal for a National Institute for School Leadership, An In Principle Position. Available online at www.aspa.asn.au (accessed 8 January 2005).

Australian Principals Associations Professional Development Council (2004) Leaders Lead. Succession Planning; Building Leadership Capacity. Discussion Paper. Available online at www.apapdc.edu.au/ (accessed 19 February 2005).

Boston, K. (1999) Culture and power, *Unicorn*, 27(1), 16–23.

Bush, T. and Jackson, D. (2002) A preparation for school leadership: international perspectives, *Educational Management and Administration*, 30(4), 417–429.

Byrne, P. (2006) How Howard's national agenda is affecting education. *The Guardian*. Issue no 1299. Available online at www.cpa.org.au/guardian/gdn2006.html (accessed 18 January 2007).

Caldwell, B. (2002) A Strategic Approach to School Culture in an Era of Transformation in Learning. Paper presented as an Invited Keynote Address at the Principal and School Development Program, 'Developing a Positive School Culture', Geelong, March 3 and 20.

Caldwell, B., Calnin, T. and Cahill, W.P. (2003) Mission possible? An international analysis of headteacher/principal training, in Bennett, N., Crawford, M. and Cartwright, M. (eds) *Effective Educational Leadership* (pp. 111–130), London: Open University.

Christie, P. and Lingard, B. (2001) Capturing Complexity in Educational Leadership. Paper presented at the American Educational Research Association, April 10–14, Seattle.

Clarke, S.R.P. (2003) Mastering the art of extreme juggling: an examination of the contemporary role of the Queensland teaching principal, Unpublished report on the Queensland Association of State School Principals (QASSP) teaching principals' survey.

Clarke, S. and Wildy, H. (2004) Context counts: viewing small school leadership from the inside out, *Journal of Educational Administration*, 42(5), 555–572.

Crowther, F. (2002) Big change question: Is the role of the principal in creating school improvement over-rated? Journal of Educational Change, (3), 167–173.

d'Arbon, T., Duignan, P. and Duncan, D. (2002) Planning for future leadership of schools: An Australian study, *Journal of Educational Administration*, 40(5) 468–485.

Dempster, N. (2001) The Professional Development of School Principals: A Fine Balance, Professorial Lecture, Griffith Public Lecture Series, 24 May, Griffith University.

Dempster, N., Freakley, M. and Parry, L. (2001) The ethical climate of public schooling under new public management, *International Journal of Leadership in Education*, 4(1), 1–12.

DEST (Department of Education, Science and Training) (2003) Australia's Teachers: Australia's Future. Advancing Innovation, Science, Technology and Mathematics Main Report, Canberra: Commonwealth of Australia.

DETYA (Department of Education, Training and Youth Affairs) (2000) Teachers for the 21st Century: Making the Difference. Available online at www.detya.gov.au/schools/publicat.htm (accessed 8 January 2005).

Duignan, P.A. (1997) *The Dance of Leadership: At the Still Point of the Turning World*, Australian Council for Educational Administration.

Hinton, F. (2005) School leadership: back on track? *EQ Australia*, (1), 15–18. Available online at www.curriculum.edu.au/eq (accessed 10 June 2005).
Kilpatrick, S., Johns, S., Mulford, B., Falk, I. and Prescott, L. (2002) More than an Education: leadership for rural school-community partnerships, a report for the Rural Industries Research and Development Corporation, Canberra: Canprint.
Lingard, B. and Porter, P. (1997) Australian schooling: the state of national developments, in Lingard, B. and Porter, P. (eds) *A National Approach to Schooling in Australia? Essays on the Development of National Policies in Schools Education* (pp. 1–25), Canberra: The Australian College of Education.
MCEETYA (Ministerial Council on Education, Employment, Training and Youth Affairs) (1999) *The Adelaide Declaration on the National Goals of Schooling for the 21st Century*, Melbourne: MCEETYA.
MCEETYA (Ministerial Council on Education, Employment, Training and Youth Affairs) (2001) Teacher Quality and Educational Leadership Taskforce. Available online at www.mceetya.edu.au/taskfrce/task2212.htm (accessed 8 January 2005).
MCEETYA (Ministerial Council on Education, Employment, Training and Youth Affairs) (2007) Improving Teacher and School Leadership Capacity Working Group. Available online at http://www.mceetya.edu.au/mceetya/default.asp?id=15810 (accessed on 13 March 2007).
Mohr, N. (2000) Small schools are not large schools. Potential pitfalls and implications for leadership, in Ayers, W., Klonsky, M. and Lyon, G. (eds) *A Simple Justice: the Challenge of Small Schools*, New York: Teachers College Press.
Mulford, B. (2004) Congruence between the democratic purposes of schools and school principal training in Australia, *Journal of Educational Administration*, 42(6), 625–639.
Nelson, B. (2004) Strengthening the Teaching Profession: Launch of the National Institute for the Quality of Teaching and School Leadership, Australian Government Minister for Education, Science and Training Media Release. 3 June. Available online at www.dest.gov.au/Ministers/Media/Nelson/2004/06/n7210 30604.asp (accessed 9 July 2005).
O'Brien, J., Murphy, D. and Draper, J. (2003) *School Leadership. Policy and Practice in Education (Number 9)*, Edinburgh: Dunedin Academic Press.
Preston, B. (2005) Teacher supply and demand to 2005: projections and issues. A report commissioned by the Australian Council of Deans of Education, Canberra. Available online at acde.edu.au/publications.htm (accessed 16 March 2005).
The Queensland Association of State School Principals Accreditation Program. Available at www.qassp.org.au/
Ramsey, G. (2000) Quality Matters. Revitalising Teaching: Critical Times, Critical Choices. Report of the Review of Teacher Education, New South Wales, NSW Department of Education and Training.
Scott, G. (2003) Learning principals. Report prepared for the State of NSW, Department of Education and Training Professional Support and Curriculum Directorate, Sydney: Quality Development Unit for the NSW Department of Education and Training.
Su, Z., Gamage, D. and Mininberg, E. (2003) Professional preparation and development of school leaders in Australia and the USA, *International Education Journal*, 4(1), 42–59.
Teaching Australia (2006) Forum on School Leadership Standards. Available online

at www.teachingaustralia.edu.au/ta/go/home/projects/pastinitiatives (accessed 18 January 2007).

Teaching Australia (2007) Leading Australia's Schools. Available online at www.teachingaustralia.edu.au/ta/go/home/projects/leadausschools (accessed 8 February 2007).

Wildy, H. and Louden, W. (2000) School restructuring and the dilemmas of principals' work, *Educational Management and Administration*, 28(3), 173–184.

Chapter 10

Capability in the leadership of teaching and learning in New Zealand

The validity and utility of a self-assessment tool

Viviane M. J. Robinson, S. Earl Irving, David Eddy and Deirdre M. Le Fevre

Introduction

Any programme of principal induction must find ways to respond to the very different school contexts to which principals are appointed and to their diverse educational and professional backgrounds. New Zealand's national principal induction programme uses a self-assessment of each principal's capability in the leadership of teaching and learning as one of its main sources of information about the very different learning needs of newly appointed principals. This chapter reports the results of a study of the reliability, validity and utility of the revised version of this self-assessment tool, known as SALTAL-II (Self-Assessment of Teaching and Learning). Scale analyses of the scores of principals confirmed the reliability of the tool. Tests of its validity revealed that in 70 per cent of cases the tool correctly identified those principals who were independently assessed by their mentors as having 'low', 'moderate' or 'high' development needs. Analysis of the principals' professional learning plans showed that the principals' priority goals were strongly aligned with their scores on the SALTAL items. Overall, the results indicate that SALTAL provides trustworthy assessments of a diverse group of principals that are useful to the principals themselves, their mentors and the programme team.

In the late 1980s New Zealand undertook an ambitious and comprehensive reform of educational administration as part of a wide-ranging public service restructuring (Fiske and Ladd, 2000). One of its main thrusts was the devolution of many previously centralized governance and management functions to the level of the local school. The resulting 1989 Education Act prescribed that every New Zealand school was to be managed by its own Board of Trustees, largely comprising elected parent representatives, one of whom was to serve as chairperson (New Zealand Government, 1989). The powers of these Boards were considerable and included the appointment and appraisal of the school's principal. At the same time, the national Department of Education was restructured as a policy making and ministerial advisory agency, and regional Education Boards were dismantled.

The 1989 education reforms, commonly known as *Tomorrow's Schools*, set a massive learning agenda for principals (Department of Education, 1989). They and their Boards were now responsible for the financial, property, human resource and health and safety aspects of their schools as well as the usual educational aspects. Principals had to learn to manage these new responsibilities in an environment where prior support systems had been disrupted and where they were accountable to largely unsupervised and inexperienced lay boards (Robinson *et al.*, 2003). Predictably enough, for the first ten years of the reforms, Boards and principals concentrated on ensuring they complied with their new management responsibilities (Wylie, 1997, 1999). Their success in these endeavours was regularly and publicly monitored by the Education Review Office (ERO), New Zealand's equivalent of OFSTED in the United Kingdom.

After ten years of focus on school management, two factors drew attention back to the state of teaching and learning in New Zealand schools. First, the ERO published a series of reports highly critical of the quality of education in several regions of the country (Education Review Office, 1996; 1997; 1998). Second, international comparisons of the achievement of New Zealand students in reading literacy (Organisation for Economic Cooperation and Development, 2001) and mathematics (Scheerens *et al.*, 1989) showed that while average achievement was high, the range of achievement was very large and lower achievement was associated with the fastest growing population groups.

One outcome of the ensuing debate was new policy initiatives designed to focus school leaders on the core business of teaching and learning. This was the policy context in which the Minister of Education announced a series of initiatives to support the development of New Zealand principals. Better leadership through more systematic professional development and support was seen as one path to improved student achievement. The 2001 budget foreshadowed expenditure of $NZ 27.4 million over the following four years for an induction programme for first-time principals and the continued professional development of experienced principals, including the provision of laptop computers and web-based resources. As a result, a significant proportion of this money was targeted for the First-time Principals Programme (for newly appointed principals) and a proposed principal professional development centre (for experienced principals).

In common with Australia and Sweden, but unlike many other countries, there are no mandatory programmes of principal preparation in New Zealand (Bush and Jackson, 2002). The minimum requirement for principalship in New Zealand is teacher registration, whereas in several states in the United States and parts of Canada (for example, British Columbia), it is an appropriate master's degree. Given the absence of specific preparation for principalship in New Zealand, the government's priority was to establish a single national induction programme open to all first-time principals appointed to any type of school. The contestable contract to inaugurate and deliver the national induction programme was granted by the Ministry of Education to The University of Auckland Principals Centre in late 2001, and it has been offered every year since 2002.

The diversity of New Zealand's schools and principals

A significant challenge in delivering an induction programme which meets the learning needs of New Zealand's first-time principals is the extraordinary diversity of the group. The diversity manifests itself along numerous dimensions including school sector, school type, language of instruction and prior experience and qualification of the principals themselves.

The programme serves principals from both Mâori medium (kura) and English medium schools. A second dimension of diversity is the inclusion of principals from all sector groups. Approximately 170 first-time principals are appointed by Boards of Trustees to New Zealand schools each year and while about 70 per cent of them are from primary schools, they also include new principals from secondary, intermediate, middle and composite schools. In addition, the programme includes principals from independent (private) schools and from state-funded special character (integrated) schools. In each cohort there will be teaching principals from schools with less than 20 students, and principals of large secondary schools with more than 1,500 students.

Compounding the diversity of school context is the wide variety of principal background. In the 2006 cohort, for example, while 36 per cent of first-time principals had over 20 years of teaching experience, 20 per cent had less than ten years. Nearly 30 per cent of these new principals had no prior senior management experience and such principals were predominantly appointed to schools with less than 50 students. There is a similarly wide range of formal qualifications in this cohort. The largest group have a bachelor's degree as their highest qualification (46 per cent), the second largest group have an undergraduate diploma (25 per cent), and only 9 per cent have a master's degree.

Responding to the diversity of first-time principals[1]

The New Zealand government wanted a single induction programme as part of its commitment to a more integrated teaching profession. At the same time, they recognized that sub-groups within each cohort would have very different learning needs. The project team delivering the First-time Principals Programme were required, therefore, to provide as much individualized and flexible provision as possible within the constraints of a single overarching programme. In the next section we describe how we have responded to this diversity by designing a programme which presents key ideas to the whole cohort while maximizing individualized, context-specific learning opportunities.

The New Zealand induction programme is voluntary and participants are not formally assessed or recognized through the award of a qualification. Despite this, almost all first-time principals enrol in and complete the programme. By mid-2007, approximately 1,050 new principals representing over one-third of New Zealand's 2,693 schools will have participated in the programme. Since the focus of the First-time Principals Programme is on their leadership of teaching and learning, participants receive additional targeted support in meeting their substantial management and compliance responsibilities from regional Leadership and Management advisors and the regional offices of the Ministry of Education.

The induction programme is currently structured and delivered as an 18-month programme comprising four interrelated components: residential courses, mentoring, online learning, research and evaluation. The residential courses pose a particular challenge because they are attended by the entire cohort at once and there is limited scope for individualized instruction within what is essentially a conference context. The project team has progressively shifted the balance between plenary sessions, option sessions and sector-based workshops so that principals can have more choice about what they attend. A separate strand for principals of Mâori medium schools (Kura) is included in the residential programme through a series of workshops facilitated in Te Reo (Mâori language).

The mentoring component currently consists of three half-day school-based visits by the mentor to the principal's school, two half-day professional learning group activities, two half-day shadowing experiences, email and telephone support. The national team of approximately 50 mentors are regionally distributed and are current school principals. They are selected for their school leadership experience and success, paid for their professional services and evaluated on the basis of confidential principal feedback. Highly experienced Mâori principals mentor new Kura principals.

The mentors attend three training days during the year to prepare them for the mentoring activities and to develop their mentoring skills. They also attend one residential course so that they have the opportunity to hear the keynote addresses, facilitate workshops, provide individual assistance, and build supportive relationships with the new principals. While the mentoring programme has some common tasks and structure, such as the completion of a professional learning plan (PLP), the structure enables each pair to determine priority learning needs and how best to address them.

A dedicated password protected website called First-time Principals Online (FPO) hosted by the Ministry of Education provides further opportunities for principals to tailor their induction programme. The site provides selected resources, discussion forums, sector-based learning communities and dialogue opportunities with some keynote presenters. The First-time Principals Programme project team has developed online curriculum modules to enhance the delivery of the induction programme. Participants also have access to multiple electronic resources in the Ministry of Education school leaders' website LeadSpace. In addition, the project has its own website which, as well as providing general information about the programme, includes web-based enrolment, selected residential courses presentations, other useful resources, and the self-evaluation tool that is the subject of this chapter.

The fourth component of the induction programme is formative evaluation and research. The formative evaluation strand involves detailed participant evaluation of every residential course, and of the mentoring and online learning to identify which components of the programme are working for which groups of principals. Apart from the first year of the programme, every residential course has attracted median levels of satisfaction ranging from 'high' to 'very high'. The overall satisfaction ratings are routinely disaggregated by school type to check the extent to which the residential courses have catered for principals from the different sector groups.

While the formative evaluation has been an invaluable source of information about how participants experience the programme, the project team has lacked solid evidence about the learning needs of individual principals and principal subgroups. It has relied on participant-appointed representatives at each residential course to indicate what they think is important for each school type and sub-group, and on widely shared assumptions about what is needed by principals from each sector. This strategy does not attend to the individual, and does not help each principal reflect systematically about their own learning needs. For these reasons we have developed a self-evaluation tool, which we now call the Self-Assessment of Leadership of Teaching and Learning (SALTAL), to assess principals' current capability as leaders of teaching and learning.

After administering SALTAL to two cohorts of first-time principals, we completed a study of its factor structure, reliability and validity (Robinson *et al.*, 2006). Factor analysis showed that SALTAL incorporated four leadership dimensions (Table 10.1) rather than the six that were used to develop the original instrument. While the four dimensions had acceptable levels of reliability, the validity of SALTAL, as judged by its ability to predict an independent measure of each principal's learning needs, was not strong enough (Robinson *et al.*, 2006). The independent measure had been obtained from each principal's mentor, and we believed that the modest validity was mostly attributable to the procedures we had used to gain their judgments about the principals' learning needs.

In this chapter, we report our second study of the properties of the revised tool, now called SALTAL-II, in which we focus on the tool's reliability,

Table 10.1 The four dimensions of leadership in SALTAL-II

Leadership dimension	*Definition*
1 Knowledge and Skills for Leading Teaching and Learning	Has a deep understanding of the relationship between teaching, learning and leadership
2 Commitment to Ensuring Positive Learning Outcomes for all Students	Focuses on and prioritises the core business of student learning
3 Collaborative Leadership	Works through and with others to effectively lead and manage the operations of the school, informed by the impact of all decisions on students' learning and needs
4 Ethical Leadership	Models personal and professional integrity

validity and utility. The validity study incorporated improved procedures for gaining mentors' judgements of principals' learning needs, and the study of the tool's utility focussed on how it was used to formulate the professional learning plan that guided each principal's development over the 18-month induction period.

We begin with a brief description of SALTAL's purposes and development (for a more detailed description, see Robinson *et al.*, 2006), and then outline the research methods and findings.

The development of SALTAL

SALTAL has been designed over a period of five years to give principals, their mentors and the project team an early indication of the extent to which each new principal meets criteria of good practice in their leadership of teaching and learning (Council of Chief State School Officers, 1996; Hay Group, 2001). The focus is on educational leadership (i.e. the leadership of teaching and learning) because the development of such leadership is the overarching strategic objective of the First-time Principals Programme. Within this strategic objective, SALTAL serves several purposes.

First, it provides clear benchmarks to new principals about what is meant by good practice in leading teaching and learning. The four dimensions of leadership in the current version of SALTAL and the 24 leadership items, are provided in Table 10.2. Each item is accompanied by between two and four examples to illustrate how a principal might demonstrate the particular capacity assessed by the item.

The second purpose of SALTAL is to provide each principal with an opportunity for systematic reflection about how well they currently lead teaching and learning. The completed self-assessment provides the basis for principals to write an individual Professional Learning Plan (PLP), in discussion with their mentor.

Table 10.2 Leadership dimensions and items for SALTAL-II

Leadership dimension	*Item wording: To what degree do you…*
Knowledge and Skills for Leading Teaching and Learning	1 Have a sound and up-to-date knowledge of effective teaching and learning. 2 Possess a thorough understanding of the New Zealand Curriculum Framework. 3 Demonstrate *a good* understanding of key concepts used in the current assessment debates. 4 Use ongoing school-wide assessment to improve teaching and learning. 5 Lead Information Technology (IT) developments in ways that enhance teaching and learning. 6 See the development of a school culture focused on learning as a critical factor in creating an effective school.
Commitment to Positive Learning Outcomes for All Students	7 Value the whole student, and use their cultural background to promote engagement with the curriculum. 8 Believe that, for all students, learning can be positively enhanced through the principal's influence on the quality of teaching. 9 Demonstrate a strong sense of personal responsibility and accountability for the learning outcomes of all students. 10 Create opportunities for staff to innovate and experiment with strategies to enhance student learning. 11 Provide, or ensure, feedback to teaching staff on teaching effectiveness and student learning.
Collaborative Leadership	12 Work effectively with the Board of Trustees (BOT) to develop and achieve important school-wide goals. 13 Welcome feedback and challenge. 14 Align school and local community objectives and cultures to support positive outcomes for students. 15 Allocate resources, including funds and time, to enhance effective teaching. 16 Ensure parents and caregivers are well informed about the school and the ways they can support student learning processes. 17 Facilitate the creation of a collaborative and ambitious vision for the school that is shared by students, staff, parents, the board of trustees and the community. 18 Plan and adopt a key set of strategies to ensure the ongoing professional development of the staff. 19 Develop and maintain systems to support the effective operation of the school, based on good management practice and in compliance with all statutory reporting requirements. 20 Facilitate change by using sound problem solving skills.
Ethical Leadership	21 Lead with integrity. 22 Effectively manage your own workload. 23 Make and explain the reasons for difficult decisions. 24 Hold others accountable, where appropriate.

The third purpose of SALTAL is to provide information to the project team about the development needs of the entire cohort. Finally, the anonymous aggregated information is reported to the Ministry of Education, so that officials and policy makers can be better informed about the level and distribution of development needs among principals and, hence, about the level of support they require. Although the tool serves these multiple purposes, it is important to stress that its primary purpose is to provide first-time principals themselves with the opportunity to reflect on the match between their current capabilities and those that are required to become excellent leaders of teaching and learning.

The limitations of self-assessment

Ideally, the measurement of learning needs is accomplished through a paper-and-pencil test or a performance assessment. The former was ruled out by the perceived incompatibility of administering a test and establishing the level of trust required to run a successful development programme. The latter was ruled out by the expense involved. It is acknowledged that there are problems with asking principals who are new to their role to self-evaluate their development needs. One could legitimately ask whether new principals know enough to know what they do not know. This is particularly the case for New Zealand principals of small rural primary schools, where so many appointees have no prior senior management experience.

Two strategies were used to mitigate the problem of using a self-evaluation. First, every questionnaire item was illustrated with between two and four examples of good practice. The examples made the meaning of the items and their underlying competencies more concrete by signalling the type of leadership knowledge and skill that met the requirements of the item and, thereby, of the competency. For example, the somewhat abstract indicator 'leads with integrity' was made more concrete by the inclusion under the item of the following illustrative examples: 'has a reputation for fairness and integrity' and 'can explain the rationale for decisions based on ethical principles'.

The second mitigating strategy was an explicit instruction about the standard we wanted the respondents to use in judging their current capability. We explained that the items and examples described things we would expect an experienced principal to demonstrate consistently, and that there was no expectation that respondents would currently demonstrate these competencies at a high level. Furthermore, the instructions stated that the items and examples signalled the types of practice that we hoped they would develop during and following the induction programme. In summary, the questionnaire provided concrete examples of leadership practices that met the competencies to a high level, and this was the benchmark we asked our respondents to use in their self-evaluation.

Methods

This section outlines the data collection and analysis procedures used for establishing the reliability, validity and utility of SALTAL-II.

Procedures for gaining principals' self-assessment

The SALTAL-II data used in these analyses were obtained from the 2006 cohort. The forms were completed independently by 121 principals, 81 per cent of whom were from primary schools, 11 per cent from secondary schools, 3 per cent from composite schools (from Years 1 to 15), and 4 per cent from special education schools. For each of the 24 items, principals were asked to rate on a five-point scale the degree to which they 'currently demonstrated the skills or knowledge described by the item'. The scale comprised: five (high degree), four (considerable degree), three (moderate degree), two (limited degree), and one (very limited degree).

The 2006 cohort was the first cohort to complete SALTAL online. Since the software would only allow a principal to enter one of the five rating values, and would not allow the principal to sign off until a response had been made to all items, there were no missing data. Information about the principals and their schools was obtained from the forms they completed when they enrolled in the programme. Ethical protocols regarding the confidentiality of individual information supplied to the project team as part of the induction programme were complied with throughout the study.

Procedures for gaining an independent assessment of learning needs

In order to establish whether SALTAL-II could accurately identify the learning needs of principals, we obtained an independent measure of the capability of each first-time principal from their mentor. Following the first mentor visit, during which the principal's self-ratings on SALTAL-II were discussed and a professional learning plan was drafted, the mentors were asked to categorize each of their principals as demonstrating either high, moderate, or low development needs depending on their capability in the leadership of teaching and learning.

The mentors were provided with the following definitions of each category: a high needs principal was one whose 'leadership skills, knowledge, and abilities require considerable development to meet the demands of the context they are working in'. This definition made clear that high needs was determined on the basis of the match between context and current capability. The same principal might not be in the high needs group if appointed to a different school context. A low needs principal was one who has 'the leadership skills, knowledge and abilities which give you confidence that as they continue to grow into their role as principal, there will be minimal need for your support and guidance'. Principals in the moderate needs category would 'develop new strengths capabilities and confidence in their own ability, so the need for your support and guidance will reduce'. The mentors were provided with a sheet with the names of each of the principals they worked with and asked to place each into one of these three categories. Mentors worked with, and therefore rated, up to five different principals. Complete mentor ratings were obtained for 90 of the 121 principals who completed SALTAL-II.

Information on how the completed SALTAL-II was used to formulate the principals' professional learning plan (PLP) was obtained from an analysis of the match between the goals that were included in each plan and the principals' SALTAL-II scores.

Data analysis procedures

The reliability of the SALTAL-II tool was assessed through scale analysis, which involved statistically examining the response patterns of the principals to determine whether the items that were grouped under a given dimension actually belonged together. If reliability is sufficiently high, the items can be summed to create one score for each dimension.

The validity of SALTAL-II was assessed through a multiple discriminant analysis to test the extent to which the SALTAL-II scores correctly identified the group in which the mentors had classified their principals. The SALTAL-II scores and mentor classifications were used to determine a formula that maximizes the difference between and minimizes differences within each criterion group. Some mismatch between the mentors' classifications and the SALTAL-II scores is to be expected.

Research findings

We turn now to the findings relevant to the reliability, validity and utility of SALTAL-II. Analysis of the reliability of each dimension showed that the items associated with Factor 2 (Commitment to Ensuring Positive Learning Outcomes), Factor 3 (Collaborative Leadership) and Factor 4 (Ethical Leadership) have strong internal consistency (0.86, 0.88 and 0.83, respectively), all exceeding Nunnally's (1978) criterion of 0.8. The remaining factor (Factor 1, Knowledge and Skills for Leading Teaching and Learning) has a smaller but still very acceptable level of consistency (0.75). We can have confidence, therefore, that these items reliably measure the four SALTAL-II dimensions of leadership and that we can sum the scores within each dimension.

The criterion groups, needed to judge the validity of SALTAL-II, were formed on the basis of mentors' judgements of principals' learning needs. The mentors placed a total of 43 principals in the low needs group, 30 principals in the moderate needs group, and 17 in the high needs group. There were no significant differences between these three groups on the following personal and school characteristics: age; gender; ethnicity; type of qualification; type of school, decile level of school and predominant ethnicity of enrolled students.[2] There were significant differences, however, between the three mentor classified groups on two additional characteristics.

There was a significant relationship between the position principals held prior to appointment and the mentors' classification of their learning needs (chi-square (10) = 19.2, $p < 0.05$*). Approximately 80 per cent of low needs principals had been appointed from a senior management position, whereas just over a half of all the high needs principals had such experience (Table 10.3). There was also a significant relationship between the number of years of teaching experience and the mentor classifications (chi-square (8) = 16.1, $p < 0.05$*), with those with more teaching experience much more likely to be classified in the low needs group.

Table 10.4 shows the mean SALTAL-II and dimension scores of the three groups of principals based on the mentor classification (criterion groups) and of the total group. The first point to note about Table 10.4 is that the principals' self-assessments were modest and realistic, given the high standard of leadership incorporated into SALTAL-II. Their mean scores of between three and four on a five-point scale contrast with the higher self-assessments obtained on an earlier version of SALTAL in which practical examples of what counted as meeting the standard were not included in the tool.

The second point to note is the narrow range of mean scores for the high needs group (from a minimum of 2.50 to a maximum of 3.88), which contrasts with the wider range of scores for the low needs group (from a minimum of 1.83 to a maximum of 4.88). The moderate needs group fell between these two extremes. However, the mean scores for the three groups did not follow the predicted direction as we had found with the 2004 and 2005 cohorts.

Table 10.5 answers our question about the ability of SALTAL-II to predict the independent judgements of mentors about their principals' learning needs. It shows the match between the way the principals are classified by the mentors and the way they were classified by SALTAL-II. Of the three groups that the mentors were asked to identify, discriminant analysis successfully classified 76.5 per cent of the high needs principals, 66.7 per cent of the moderate needs principals, and 69.8 per cent of the low needs principals. This was a considerable improvement on our prior study in which 70 per cent, 46.8 per cent and 65.5 per cent respectively were correctly classified. Of the original 90 cases, just on 70 per cent of the principals were correctly classified. We attribute this improvement to the revised procedures for obtaining the mentors' classifications.

One of the main purposes of SALTAL was to determine the diverse learning needs of the principals in each of the three criterion groups. A

Table 10.3 Principals' learning needs by position held prior to appointment

Prior position of principal	*Mentor classification of principal*							
	Low needs		*Moderate needs*		*High needs*		*Total cohort*	
	N	%	N	%	N	%	N	%
Senior management	35	81.4	21	70.0	8	47.1	64	71.1
Middle management	2	4.7	4	13.3	3	17.6	7	7.8
Classroom teacher	2	4.7	5	16.7	5	29.4	12	13.3
Government agency	1	2.3	0	0.0	0	0.0	1	1.5
Teacher training	3	7.0	0	0.0	0	0.0	3	3.3
Tertiary	0	0.0	0	0.0	1	5.9	3	3
Total	43	100.0	30	100.0	17	100.0	90	100.0

Note
* $p < 0.05$.

Table 10.4 Mean scores and standard deviations (SD) for SALTAL-II scores as a function of criterion group membership

Criterion group	*Dimension 1*	*Dimension 2*	*Dimension 3*	*Dimension 4*	*Total*	*Min.*	*Max.*
High Needs	3.02 (0.53)	3.24 (0.66)	2.92 (0.55)	3.15 (0.59)	3.05 (0.51)	2.50	3.88
Moderate Needs	3.39 (0.50)	3.71 (0.68)	3.30 (0.61)	3.49 (0.65)	3.44 (0.52)	2.50	4.67
Low Needs	3.46 (0.56)	3.51 (0.67)	3.27 (0.67)	3.38 (0.63)	3.39 (0.57)	1.83	4.88
Combined Cohort	3.35 (0.55)	3.52 (0.68)	3.22 (0.64)	3.37 (0.63)	3.34 (0.56)	1.83	4.88

Note
The response scale ranged from '1' indicating the quality was present to a 'very limited degree' to '5' indicating a 'high degree'.

Table 10.5 Classification analysis using SALTAL scores

Mentor's classification		*Predicted group membership* (n = 90)			
		High needs	*Moderate needs*	*Low needs*	*Total*
Frequency	High needs	13	2	2	17
	Moderate needs	5	20	5	30
	Low needs	3	10	30	43
Percentage	High needs	76.5	11.8	11.8	100.0
	Moderate needs	16.7	66.7	16.7	100.0
	Low needs	7.0	23.3	69.8	100.0

comparison of the average scores of those in each group showed that the high needs principals rated themselves as less capable than the other groups on all four leadership dimensions, but the low needs group rated themselves as more capable only on the first dimension (Table 10.5). The moderate needs group had the highest average score on the remaining three dimensions.

A secondary analysis was completed using the classification derived from the SALTAL scores rather than from the mentors. In this case, the three groups were distinguishable from each other on two of the four leadership factors – Factor 1 (Knowledge and Skills for Leading Teaching and Learning) and Factor 2 (Commitment to Positive Learning Outcomes for all Students). These analyses suggest that whether principals are classified on the basis of self-assessment or independent judgements, they have different learning needs on many if not all aspects of the leadership of teaching and learning.

The utility of SALTAL

Each first-time principal worked with their mentor to develop a Professional Learning Plan (PLP) comprising from three to five SMART (Specific, Measured, Achievable, Relevant, Timed) developmental goals. Since it was intended that the principals' self-ratings on SALTAL would inform their identification of appropriate goals, the guidelines for PLP development included the four SALTAL dimensions listed below them.

Our analysis of the 82 available plans was designed to check:

1 how the completed SALTAL-II tool informed the plan;
2 the items that were most and least likely to be used as the basis of goal selection;
3 the extent to which goal selection matched the pattern of SALTAL scores.

Inspection of the plans showed a close alignment between principals' PLP goals and the items and examples provided in SALTAL. The examples were initially included to increase the validity of the SALTAL instrument, but it would appear that they serve the additional purpose of providing a framework for principals to use in designing their own developmental goals within the PLP. For example, the item 'Make and explain the reasons for difficult decisions' (item no. 23) was illustrated by the following examples: you seek advice prior to decision-making; you deliberate without undue procrastination; you consider options and their likely outcomes, and then decide on a course of action; you are not afraid to make decisions in the interest of the whole school that may upset particular interest groups or individuals.

Some principals decided to use these examples, with a slight change of wording, as goal statements. Others modified the SALTAL items to describe more specific foci relevant to their school. For example, the item 'Align school and local community objectives and cultures to support positive outcomes for students' (item no. 14) was used in the following ways by one principal:

1 PLP Goal: to improve the transition between preschools and school.
2 PLP Actions: invite all contributing early childhood teachers and parents to a junior school information evening, focusing on the literacy and numeracy programmes we deliver; deputy principal and principal to maintain regular contact with the early childhood centres and prospective parents; review information booklet/enrolment pack for parents; initiate two-way visits between school and early childhood centre.

Contrary to expectations, there was no relationship between the average scores for the whole group on each leadership dimension and the proportion of goals that fell under each dimension. There was, however, a strong relationship between the specific items identified as goals in the PLP and the principals' average self-ratings of those SALTAL-II items ($r_{pearson} = -0.44$, $p < 0.05*$). The lower the principals' average self-rating on a SALTAL-II item, the more likely it was to be included as a PLP goal. This indicates that the principals, on average, are using their understanding of their learning needs (as identified by SALTAL-II) to prioritize their professional learning goals.

There were 19 occasions, however, on which a principal rated a SALTAL-II item as 1 (high need) but did not include it as a PLP goal. This would suggest that the principals are not *always* prioritizing their highest need areas (as defined by SALTAL-II) as professional learning goals. Discussion with mentors indicates there may be several reasons for this, including the fact that SALTAL-II is designed to assess the learning needs of the principal rather than identify all the school issues that require attention. The need to integrate school issues with professional learning goals accounts for some of the mismatch between PLP goals and SALTAL-II ratings.

Discussion

One of the challenges to be met by any programme of principal induction is how to cater for the diversity of participants. This challenge is particularly relevant to New Zealand's national programme because principals from all school sectors and types, and from both Mâori and English medium schools, participate in the same programme.

The SALTAL-II tool is one of the most important strategies we use for providing a more individualized induction experience. The factor structure, reliability and validity have been improved in the five years of its development. The analysis reported has confirmed the high reliability of SALTAL-II. This means that scores for every principal can be derived for each of the four dimensions and taken into account when principals work with their mentors to develop their individualized learning plan.

The validity of SALTAL-II was established by showing that it can distinguish between those principals who are classified by their mentors as having low, moderate or high learning needs in seventy per cent of cases. This represents a considerable improvement on the previous classification using SALTAL, in which only 54 per cent of the cases were correctly classified. The improvement is due to some revisions to the tool and to clearer definitions and procedures for completing the mentor classifications.

The analysis of the PLP data showed that the tool is not only a valuable form of self-assessment but also a guide to the formulation of learning goals. The detailed examples that accompany each item were originally included to reduce the likelihood of inflated self-assessments. The modest average scores suggest that the tool is succeeding in that respect, and, in addition, the examples are providing a powerful guide to the selection and formulation of goals.

More research on the use of SALTAL by mentor–principals pairs is planned. We are keen to conduct more qualitative studies of the discussions in which principals and their mentors set, monitor and evaluate goal achievement over the course of the induction experience. We also want to investigate why three of the four indicators of ethical leadership were so rarely selected as goals.

Overall, the study confirmed that New Zealand's first-time principals have very different learning needs, and that the emphasis on differentiation and choice within a common induction programme and curriculum needs to be continued. Depending on whether mentors' classification of the principals, or an adjusted classification based on the discriminant analysis is used, there are significant differences in the way the three principal groups rate themselves on between one third and one half of the leadership indicators. This suggests that a continued emphasis within the induction programme on choice, individual mentoring, goal-setting, and targeted support is essential.

Acknowledgements

The authors are grateful to Debbie Waayer and Claire Lloyd for their assistance in the development and administration of the SALTAL tool, to John Hattie for statistical advice and to Claire Lloyd for her help in manuscript preparation. Although funding for this study was provided by the New Zealand Ministry of Education, the views expressed in this paper are those of the authors alone.

Notes

1 Further information about the programme can be found at www.firstprincipals.ac.nz.
2 Figures for distribution of principals across age, gender, ethnicity, years of teaching experience, type of qualification, decile level of school and predominant ethnicity of enrolled students are available from the first author.

References

Bush, T. and Jackson, D. (2002) A preparation for school leadership: international perspectives. *Educational Management and Administration,* 30(4), 417–429.

Council of Chief State School Officers (1996) *Interstate Leaders Licensure Consortium: Standards for School Leaders.* Washington, DC: CCSSO.

Department of Education (1989) *Tomorrow's Schools: The Reform of Education Administration in New Zealand.* Wellington: Department of Education.

Department for Education and Skills (2004) *Guidance on the Mandatory Requirement to hold the National Professional Qualification for Headship.* Retrieved 21 January 2006, publications.teachernet.gov.uk/eOrderingDownload/0087–2004.pdf

Education Review Office (1996) *Improving Schooling in Mangere and Otara.* Wellington: Author.

Education Review Office (1997) *Improving Schooling on the East Coast.* Wellington: Author.

Education Review Office (1998) *Schooling in the Far North.* Wellington: Author.

Fiske, E. B. and Ladd, H. F. (2000) *When Schools Compete: A Cautionary Tale.* Washington, DC: Brookings Institution Press.

Hay Group (2001) *Identifying the Skills, Knowledge, Attributes and Competencies for First-Time Principals: Shaping the Next Generation of Principals.* Wellington: Hay Acquisitions Inc.

New Zealand Government (1989) *Education Act (Public Act 1989, No. 80).* Retrieved 21 October 2002, from rangi.knowledge basket.co.nz/gpacts/public/text/1989/an/080.html

Nunnally, J. O. (1978) *Psychometric Theory.* New York: McGraw-Hill.

Organisation for Economic Co-operation and Development (2001) *Knowledge and Skills for Life: First Results from the OECD Programme for International Student Assessment (PISA) 2000.* Paris: OECD.

Robinson, V. M. J., Eddy, D. and Irving, E. (2006) Catering for diversity in a principal induction programme. *School Leadership and Management*, 26(2), 149–167.

Robinson, V. M. J., Ward, L. and Timperley, H. (2003) The difficulties of school governance: a layperson's job? *Educational Management & Administration*, 31, 263–281.

Scheerens, J., Vermeulen, C. and Pelegrum, W. J. (1989) Generalizability of instruction and school effectiveness indicators across nations. *International Journal of Educational Research*, 13(7), 789–799.

Wylie, C. (1997) *The Role of New Zealand School Boards in 1997* (Report to the New Zealand Schools' Trustees Association No. NZP 379.1531 W98). Wellington: New Zealand Council for Educational Research.

Wylie, C. (1999) *Ten Years on: How Schools View Educational Reform.* Wellington: New Zealand Council for Educational Research.

Chapter 11

University-based leader preparation in the US

A brief history and emerging trends

Joseph Murphy

Introduction

For much of the last quarter century, academics and practitioners have been engaged in an unbroken quest to understand the school improvement algorithm (Teddlie and Reynolds, 2000). That is, there have been ongoing efforts, sometimes systematic and often ad hoc, to isolate the variables in the school performance equation and to understand how they work, both as individual components and as parts of the system of schooling. Across this time, investigators have paid special attention to conditions in schools that help explain the dramatic overrepresentation of selected groups of youngsters in the underperforming and failing categories of the school success taxonomy.

From this work, we have discovered a good deal about how schools work to promote, or fail to promote, student achievement. For example, we know that quality instruction and opportunity to learn (time, content and success rate) explain a good deal of student performance. In a similar vein, we have learned that robust connections between home and school focusing on academic mission and thoughtful professional development in the context of communities of practice are important links in the school improvement chain (Murphy *et al.*, in press a).

Research throughout the last quarter century in education has also underscored leadership as a critical theme in the school improvement narrative (Wellisch *et al.*, 1978). Indeed evidence from nearly every realm of investigation beginning with effective schools studies through the most recent work on comprehensive school reform confirms leadership as an explanatory variable in schools where all students meet ambitious achievement targets (Leithwood *et al.*, 2004).

As is often the case, enhanced recognition has been accompanied by increased scrutiny. And, not unexpectedly, the spotlight has revealed both positive attributes and flaws in how we think about and practice leadership in schools. For example, at the same time that some researches were uncovering the importance of learning-centred work for school administrators, other analysts were documenting that leadership, as commonly enacted, had little to do with education – that the calculus of leadership in schools has been a composite of management, politics and organization (Bates, 1984).

As understanding of leadership in the work of school reform began to deepen, more and more attention was directed to the qualifications of the women and men who occupy leadership roles in schools. Consequently, considerable interest was devoted to the preparation of those leaders. And analyses of the preparation function in the US exposed a profession in need of major improvements – in how it recruited and selected students, in the content it stressed, in the ways it provided learning opportunities, in the procedures used to assess student learning, and in the strategies engaged to evaluate its own performance.

The analysis in this chapter is devoted to this last link in the discussion, that is, to the education of school leaders. The first part of the chapter provides a brief historical treatment of the education of school leaders in the US. In the second part, we examine emerging trends in the current era of leadership development for new school administrators.

An historical overview of preparation for school leaders – preparing school administrators, 1900–1946: the prescriptive era

Although school administrators were in evidence before the turn of the century, little was written on the topic of school leadership in the US 'and formal preparation programs for school administrators had not yet developed' (Gregg, 1960, p. 20). Prior to 1900, character (Tyack and Hansot, 1982) and ideology (Glass, 1986) were important characteristics of school leaders. Administrators of this era have been described as philosopher educators (Callahan and Button, 1964) and as teachers of teachers (Button, 1966).

The twentieth century ushered in the beginning of the 'prescriptive era' in school administration (Campbell *et al.*, 1987), a nearly 50-year period of expansion in training programmes for school leaders. In 1900, no institutions in the US were offering systematic study in the area of school management. By the end of the Second World War, 125 institutions were actively engaged in preparing school administrators (Silver, 1982). A first generation of educational administration professors – men like Cubberly, Strayer and Mort – were actively engaged in laying the foundations of the field and in training a second generation of professors to take their place. Many states were requiring formal course work in educational leadership for administrative positions and were certifying graduates of preparation programmes for employment (Moore, 1964). As these elements of the profession began to find acceptance, more and more principals and superintendents in the US embarked on their careers with university training in the practice of school administration.

This shift from an era of teaching, ideology, character and philosophy to one of prescription in the early 1900s represents the first era of ferment in school administration – one marked by a number of trends that we see repeated during later periods of unrest in the profession. There was much critical analysis about the health of educational administration in general and the status of leadership development in particular. There was considerable muckraking literature about the way practicing administrators were managing schools. In addition, new views of leadership that reflected dominant social and cultural forces were held up as desirable alternatives for training educational administrators.

Information on the preparation of school leaders during the first half of the twentieth century is limited and uneven (see McCarthy, 1999; Murphy 1992). Faculty of this era were drawn almost exclusively from the superintendency. They carried heavy teaching loads and showed little proclivity for research. A similar homogeneity characterized students of this period. Most were white males holding full-time positions as school administrators while attending school on a part-time basis (Campbell *et al.*, 1987). Some trained for the professoriate, most for the superintendency (Silver, 1982).

The education received by superintendents and principals was largely undifferentiated from that of teachers until the onslaught and widespread acceptance of the scientific management movement throughout the corporate world between 1910 and 1915. For the next 20 years, business was to exert considerable influence over preparation programmes for school administrators in the US. During this time, 'preservice education for school executives tended to stress the technical and mechanical aspects of administration' (Gregg, 1969, p. 994); 'specific and immediate tasks' (Callahan and Button, 1964, p. 87); and the practical aspects of the job (Newlon, 1934). The objective was to train students to understand the job of administration as it was and to perform successfully in the roles they undertook – what Campbell and his colleagues (1987) label preparation for the role – as opposed to studying what might need to be done differently and preparing for roles as change agents, i.e. preparing the person.

While the Great Depression and the Second World War saw the incorporation of new material into training programmes in the US – 'human relations in cooperative educational activities' (Gregg, 1969, p. 994), social foundations, and the human factor in general – by the end of the prescriptive era initial leader development was still highly technical in nature. Almost no attention was given to the theoretical underpinnings of the work of school leaders: the scholarship that informed course content throughout this era was characterized as little more than 'naked empiricism' (Griffiths, 1965, p. 34; Halpin, 1957, p. 197) or 'factualism' (Griffiths, 1959, p. 9), resulting in the development of: 'fuzzy concepts' (Griffiths, 1988, p. 29); 'inadequately field-tested principles' (Crowson and McPherson, 1987, p. 47); and a mere 'encyclopedia of facts' (Griffiths, 1959, p. 9) that lacked 'the power of unifying interpretive theories' (Tyack and Cummings, 1977, p. 62; Goldhammer, 1983). The knowledge base, it was held, comprised: 'folklore, testimonials of reputedly successful administrators, ... the speculation of college professors' (Griffiths, 1959, p. v); 'personal success stories and lively anecdotes' (Marland, 1960, p. 25); 'personal accounts or "war stories", and prescriptions offered by experienced practitioners' (Silver, 1982, p. 51); 'experiences of practicing administrators as they managed the various problem areas of school administration' (Gregg, 1969, p. 996); 'maxims, exhortations, and several innocuous variations on the theme of the Golden Rule' (Halpin, 1960, p. 4); and 'preachments to administrators about ways in which they should perform' (Goldhammer, 1983, p. 250).

Preparing school administrators, 1947–1990: the scientific era

Beginning in the late 1940s and continuing for much of the next four decades in the US, prescriptions drawn from practice came to be overshadowed in preparation programmes by theoretical and conceptual material drawn from the various social sciences. Like the prescriptive era before it, the 'scientific era', in its emergence, drew support because of its harsh attacks on the status quo in the area of administrative training, its critical analyses of the performance of existing school leaders, and its lure of an alternative vision – science in this case – that held forth the promise of dramatically improving the education available to prospective school leaders.

At the onset of the scientific era, as we just reported, considerable criticism was levelled against the naked empiricism, personal success stories and maxims or untested principles that constituted the knowledge base of educational administration at the time. It was also argued by many that the explicit values framework of the latter half of the prescriptive era – the human relations era – was inappropriate in a scientific world. In the period of ferment at the beginning of the twentieth century, practicing administrators were chastised for their lack of grounding in the management principles of the corporate world, especially those developed by Frederick Taylor and his peers. In the era of ferment following the Second World War, they came under attack for their unscientific, non-theoretical approach to administration (McCarthy, 1999). Throughout this time, training institutions in the US were being exhorted to develop better preparation programmes 'to protect the public against ill-prepared or indifferent practitioners' (Goldhammer, 1983, p. 253). In addition, as has been the case throughout the history of school management in the US, professors began to reweave the fabric of preparation programmes to mirror the high-status professions in the larger society, thereby creating an alternative vision of the role of school administrators (Callahan, 1962; Callahan and Button, 1964). Since scientists, not business people, held centre stage at this time (Halpin, 1960), a quest for a science of school administration was undertaken (Greenfield, 1988; Griffiths, 1988).

The post-Second World War ferment in school administration was characterized by considerable enthusiasm, activity, growth and dramatic changes in the structure and content of training programmes (Crowson and McPherson, 1987; Willower, 1983; Wynn, 1957). It was a period which many believed would lead to the full professionalization of school administration (Farquhar, 1977; Goldhammer, 1983).

Four major events mark the era of turmoil following the Second World War in the US. The first of these was the formation of the National Conference of Professors of Educational Administration (NCPEA) in 1947. By linking professors throughout the country for the first time, the NCPEA exercised considerable influence over emerging conceptions of the profession and over school administration training programmes (Campbell *et al.*, 1987; Gregg, 1960). The second defining event in the transition from the prescriptive to the scientific era was the creation of the Cooperative Project in Educational Administration (CPEA) – a consortium of eight universities funded by the Kellogg Foundation whose primary purpose was to institute changes in preparation programmes. Continuing initiatives charted at earlier NCPEA meetings, especially the 'benchmark' 1954 gathering in Denver (Getzels, 1977, p. 8), the CPEA encouraged multidisciplinary approaches to analyses of administration and to the education of school leaders. As Gregg concluded in his 1969 review, the CPEA had a profound influence on preparation programmes and on the practice of school administration. The establishment of the Committee for the Advancement of School Administration (CASA) in 1955 and of the University Council for Educational Administration (UCEA) in 1956 represent the final milestones that helped shape evolving conceptions of initial leader development during the second era of ferment (Forsyth, 1999; Griffiths, 1959; Moore, 1964). The CASA's most important work focused on the development of professional standards of performance. The UCEA's influence has been more pervasive (Culbertson, 1995; Forsyth, 1999; Willower, 1983). Throughout the 1960s and 1970s, it 'became the dominant force in shaping the study and teaching of educational administration ... [and] a major force in the advancement of preparation programs' (Campbell *et al.*, 1987, pp. 182–183).

Under the pull of these forces, there was a considerable flurry of activity in preparation programmes throughout the US during the scientific era, especially during the 1950s and 1960s. This was a period of rapid growth in educational administration. While in 1946 approximately 125 institutions were in the business of preparing school leaders, 40 years later, over 500 were involved (National Commission on Excellence in Educational Administration, 1987). The number of doctoral degrees doubled during each decade throughout this period (Farquhar, 1977). The size of the typical programme – defined in terms of number of faculty – increased substantially during the heyday of the scientific era, doubling in size from five to ten full-time faculty members (Farquhar, 1977) before falling back to its original size by the mid-1980s (McCarthy *et al.*, 1988).

The average faculty member in 1945 was most likely to be a generalist, drawn from the superintendency, and oriented primarily toward the practice dimensions of the profession. By the mid-1980s, that picture had changed considerably. The typical faculty member in educational administration, especially those in UCEA institutions, at the end of the scientific era was likely to be a discipline-focused specialist with little or no practical experience, concerned primarily with the professorial (if not scholarly) aspects of the profession (McCarthy and Kuh, 1997). While there was considerably more diversity among students in preparation programmes in 1985 than in 1945 in terms of gender, and to a lesser extent race, there were still many commonalities. Most students continued to be drawn from the bottom quartile on national entrance exams, self-selected their programmes, attended local institutions on a part-time basis, and exercised little control over their lives as students (Murphy, 1992).

Consistent with the guiding vision of the scientific era, the predominant trend during this 40-year period was the infusion of content from the social sciences into preparation programmes (McCarthy, 1999; Murphy, 1992). The infrastructure for this activity was the expansion of the conceptual and theoretical knowledge base of the profession through the development of a science of administration. This was a movement intended 'to produce a foundation of scientifically supported (hypothetico-deductive) knowledge in educational administration in place of the hortatory, seat-of-the-pants literature already in place' (Crowson and McPherson, 1987, pp. 47–48) and a trend 'away from technique-oriented substance based upon practical experience and toward theory-oriented substance based on disciplines "external" to education' (Culbertson and Farquhar, 1971, p. 9). The scientific movement led to: a conception of educational administration as 'an applied science within which theory and research are directly and linearly linked to professional practice [and in which] the former always determine the latter, and thus knowledge is superordinate to the principal and designed to prescribe practice' (Sergiovanni, 1991, p. 4); the acceptance of a heavy reliance on social science content 'as an indicator of a high quality program' (Miklos, 1983, p. 160); 'the borrowing and adopting of research techniques and instruments from the behavioral sciences' (Culbertson, 1965, p. 7); and a multidisciplinary (if not interdisciplinary) approach to preparation (Culbertson, 1963; Hodgkinson, 1975).

Emerging trends, 1990–2008

For the last 20 years, educational administration in the US has again been in the throes of still another period of ferment, turmoil that appears to be accompanying the shift from a scientific to a post-scientific or 'dialectic era' in school administration. As was true in each of the preceding periods, ferment here is being fuelled by devastating attacks on the state of preparation programmes, critical analyses of practicing school administrators, and references to alternative visions of what programmes should become. If anything, the rhetoric in this third period of ferment seems both more strident and more comprehensive than that found in earlier eras of reform.

Critique

Although over the life of the scientific era the profession 'increased in formality, structure, and complexity – from amateur to professional, from simple to complicated, and from intuitive to "scientific"' (Cooper and Boyd, 1987, p. 7) – the outcomes of the quest for a science of administration were considerably less robust than had been anticipated (Donmoyer, 1999; Murphy, 2006b). By the mid-1970s, this failure of the theory movement to deliver on its promises was brought to a head in a landmark paper delivered by T. B. Greenfield (1975) at the Third International Intervisitation Program in Bristol, England (Griffiths, 1988). Although other scholars had been drawing attention to the limitations of a near-exclusive emphasis on a scientific approach to training for some time, Greenfield unleashed the first systemic, broadside attack on the central tenets of the theory movement, especially on its epistemological roots and guiding values. In a word, he found the scientific era of educational administration to be impoverished. Greenfield's paper went a long way in galvanizing critique of the field that began to wash over the profession of school leadership in the US in the 1990s.

Over the past quarter century, other thoughtful analysts have joined the debate about the appropriate value structure and cognitive base for educational administration (see Culbertson, 1988; Donmoyer, 1999; Griffiths, 1988). On the knowledge base issue, there has been increasing agreement – although with noticeable differences in explanations – that 'a body of dependable knowledge about educational administration' (Crowson and McPherson, 1987, p. 48) did not emerge during the behavioural science era. This condition means that upon exiting the behavioral science era, there was not much 'conceptual unity' to the field (Erickson, 1979, p. 9). In practical terms, Erickson concluded that 'the field consist[ed] of whatever scholars associated with university programs in "educational administration" consider[ed] relevant. It is, to say the least, amorphous' (p. 9). In his review, Boyan (1988) concurred, arguing that 'the explanatory aspect of the study of administrator behavior in education over 30 years appears to be an incomplete anthology of short stories connected by no particular story line or major themes' (p. 93). Given this absence of conceptual unity, until quite recently there has not been much common agreement about the appropriate foundation for the profession (Murphy, 1999a). Thus, as the behavioural science era drew to a close, Goldhammer (1983) reported that although there were 'general areas of concern that might dictate to preparatory institutions the names of courses that should be taught, ... there [was] less agreement on what the content of such courses should actually be' (p. 269).

At the same time, a pattern of criticism was forming about both the definition of legitimate knowledge and the accepted ways in which it could be generated (Murphy, 1999a). As Crowson and McPherson (1987) reported, during this transition phase, critics 'questioned with increasing vigor the appropriateness of traditional research methods and assumptions as a guide to an understanding of practice' (p. 48). Analysts called for both relegitimization of practice-based knowledge and the acceptance of:

> An increasing diversity of research methods, including attempts at qualitative ethnographic, naturalistic, phenomenological, and critical studies ... [and] an *effort* to generate 'theories of practice' that incorporate both objective and subjective ways of knowing, both fact and value considerations, both 'is' and 'ought' dimensions of education within integrated frameworks for practice.
>
> (Silver, 1982, pp. 56, 53)

Finally, there was a deepening recognition that the knowledge base employed in preparation programmes had not been especially useful in solving real problems in the field (Bridges, 1982; Hills, 1975). This questioning of the relevance of theory to practice can be traced to a number of causes (Murphy 2006a). Deeply ingrained methods of working that assumed that one could discover theory that would automatically apply itself to situations of practice was the first. A second was the emergence of a 'parochial view of science' (Halpin, 1960, p. 6) – one in which social scientists became 'intent upon aping the more prestigious physical scientists in building highly abstract, theoretical models' (p. 6) at the expense of clinical science. A third was the proclivity of educational researchers employing social and behavioural sciences to contribute to the various disciplines rather than to administrative practice – administrative 'structure and process were studied mostly as a way of adding to disciplinary domains' (Erickson, 1977, p. 136): 'Indeed, the evolution of the field of educational administration reveals a pattern of attempts to resemble and be accepted by the more mature disciplines on campus' (Björk and Ginsberg, 1995, p. 23; Campbell, 1981). Along these same lines, during this entire era there was a lack of effort on the part of professors to distinguish systematically those aspects of the social and behavioural sciences that were most appropriate for practitioners (Gregg, 1969). In particular, insufficient attention was directed toward educational organizations as the setting for administration and leadership (Greenfield, 1995). Largely because of the overwhelming nature of the task

(Culbertson, 1965), the weakness of the theory movement noted by the American Association of School Administrators (AASA) in 1960 – the failure 'to work out the essentials in the social sciences for school administrators and to develop a program containing these essentials' (p. 57) – was still a problem as the sun set on the behavioural science era in the 1990s. It remains a problem for the field as we embark on a new millennium in the education of school leaders (Murphy, 2006a).

A number of critics have also pointed out that regardless of its usefulness, the knowledge base constructed during the scientific era in the US gave rise to a 'narrowly defined concept of administration' (Greenfield, 1988, p. 147). This line of analysis spotlights the failure of the profession to include critical concepts, materials and ideas (Donmoyer, 1999). To begin with, by taking a 'neutral posture on moral issues' (Culbertson, 1964, p. 311), the theory movement 'actively de-centered morality and values in the quest for a science of organization' (English, 1997, p. 18). When the term value judgement did surface, it was 'frequently as an epithet indicating intellectual contempt' (Harlow, 1962, p. 66). Throughout the behavioural science era, there was 'little serious, conscious effort to develop demonstrably in students the skills or behavioral propensities to act in ways that could be considered ethical' (Farquhar, 1981, p. 199; Beck and Murphy, 1994). Attention to the 'humanities as a body of "aesthetic wisdom" capable of contributing its own unique enrichment to the preparation of school administrators' (Popper, 1982, p. 12) was conspicuous by its absence.

Also neglected during this period of administration qua administration were educational issues (Callahan, 1962; Erickson, 1977, 1979) – a phenomenon exacerbated by efforts to professionalize administration and thereby distinguish it from teaching (Murphy *et al.*, 1987). What Anderson and Lonsdale reported in 1957 – that 'few items in the literature of educational administration ... say much about the psychology of learning' (p. 429) – and what Boyan concluded in 1963 – that 'the content of the advanced preparation tends to focus on the managerial and institutional dimensions as compared to teaching, the technical base of educational organizations' (pp. 3–4) – were still true at the onset of the twenty-first century (Murphy, 1990, 1999a).

In summary, by the early 1990s, a multifaceted assessment of the intellectual foundations of educational leadership had produced a good deal of disquiet in the profession (Donmoyer *et al.*, 1995). This unease, in term, is continuing to fuel the turmoil that characterizes the academic wing of the field. It has also served – directly and indirectly – as a foundation for many of the reform initiatives that have sprung up in the profession, especially around the preparation and professional development functions.

A changing landscape of leadership development in the US

The story of changes underway in preparation programmes in school leadership in the US is constructed from information from four areas of work. Chronicles of reformation in individual programmes or groups of departments engaged in related reforms provide the richest repository of knowledge to date. Second, but less prevalent, are analyses of activities on specific pieces of the reform agenda (e.g. cohort programmes, problem-based instructional strategies, the use of technology). Treatments of the strategies that important professional bodies have used to reshape the profession furnish a third useful lens for drawing conclusions about changes afoot in departments of educational leadership. Finally, there are a number of macrolevel analyses of the recontoured landscape of the profession. These, in turn, are of two types: synthetic reviews and empirical studies. Building on this collective work, we discern that some distinct patterns in the reform of preparation programmes have begun to emerge in the last few years. We review the most important of these trends below, concentrating on those with deepest roots and/or with greatest implications for the redevelopment of the preparation function.

We begin, however, with a few cautionary notes to guide our analyses. In *Life on the Mississippi*, Mark Twain reminds us that 'partialities often make people see more than really exists'. Thus, an analysis of trends in preparation may encourage the reader to arrive at firmer conclusions than might be desirable. A thoughtful review of the history of innovation in preparation programmes for school leaders in the US would lead one to be careful here. The literature is replete with inaccurate claims of the importance and the magnitude of incipient movements in the training of school administrators. Whether or not the changes described herein represent the crest of a wave that will break across all of educational leadership is an empirical question which can be answered only at some time in the future. Even if our inchoate chronicle here faithfully portrays the right set of actors and themes, it is difficult to imagine that the storyline will not evolve over time, changing in ways that will, perhaps, make them unrecognizable to today's viewers.

An awakening: new energy for reform work

One central conclusion of our analysis is that considerable energy is flowing into the reformation of preparation programmes in school administration in the US. A second finding is that the pressure is having a noticeable impact on administrator preparation programmes.

Earlier reports on the readiness of the field for change in its preparation programmes were disheartening. Studies by McCarthy and her colleagues (McCarthy *et al.*, 1988; McCarthy and Kuh, 1997) and by Murphy (1991) found a general level of complacency about preparation programmes among professors of educational administration. The assumption by the profession of a more active stance (see Murphy, 1999b, 1999c) is, therefore, worthy of note. We expect that time is one variable in play in this shift in expectations. That is, unlike in the earlier studies, most of the reform reports in the area of leadership have had a chance to spread across the profession. There has also been sufficient time for programmes to engage change initiatives and for some of those efforts to take root.

It may also be the case that the buffering these programmes have historically enjoyed – buffering employed to fend off external influences – may be thinning considerably. In short, their option not to act may be becoming reduced. In particular, the resurgence of more vigorous state control over preparation programmes may be propelling reform efforts (Murphy *et al.*, in press a). Concomitantly, the introduction of market dynamics into the licensure system may be influencing departments to strengthen training programmes (Murphy and Hawley, 2003). At least two such forces have surfaced over the past decade – the creation of alternative avenues for licensure and the growth of alternative providers of programmes leading to licensure, especially those offered by professional associations, local educational agencies, and entrepreneurial developers (Murphy, 2006b).

Professional forces may also lie behind recent reform work in the US. There is a sense that the earlier widespread complacency about preparation programmes among professors of educational administration is being challenged as older members of the professoriate retire and new faculty begin to assume the reins of the profession. If, indeed, we are witnessing a lifting of the veil of complacency, it may be attributable to the influx of more women professors and of more faculty members who are joining the professoriate from practice (McCarthy, 1999) than was the case in earlier decades.

The growth of professional groups dedicated to programme reform, such as the new AERA special interest groups on problem-based learning and learning and teaching in educational administration, are noteworthy markers in the professional area. So, too, has been the development of professional networks of reformers, such as those nurtured through the Danforth initiatives of the late 1980s and early 1990s and the work of Kottkamp, Orr and Pounder on programme evaluation and Marshall on social justice over the last few years. In short, it may be that the rather inhospitable landscape of the profession in the US is being remoulded to be more receptive to the seeds of change. It is worth noting that many more colleagues than was the case 15 years ago have staked at least part of their professional reputations on work related to preparation programme development and reform.

Finally, it is possible that shifting norms in universities in general and in colleges of education in particular in the US may be responsible for some of the increased attention to programme reform. Specifically, at least two forces operating in education schools may be directing, or at least facilitating, programme improvement. The first is the increased emphasis 'on enhancing the quality of instruction [in] most colleges and universities' (McCarthy and Kuh, 1997, p. 245). The second is the demand by many colleges of education that meaningful connections to practice be established and nurtured. Although sometimes offset by other forces (e.g. the press for research respectability), these two dynamics may be helping to energize efforts to strengthen preparation programmes in the area of educational leadership.

A reforging of the technical core: alterations in the programme content and instruction

On the instructional front, a renewed interest in teaching is embedded in the leadership development reform narrative in the US. There is evidence of an increase in the use of technology in instruction – in redefining the classroom (e.g. distance learning), in classroom activities (e.g. teaching simulations), and in building working relationships with students outside the class (e.g. email communications). There appears to be greater stress on applied approaches and relevant materials in general and on the additional use of problem- and case-based materials specifically. The emergent cognitive perspectives that are helping to redefine learning more generally seem to be slowly working their way into instructional designs in leadership preparation programmes (Murphy, 1999b, 1999c).

A number of issues in the area of curriculum stand out. To begin with, there is greater interest on matters of teaching and learning, including connections between principals' actions and the core technology. Ethics and values are featured in newly designed preparation programmes, coursework related to the normative dimensions of educational leadership. Closely connected to the growing interest in values is an expanded concern for the social and cultural influences shaping schooling, what we referred to earlier as the social context of education. A sub-theme that cuts across both of these areas – values and social context – is heightened attention to issues of diversity, race and gender. Closely related to this last focus, programmes for preparing school leaders are devoting more attention to topics related to underserved children and their families, especially to the equity agenda. There is some movement from the discipline-based courses that dominated preparation programmes throughout the theory era of the profession. Finally, approaches to inculcating habits of reflection and critical analysis are finding life in preparation programmes as we push into the twenty-first century (Murphy, 2006b).

A reunification of the profession: reconnecting the practice and academic arms of the profession

A central strand in the preparation reform tapestry in the US illuminates efforts to reweave the somewhat tattered fabric that represents the profession of school administration. While the practice and academic spheres of the profession have been estranged for nearly 50 years, preparation programmes are being redesigned to repair that gap. These endeavours are of two types: stronger field-based elements in preparation programmes and more robust linkages between university faculty and district- and school-based administrators. On the first topic, preparation programmes feature the use of practice-anchored materials to a much greater extent than had been the norm in earlier times. There has been a revitalization of the internship. We also see more attention to related clinical activities – shadowing, interviewing administrators, working with practitioners on projects. In general, reforging content has surfaced an underlying dynamic for redirecting energy toward the practice aspects of school leadership (Murphy, 1999c).

On the second topic, university-field connections, a number of trends are visible. The most evident is an enhanced emphasis on forging partnerships in preparation programmes between university-based and school-based educators, including the legitimization of practitioner-based advisory groups to help inform preparation programme design and content. Another piece of the university-field matrix underscores the rejuvenation of adjunct and clinical faculty roles (Murphy, 2006b).

Cracks in the monopoly structure of delivery: alternative preparation models

During its short history, formal preparation for the role of school leader in the US has been the purview of universities, with the imprimatur of state government agencies. As noted above, under the onslaught of critical analysis and the renewed interest in the power of markets, the monopolistic position of universities has come under attack (Hess, 2003). It is increasingly being asserted that preparation might occur more productively in venues other than universities and be provided more effectively by other agents than faculty members in departments of educational leadership.

In response to these forces, alternative pathways to the role of formal school leader are emerging, again with the warrant of the state. New pathways feature providers not historically associated with the preparation of school administrators.

Under alternative *university models*, the preparation function remains in institutions of higher education but it is no longer restricted to colleges of education, or, if it is so restricted, departments other than school leadership are brought into the picture. For example, focusing on the former scenario, New Jersey allows anyone with a degree in administration (e.g. business administration, public administration) to receive a license to become a school leader. Under the latter scenario, one could become a school administrator with a degree in psychology or curriculum and instruction for example.

Professional models transfer responsibility for preparation from universities to professional associations. For example, professional groups in California, Massachusetts and New Jersey are all in the business of preparing newly minted school leaders. *District models*, in turn, make the employer the prime actor in the preparation drama, as is the case in Houston and other districts throughout the US, especially large-city school systems.

Entrepreneurial models combine the insights of creative individuals outside the university and the resources of committed reformers, almost always philanthropic foundations. The best known examples here are Dennis Litkey and his Big Picture Company with its school-based, mentoring model of preparation and Jon Schnur and Monique Burns and the New Leaders for New Schools programme to prepare non-traditional actors as school administrators for urban school systems.

The efforts of for-profit firms fall into the category of *private models*. The most extensive and visible example here is the Leadership for Learning masters programme developed by Canter and Associates, which it developed in partnership with the American Association of School Administrators. *Experiential models* permit potential administrators to substitute work experience for coursework. Although to date almost all initiatives in this area have been ad hoc (e.g. a waiver to certification regulations) it is likely that the profession will see more systematic initiatives to allow work experience to substitute for formal preparation in the future.

References

Bates, R. J. (1984). Toward a critical practice of educational administration. In T. J. Sergiovanni and J. E. Corbally (eds), *Leadership and organizational culture: New perspectives on administrative theory and practice* (pp. 360–374). Urbana: University of Illinois Press.

Beck, L. G. and Murphy, J. (1994). *Ethics in educational leadership programs: An expanding role.* Newbury Park: Corwin Press.

Björk, L. G. and Ginsberg, R. (1995, February). Principles of reform and reforming principal training: A theoretical perspective. *Educational Administration Quarterly*, 31(1), 11–37.

Boyan, N. J. (1963). Common and specialized learnings for administrators and supervisors: Some problems and issues. In D. J. Leu and H. C. Rudman (eds), *Preparation programs for school administrators: Common and specialized learnings* (pp. 1–23). East Lansing: Michigan State University.

Boyan, N. J. (1988). Describing and explaining administrator behavior. In N. J. Boyan (ed.), *Handbook of research on educational administration* (pp. 77–97). New York: Longman.

Bridges, E. M. (1982, Summer). Research on the school administrator: The state of the art, 1967–1980. *Educational Administration Quarterly*, 18(3), 12–33.

Button, H. W. (1966). Doctrines of administration: A brief history. *Educational Administration Quarterly*, 2(3), 216–224.

Callahan, R. E. (1962). *Education and the cult of efficiency.* Chicago: University of Chicago Press.
Callahan, R. E. and Button, H. W. (1964). Historical change of the role of the man in the organization: 1865–1950. In D. E. Griffiths (ed.), *Behavioral science and educational administration* (Sixty-third NSSE yearbook, Part II, pp. 73–92). Chicago: University of Chicago Press.
Campbell, R. F. (1981). The professorship in educational administration: A personal view. *Educational Administration Quarterly*, 7(1) 1–24.
Campbell, R. F., Fleming, T., Newell, L. J. and Bennion, J. W. (1987). *A history of thought and practice in educational administration.* New York: Teachers College Press.
Cooper, B. S. and Boyd, W. L. (1987). The evolution of training for school administrators. In J. Murphy and P. Hallinger (eds), *Approaches to administrative training* (pp. 3–27). Albany: SUNY Press.
Crowson, R. L. and McPherson, R. B. (1987). The legacy of the theory movement: Learning from the new tradition. In J. Murphy and P. Hallinger (eds), *Approaches to administrative training in education* (pp. 45–64). Albany: SUNY Press.
Culbertson, J. A. (1963). Common and specialized content in the preparation of administrators. In D. J. Leu and H. C. Rudman (eds), *Preparation programs for administrators: Common and specialized learnings* (pp. 34–60). East Lansing: Michigan State University.
Culbertson, J. A. (1964). The preparation of administrators. In D. E. Griffiths (ed.), *Behavioral science in educational administration* (Sixty-third NSSE yearbook, Part II, pp. 303–330). Chicago: University of Chicago Press.
Culbertson, J. A. (1965). Trends and issues in the development of a science of administration. In Center for the Advanced Study of Educational Administration, *Perspectives on Educational Administration and the Behavioral Sciences* (pp. 3–32). Eugene: Center for the Advanced Study of Educational Administration.
Culbertson, J. A. (1988). A century's quest for a knowledge base. In N. J. Boyan (ed.), *Handbook of research on educational administration* (pp. 3–26). New York: Longman.
Culbertson, J. A. (1995). *Building bridges: UCEA's first two decades.* University Park: University Council for Educational Administration.
Culbertson, J. A. and Farquhar, R. H. (1971, January). Preparing educational leaders: Content in administration preparation. *UCEA Newsletter*, 12(3), 8–11.
Donmoyer, R. (1999). The continuing quest for a knowledge base: 1976–1998. In J. Murphy and K. S. Louis (eds), *Handbook of research on educational administration* (2nd ed., pp. 25–43). San Francisco: Jossey Bass.
Donmoyer, R., Imber, M. and Scheurich, J. J. (eds) (1995). *The knowledge base in educational administration: Multiple perspectives.* Albany: The State University of New York Press.
English, F. W. (1997, January). The cupboard is bare: The postmodern critique of educational administration. *Journal of School Leadership*, 7(1), 4–26.
Erickson, D. A. (1977). An overdue paradigm shift in educational administration, or how can we get that idiot off the freeway. In L. L. Cunningham, W. G. Hack and R. O. Nystrand (eds), *Educational administration: The developing decades* (pp. 114–143). Berkeley: McCutchan.
Erickson, D. A. (1979, March). Research on educational administration: The state-of-the-art. *Educational Researcher*, 8, 9–14.

Farquhar, R. H. (1977). Preparatory program in educational administration. In L. L. Cunningham, W. G. Hack and R. O. Nystrand (eds), *Educational Administration: The developing decades* (pp. 329–357). Berkeley: McCutchan.

Farquhar, R. H. (1981, June). Preparing educational administrators for ethical practice. *The Alberta Journal of Educational Research*, 27(2), 192–204.

Forsyth, P. (1999). A brief history of scholarship on educational administration. In J. Murphy and P. Forsyth (eds), *Educational administration: A decade of reform* (pp. 71–92). Newbury Park: Corwin Press.

Getzels, J. W. (1977). Educational administration twenty years later, 1954–1974. In L. L. Cunningham, W. G. Hack and R. O. Nystrand (eds), *Educational administration: The developing decades* (pp. 3–24). Berkeley: McCutchan.

Glass, T. E. (1986). *An analysis of texts on school administration 1820–1985*. Danville: Interstate.

Goldhammer, K. (1983, Summer). Evolution in the profession. *Educational Administration Quarterly*, 19(3), 249–272.

Greenfield, T. B. (1975). Theory about organization: A new perspective and its implications for schools. In M. G. Hughes (ed.), *Administering education: International challenge* (pp. 71–99). London: Athlone.

Greenfield, T. B. (1988). The decline and fall of science in educational administration. In D. E. Griffiths, R. T. Stout and P. B. Forsyth (eds), *Leaders for America's schools* (pp. 131–159). Berkeley: McCutchan.

Greenfield, W. (1995, February). Toward a theory of school administration: The centrality of leadership. *Educational Administration Quarterly*, 31(1), 61–85.

Gregg, R. T. (1960). Administration. In C. W. Harris (ed.), *Encyclopedia of educational research* (3rd ed., pp. 19–24). New York: MacMillan.

Gregg, R. T. (1969). Preparation of administrators. In R. L. Ebel (ed.), *Encyclopedia of educational research* (4th ed., pp. 993–1004). London: MacMillan.

Griffiths, D. E. (1959). *Administrative theory.* New York: Appleton-Century-Crofts.

Griffiths, D. E. (1965). Research and theory in educational administration. In CASEA, *Perspectives on educational administration and the behavioral sciences* (pp. 25–48). Eugene: University of Oregon, Center for the Advanced Study of Educational Administration.

Griffiths, D. E. (1988). Administrative theory. In N. J. Boyan (ed.), *Handbook of research on educational administration* (pp. 27–51). New York: Longman.

Halpin, A. W. (1957). A paradigm for research on administrative behavior. In R. F. Campbell and R. T. Gregg (eds), *Administrative behavior in education* (pp. 155–199). New York: Harper.

Halpin, A. W. (1960). Ways of knowing. In R. F. Campbell and J. M. Lipham (eds), *Administrative theory as a guide to action* (pp. 3–20). Chicago: University of Chicago, Midwest Administrative Center.

Harlow, J. G. (1962). Purpose-defining: The central function of the school administrator. In J. A. Culbertson and S. P. Hencley (eds), *Preparing administrators: New perspectives* (pp. 61–71). Columbus: University Council for Educational Administration.

Hess, F. M. (2003). *A license to lead? A new leadership agenda for American schools.* Washington, DC: Progressive Policy Institute.

Hills, J. (1975, Autumn). The preparation of administrators: Some observations from the 'firing line'. *Educational Administration Quarterly*, 11(3), 1–20.

Hodgkinson, C. (1975, Winter). Philosophy, politics, and planning: An extended rationale for synthesis. *Educational Administration Quarterly*, 11(1), 11–20.

Leithwood, K., Louis, K. S., Anderson, S. and Wahlstrom, K. (2004). *How leadership influences student learning* (paper commissioned by the Wallace Foundation). Minneapolis: University of Minnesota.

McCarthy, M. M. (1999). The evolution of educational leadership preparation programs. In J. Murphy and K. S. Louis (eds), *Handbook of research on educational administration* 2nd ed., pp. 119–139). San Francisco: Jossey-Bass.

McCarthy, M. M. and Kuh, G. D. (1997). *Continuity and change: The educational leadership professoriate.* Columbia: The University Council for Educational Administration.

McCarthy, M. M., Kuh, G. D., Newell, L. J. and Iacona, C. M. (1988). *Under scrutiny: The educational administration professoriate.* Tempe: University Council for Educational Administration.

Marland, S. P. (1960). Superintendents' concerns about research applications in educational administration. In R. F. Campbell and J. M. Lipham (eds), *Administrative theory as a guide to action* (pp. 21–36). Chicago: University of Chicago, Midwest Administration Center.

Miklos, E. (1983, Summer). Evolution in administrator preparation programs. *Educational Administration Quarterly*, 19(3), 153–177.

Moore, H. A. (1964). The ferment in school administration. In D. E. Griffiths (ed.), *Behavioral science and educational administration* (Sixty-third NSSE yearbook, Part II, pp. 11–32). Chicago: University of Chicago Press.

Murphy, J. (1990). Restructuring the technical core of preparation programs in educational administration. *UCEA Review*, 31(3), 4–5, 10–13.

Murphy, J. (1991, Spring). The effects of the educational reform movement on departments of educational leadership. *Educational Evaluation and Policy Analysis*, 13(1), 49–65.

Murphy, J. (1992). *The landscape of leadership preparation: Reframing the education of school administrators.* Newbury Park: Corwin Press.

Murphy, J. (1999a). *The quest for a center: Notes on the state of the profession of educational leadership.* Columbia: University Council for Educational Leadership.

Murphy, J. (1999b). The reform of the profession: A self portrait. In J. Murphy and P. Forsyth (eds), *Educational administration: A decade of reform* (pp. 39–68). Newbury Park: Corwin.

Murphy, J. (1999c). Changes in preparation programs: Perceptions of department chairs. In J. Murphy and P. Forsyth (eds), *Educational administration: A decade of reform* (pp. 170–191). Newbury Park: Corwin Press.

Murphy, J. (2006a, Fall). *Of dubious efficacy – questioning the core of university-based preparation programs for school leaders: A reflective essay.* (AERA Division A Newsletter).

Murphy, J. (2006b). *Preparing school leaders: An agenda for research and action.* Lanham: Rowman & Littlefield.

Murphy, J. and Hawley, W. (2003, Fall). The AASA 'Leadership for Learning' masters program. *Teaching and Learning in Educational Administration*, 10(2), 1–6.

Murphy, J. and Hallinger, P., Lotto, L. S. and Miller, S. K. (1987, December). Barriers to implementing the instructional leadership role. *Canadian Administrator*, 27(3), 1–9.

Murphy, J., Moorman, H. and McCarthy, M. M. (in press a). A framework for rebuilding initial certification and preparation programs in educational leadership: Lessons from whole-state reform initiatives. *Teachers College Record*.

Murphy, J., Elliott, S., Goldring, E, and Porter, A. (in press b). Leadership for learning: A research-based model and taxonomy of behaviors. *School Leadership & Management*.

National Commission on Excellence in Educational Administration (1987). *Leaders for America's schools*. Tempe: University Council for Educational Administration.

Newlon, J. H. (1934). *Educational administration as social policy*. New York: Scribner.

Popper, S. H. (1982, Winter). An advocate's case for the humanities in preparation programs for school administration. *Journal of Educational Administration*, 20(1), 12–22.

Sergiovanni, T. J. (1991). *The principalship: A reflective practice perspective* (2nd ed.). Boston: Allyn & Bacon.

Silver, P. F. (1982). Administrator preparation. In H. E. Mitzel (ed.), *Encyclopedia of educational research* (5th ed., Vol. 1, pp. 49–59). New York: Free Press.

Teddlie, C. and Reynolds, D. (2000). *The international handbook of school effectiveness research*. London: Falmer.

Tyack, D. B. and Cummings, R. (1977). Leadership in American public schools before 1954: Historical configurations and conjectures. In L. L. Cunningham, W. G. Hack and R. O. Nystrand (eds), *Educational administration: The developing decades* (pp. 46–66). Berkeley: McCutchan.

Tyack, D. B. and Hansot, E. (1982). *Managers of virtue: Public school leadership in America, 1920–1980*. New York: Basic Books.

Wellisch, J. B., MacQueen, A. H., Carriere, R. A. and Duck, G. A. (1978). School management and organization in successful schools. *Sociology of Education*, 51, 211–226.

Willower, D. J. (1983, Summer). Evolutions in the professorship: Past philosophy, future. *Educational Administration Quarterly*, 19(3), 179–200.

Wynn, R. (1957). Organization and administration of the professional program. In R. F. Campbell and R. T. Gregg (eds), *Administrative behavior in education* (pp. 464–509). New York: Harper.

Index

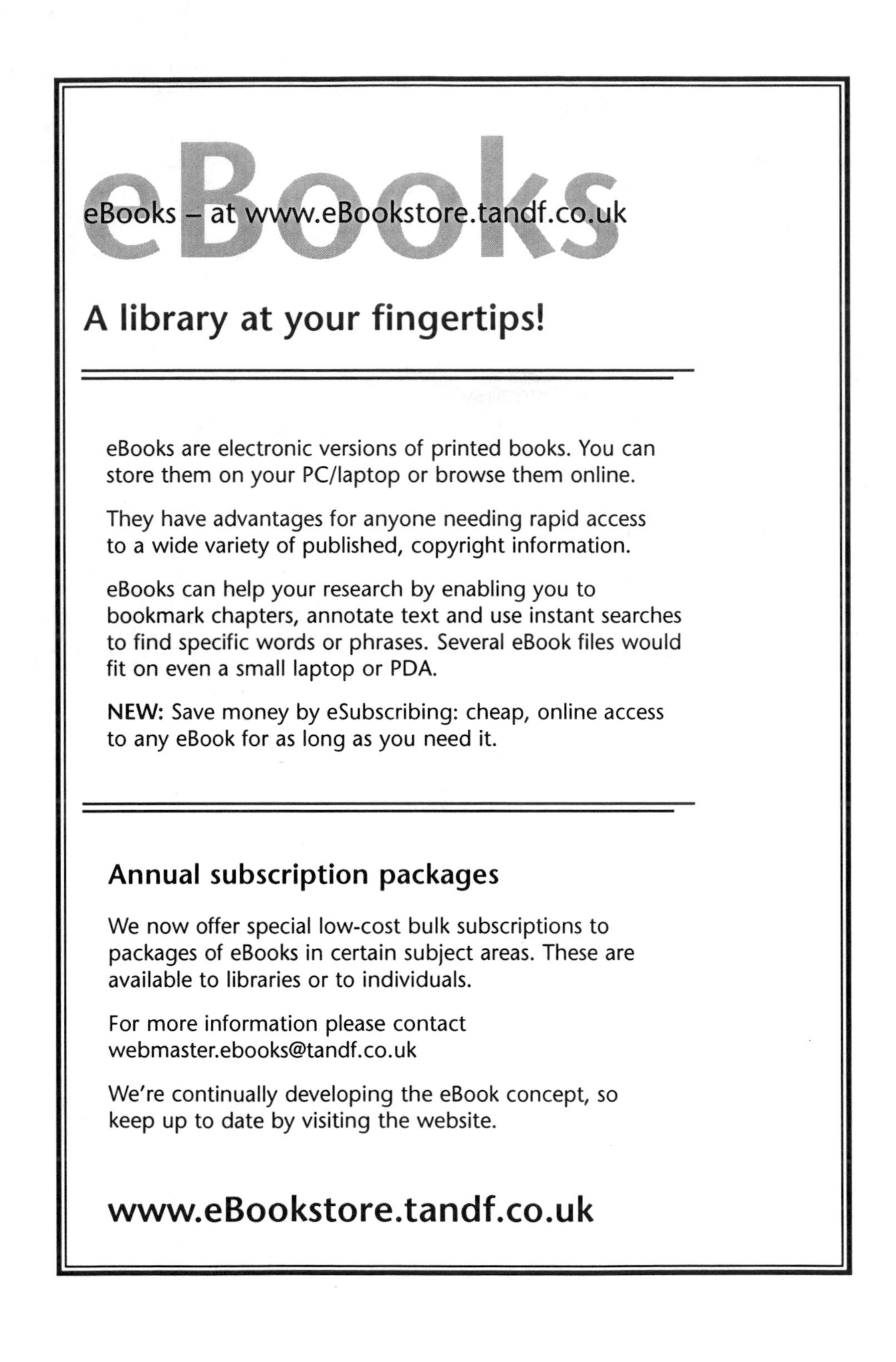
eBooks
eBooks – at www.eBookstore.tandf.co.uk
A library at your fingertips!
eBooks are electronic versions of printed books. You can store them on your PC/laptop or browse them online.
They have advantages for anyone needing rapid access to a wide variety of published, copyright information.
eBooks can help your research by enabling you to bookmark chapters, annotate text and use instant searches to find specific words or phrases. Several eBook files would fit on even a small laptop or PDA.
NEW: Save money by eSubscribing: cheap, online access to any eBook for as long as you need it.
Annual subscription packages
We now offer special low-cost bulk subscriptions to packages of eBooks in certain subject areas. These are available to libraries or to individuals.
For more information please contact webmaster.ebooks@tandf.co.uk
We're continually developing the eBook concept, so keep up to date by visiting the website.
www.eBookstore.tandf.co.uk